The Kabbalah & Magic
OF ANGELS

About the Author

Migene González-Wippler was born in Puerto Rico and has degrees in psychology and anthropology from the University of Puerto Rico and from Columbia University. She has worked as a science editor for the Interscience Division of John Wiley, the American Institute of Physics, and the American Museum of Natural History, and as an English editor for the United Nations in Vienna, where she lived for many years. A cultural anthropologist, she lectures frequently at universities and other educational institutions.

. . . .

The Kabbalah & Magic
OF ANGELS

MIGENE GONZÁLEZ-WIPPLER

· · · · · · · · · · · ·
LLEWELLYN PUBLICATIONS
Woodbury, Minnesota

FIRST EDITION
Thirteenth Printing, 2020

Cover design by Adrienne Zimiga
COVER CREDITS:
St. Michael Archangel Nostalgia Cards Color Lithograph: © SuperStock;
ornate oval panel: iStockphoto.com / Gary Godby;
background texture: iStockphoto.com / Duncan Walker
Interior angel and decorative illustrations from
1167 Decorative Cuts CD-ROM and Book (Dover Publications, 2007);
illustrations in appendix 6 from the author's archives

Llewellyn Publications is a registered trademark of Llewellyn Worldwide Ltd.

Library of Congress Cataloging-in-Publication Data
The Library of Congress has already cataloged an earlier printing under LCCN:
2012048931

Llewellyn Publications
A Division of Llewellyn Worldwide Ltd.
2143 Wooddale Drive
Woodbury, MN 55125-2989
www.llewellyn.com
Printed in the United States of America

*This book is dedicated
to Joey and Noël*

Contents

Introduction

Belief in angels is on the rise, at least in the United States. According to a 1994 Gallup poll, 72 percent of Americans said they believed in angels. By 2004 the numbers had grown to include 78 percent of the population. More Americans believe in angels than they do in global warming, and the number of believers is on the increase (Gallup Poll Survey, May 10, 2007).

Interestingly enough, belief in the devil has also increased dramatically, from 55 percent in 1990 to 70 percent in 2004. Clearly, Americans believe that there is a struggle going on between the forces of good and the forces of evil. The terrifying specter of proliferating wars, a disturbing rise in crime statistics, family problems, drug and alcohol–related tragedies, economic turmoil, unabated unemployment, natural and man-made disasters, outspread poverty throughout the world, and many other problems lead many people to believe we are on the receiving end of a demonic onslaught of Machiavellian proportions. And, as God's celestial hosts, the angels are viewed as the most powerful deterrents to this hellish devastation (Gallup Poll Survey, May 10, 2007).

This growing interest in the angelic realm can be seen in the vast array of novels, films, and TV series that have made their recent appearance in bookstores and on screens throughout the country. Films are especially abundant, with tantalizing titles like *Angels in the Outfield*, *Wings of Desire* (newly remade as *City of Angels*), *Dogma*, *Michael*, *Fallen*, *Legion*, *The Devil's Advocate*, *The Prophecy Series* (about a rebellious Gabriel), *Angels and Demons*, *Constantine*, *The Preacher's Wife* (a remake of *The Bishop's Wife*), and many others. Older films featuring angels include classics like *It's a Wonderful Life*, *Here Comes Mr. Jordan*, *Angel on My Shoulder*, and *Heaven Can Wait*.

The small screen gave us several popular angel series like *Touched by an Angel* and *Angels in America*.

The angel theme can also be found in many American homes in the form of angel jewelry, angel clothing, angel linens, all sorts of angel ornaments, and even angel water and angel wine. We seem to be reaching up to Heaven for celestial protection, and the angels are our preferred link to that divine realm.

But can we contact the angels? Can we get their protection? Can they help us achieve our goals? Are there special rites and invocations that can bridge the unfathomable distances between our material world and the divine realms where angels dwell? The answer to all these questions is yes, and that is the reason this book was written. Angel magic is the way we connect with angels and get their undivided attention. For, rest assured, angels exist, they are real, and they want to help us. Indeed, they were created for that purpose. But you have to know how to contact them and let them know you want their help.

Kabbalah is a vast storehouse of lore about angels and their cosmic importance. It reveals not only who and what they are but also how we may establish a link with their immense powers. Ultimately, Kabbalah is the key to the magic of angels. Based on secret kabbalistic techniques, this book will explain to you who and what the angels are, how they interact with us, and, most importantly, how to work with them to lead richer and more productive lives. That is what the magic of angels is all about.

A Note from the Author

Although this is a book about angels and the Kabbalah, it also includes a great deal of scientific information pertinent to the book's central theme. The reason I have used so much science in the book is because I believe that science will find tangible evidence of the existence of an intelligent, omniscient force behind the creation of the universe. Everything that exists is based on very powerful and very real natural laws. The Creative Mind that brought the cosmos into being used these laws to achieve a purpose; therefore, the universe is based on logic, reason, and mathematical precision. Plato said, "God forever geometrizes." It is on science that we must depend to validate and ultimately prove the existence of a creator.

Recently the scientific world was stunned with the news that the Higgs boson, best known as the "god particle," is probably a reality. This does not mean that physics has proven the existence of God, but that it has found the particle that gives mass to matter and therefore makes the universe possible. The Higgs boson is so subtle and ethereal that it is practically impossible to detect. It is more an impulse than a true particle. In my book *A Kabbalah for the Modern World* (1974), I expressed my belief that science has already proven the existence of God. The proof is subtle, like the Higgs boson, but it is there.

Scientists are understandably reticent to express definite opinions on the "God question," but they are continuously engaged in trying to find the definite answer to the creation problem. Otherwise, why should they have called the Higgs boson the "god particle"? It is important that we keep science in mind when we talk about God and the angels, because what cannot be proven by science simply does not exist. Science is the ultimate religion. It must function on strict empirical proof because its quest is a holy quest. Famed astronomer Robert Jastrow, in his book *God and the Astronomers*, made this strange and now legendary prediction:

> *For the scientist who has lived by his faith in the power of reason, the story ends like a bad dream. He has scaled the mountains of ignorance; he is about to conquer the highest peak; as he pulls himself over the final rock, he is greeted by a band of theologians who have been sitting there for centuries.*

CHAPTER I

Who Are the Angels?

The angels come to visit us, and we only
know them when they are gone.

. . . .

GEORGE ELIOT

The study of angels is known as angelology. The word *angel* comes from the Latin *angelus,* which in turn is a romanization of the Greek *angelos*. The earliest form of the word is the Mycenaean *akero*. Many angelologists believe *angelos* is a Greek translation of the Hebrew *mal'akh*, meaning "messenger." The etymology suggests a being or entity acting as an intermediary between the material world and the world of the Divine.

The first conceptualization of angels can be traced to ancient Sumer, a civilization that flourished in southern Mesopotamia in what is known today as modern Iraq. It began its first settlements on the region over 5,000 years ago. It was the earliest society in the world, and it is known as the cradle of civilization.

. . . .

WHO ARE THE ANGELS?

The Sumerians were the first to use a winged human form in the many statues and relief carvings that were expressions of their religious beliefs. The Sumerians embraced a great variety of gods, but one of the basic tenets of their religion was their belief in messengers of the gods, celestial entities who ran errands between gods and humans. They also believed in the concept of "guardian angels," who were assigned to human beings at birth and remained by their side throughout their life. They dedicated altars to these forces, some of which have been found in excavations.

Around 1900 BCE, polytheistic Semitic tribes conquered the Sumerians and incorporated the concept of angels into their own mythical cosmologies. Among them were the Assyrians and the Babylonians. These peoples later developed the idea of groups of angels that served the many Semitic gods, subdividing the angels into hierarchies; this notion was preserved in Zoroastrianism, monotheistic Judaism, and other cultures. The Egyptians also may have borrowed some of the religious concepts of the Sumerians, but theologians are divided on the subject.

How did the images of angelic beings find their way into the iconography of the Sumerians? It is almost certain that the concept of a winged human figure must have been borrowed by them from an earlier, unknown civilization that has long disappeared in the sands of time—or perhaps the concept came to them in the form of a revelation from the angels themselves.

Zoroaster, or Zarathushtra, was an ancient Iranian prophet and philosopher who founded the Zoroastrian religion. He lived around the tenth or eleventh century BCE. Most information about Zoroaster derives primarily from the Avesta, the Zoroastrian scriptures, of which the Gathas—hymns attributed to Zoroaster himself—are a part. Elements of Zoroastrian philosophy deeply influenced Judaism and the classic Greek philosophers.

As a result of what he called "angelic communications," Zoroaster created a monotheistic religion that spread throughout the Persian Empire.

Zoroaster taught that there are hierarchies of angels considered to be divine gifts, all of them aspects of the Lord of Light, Ahura Mazda. The counterpart of the Lord of Light is the Lord of Darkness, Angra Nainyu.

According to Zoroaster, there are six main Archangels: the Archangel of Good Thought, the Archangel of Right, the Archangel of Dominion, the Archangel of Piety, the Archangel of Prosperity, and the Archangel of Immortality. There are also forty lesser angels identified as the Adorable Ones. Some of these angels and Archangels are believed to be male and others female. The guardian angels are a third rank of celestial beings who are assigned as guides and protectors to human beings at their birth.

Zoroaster also introduced the concept of demons, known as *daevas*.

The angelic forces were known as *ahuras*. Interestingly enough, in the ancient Hindu scriptures known as the Vedas, the demons are referred to as *assuras* while the angelic forces are called *devas*. It is from the Zoroastrian concept of a daeva that the word *devil* comes.

The influence of Zoroastrianism in Judaism can be seen in the fact that it was not until post-exilic times, after the Jews returned from captivity in Babylon, that angels were firmly incorporated into their religious beliefs. The impact of Zoroaster's teachings continued through the millennium before Christ, with many additional angels being added to the Jewish writings.

Although the Bible is a great source of angelic encounters and angelic lore, these heavenly beings are also present in the Talmud, the Midrash, the Apocrypha, the books of Enoch, the *Merkabah* literature, and throughout the Kabbalah.

The Bible uses several angelic terms to refer to the divine messengers. Among them are *mal'akh Elohim* (messenger of God), *mal'akh Adonai* (messenger of the Lord), and *ha-qodeshim* (the Holy Ones). Daniel is the first of the prophets to refer to individual angels by name. In Daniel 10:13 he identifies Michael as a warrior and advocate for Israel. In Daniel 8:15 he also mentions Gabriel.

. . . .

In post-biblical Judaism some of the angels developed specific personalities and were given especial tasks to perform. In the Kabbalah the angels exist in the higher worlds as tasks of God to produce effects in our material world. After a task is completed, the angel ceases to exist; the angel is the task. But as most of the tasks are multiple and the angels are also identified with cosmic laws, we could say that as long as the universe exists, so will the angels.

In addition, the Talmud teaches us that each angel has only one mission. The angels' missions are revealed in their names. For example, Raphael's name means "God heals." Raphael is therefore seen as the healing angel, the divine physician. But in Kabbalah Raphael is also ascribed the rulership of all written documents, such as books and contracts. That means he has a dual mission and a dual task, which seems to contradict the Talmudic teachings.

Angels appear in the Bible from the beginning to the end. They are mentioned in Genesis, the first book of the Old Testament, and in the book of Revelation, the last book of the New Testament. The concept of the guardian angel, borrowed from Zoroaster, is expressed in Psalm 91, Matthew 18, and Acts 12.

It is in the book of Genesis that angels appear most frequently. In Genesis 3:23 God stations the Cherubim in the Garden of Eden with the fiery, revolving sword to guard the way to the Tree of Life. In Genesis 18:1 three angels appear to Abraham to announce the birth of Isaac and the destruction of Sodom and Gomorrah. In Genesis 19:1 two angels appear to Lot in Sodom to foretell the destruction of the city. In Genesis 21:17 an angel of the Lord appears to Hagar in the desert and saves her son Ishmael. In Genesis 28:10 Jacob has a dream where he sees a ladder reaching up to Heaven with the angels of God ascending and descending upon it. And we must not forget Genesis 6:1, when the sons of God took wives for themselves among the daughters of men, thus becoming fallen angels.

Other angels make their appearances in Exodus 23:20 when God sends one of his heavenly messengers to lead Moses and guard him on his way. And in Tobias 12:15 Raphael identifies himself by name and asserts that he is one of the seven angelic princes who stand before the Divine Presence.

Angels of the Presence are highly exalted archons who are also known as Angels of the Face. According to the Book of Jubilees, Angels of the Presence and Angels of Sanctification are the two highest orders of angels. They were created on the first day, while the rest of the angels were created on the second. The Book of Jubilees asserts that these angels were created already circumcised so they could partake of the celebration of the Sabbath with God in Heaven and on earth. God instructed one of these angels—believed to be Michael—to write the history of creation for Moses. Other angels usually identified as Angels of the Presence are Metatron, Raphael, Gabriel, Uriel, Sandalphon, Phanuel, and Uriel, but Suriel, Sarakiel, Jehoel, Akatriel, Zagzagael, and Yefefiah are also mentioned by some biblical scholars. The Angels of the Presence are also equated with the Angels of Glory. In rabbinic tradition there are seventy tutelary angels, called Angels of the Presence.

The Midrash Tanhuma tells the story of an angel called Lailah, who brings the soul and the human seed together and plants them in the womb. While the child grows in the womb, Lailah places a candle at its head so it can see from one end of the world to the other. Then the angel proceeds to teach the baby the entire Torah and the history of its soul. When the child is born, Lailah extinguishes the candle, presses a finger on the child's upper lip, and says *shhh*. This causes the child to forget everything it learned in the womb, but the knowledge remains in its unconscious and is a subtle guide throughout its life. This also explains the indentation human beings have on their upper lip. Then, at the time of death, Lailah guides each human soul from this world to the next.

Perhaps the richest and most descriptive of the biblical encounters with angels is Ezekiel's vision of the *Merkabah*, or divine chariot. In the first chapter of Ezekiel's book he describes the *Chasmalim*, which is a radiance or fire. In the center of this fire is a gleam of amber. Out of this fire appear four living creatures (*Chayot*). Each has four faces and four wings. One of the faces is that of a lion, the second is that of an eagle, the third is that of an ox, and the fourth is that of a man. These four faces were later identified with the four elements of nature: lion as fire, eagle as water, ox as earth, and man as air.

The tips of the upper wings touch the wings of the living creature on each side, thus forming a square between them. The lower wings are used to cover the angels' bodies. Beside each of these living creatures is a wheel within a wheel (*Ophanim*), each covered with many eyes. As the living creatures move, the wheels move with them. Above the four living creatures is a crystal dome, and resting upon the dome is a throne made of a single sapphire. Seated upon the throne is God's Presence. The four living creatures with the four wheels and the dome with God and his throne upon it form the *Merkabah*, or divine chariot. The entire vision is a mystery, and its true meaning is a kabbalistic secret only revealed to high initiates. This is the only time that God and his angels are described so visually in the Bible.

Moses Maimonides counts ten ranks of angels in the celestial hierarchy (see *The Guide to the Perplexed*, 1956). They are also the orders that rule the ten sephiroth, or spheres, of the Tree of Life. Beginning with the highest ranking order, they are:

1. Chayot ha Kodesh—Powers

2. Ophanim—Thrones

3. Erelim—Principalities

4. Hasmalim (Chasmalim)—Dominions

5. Seraphim—Seraphim

6. Malachim—Virtues

7. Elohim—Archangels

8. Bene Elohim—Angels

9. Cherubim—Cherubim

10. Ishim—Souls of the Saints

According to this ranking, the Chayot and the *Ophanim*, who hold God's throne and are part of the *Merkabah*, are the highest and most exalted orders in the angelic hierarchy.

Deeply influenced by Judaism, Christianity developed its own concept of the angelic hierarchies. Although many ecclesiastical authorities have presented their versions of the angelic orders, like Saint Ambrosius, Saint Jerome, and Pope Gregory the Great, the most commonly accepted Christian version is that of Pseudo-Dionysius.

Pseudo-Dionysius is the author of many ecclesiastical writings, especially three long treatises: *The Divine Names*, *The Ecclesiastical Hierarchy*, and *The Celestial Hierarchy*. Pseudo-Dionysius presented himself as Dionysius the Aeropagite, the disciple of Paul mentioned in Acts 17:34. His writings were accepted as apostolic authority until the nineteenth century CE, when studies revealed a marked influence of Neoplatonism; thus it is now believed his writings date from around 500 CE. From that point on he became known as Pseudo-Dionysius, but he has not lost his credibility as an articulate Athenian Neoplatonist expressing an authentic Christian mystical tradition. His works rank among the classics of Western spirituality and were a source of inspiration to many theologians and Christian writers like Thomas Aquinas, Dante Alighieri, and John Milton.

According to Pseudo-Dionysius there are three angelic orders, each composed of three angelic choirs, making a total of nine celestial choirs:

First Order

FIRST CHOIR—Seraphim—fire, those who burn

SECOND CHOIR—Cherubim—messengers of knowledge, wisdom

THIRD CHOIR—Thrones—the seat of God

This order and its three choirs control the balance of the universe and the manifestation of the divine will, which they carry out.

· · · · · · · · · · · ·

Second Order

FOURTH CHOIR——Dominions——justice

FIFTH CHOIR——Virtues——courage, virility

SIXTH CHOIR——Powers——order, harmony

This order and its three choirs represent the power of God, and they also govern the planets, especially Earth. They also carry out the decrees of the angels of the first order and oversee the angels of the third order.

Third Order

SEVENTH CHOIR——Principalities——authority

EIGHTH CHOIR——Archangels——unity

NINTH CHOIR——Angels——revelation, messengers

This order and its three choirs protect and guide humanity, and bring our prayers to the Divine Presence. The Ninth Choir, the Angels, is the source of guardian angels.

Even though all the members of the celestial hierarchy are commonly known as angels, there is a specific choir that bears the same name. This means that all divine messengers are angels, but some of them occupy a more exalted position in the celestial choirs.

Each angel belongs to one or more of the choirs, and their titles reflect their position in the angelic hierarchy. For example, Michael belongs to three of the choirs: he is a Seraph, a Virtue, and an Archangel. Gabriel belongs to five of the choirs: he is a Cherub, a Virtue, a Power, an Archangel, and an Angel. Although he belongs to more choirs than Michael, Gabriel is not a Seraph, the highest-ranking choir, and therefore Michael is in a more exalted position. The only angel who belonged to the two highest choirs, the Seraphim and the Cherubim, was Satan before the Fall. He also belonged to the Powers and to the Archangels. Metatron, the Chancellor of Heaven who is known as the Lesser Jehovah, is a Seraph and an Archangel.

Another order of angels that is not part of the angelic hierarchy is the Ephemera. These are angels created by God at the dawn of each day. These angels' task is to sing the Trisagion, which are God's praises, three times a day. At the end of the day they cease to exist and are reborn again the next morning.

Many people believe that human beings who were exceptionally good during their lives become angels when they die, but this is not so. Angels were never born and have no human characteristics. They are pure energy and were created specifically to serve God and carry out his mandates.

According to medieval kabbalistic Judaism, around the fourteenth century CE a kabbalist calculated that there were 301,655,722 angels in the universe. It is not known who he was or how he reached that figure. Albertus Magnus also did some arithmetic on the subject and ended up proposing that there are 6,666 legions in each of the choirs and 6,666 angels in each legion. According to his calculations, there are more than 400 million angels floating about. But none of these numbers seem to be very accurate if we consider each star is an angel, according to John in the book of Revelation and Clement of Alexandria in *The Stromata*. Astronomers tell us that there are billions of stars in our galaxy alone, and billions of galaxies in the universe. This would indicate that if John and Clement of Alexandria are correct, the number of angels in existence runs into the billions of billions, or myriads upon myriads, according to the prophet Daniel. A myriad is an innumerable quantity.

Because most of the angels were created at the same time, their numbers are always the same. God does not create angels continuously, with the exception of the Ephemera.

Angels are very important in Christianity, and they appear frequently in the New Testament, most prominently in the book of Revelation. The distinction between angels and demons is recognized. Gabriel, as an angel of light, appears in Luke 1:19. The evil angel Abbadon/Apollyon appears in Revelation 9:11. We find Beelzebub in Mark 1:13 and Satan in Mark 1:16. Hierarchies are also acknowledged. Thus we find Archangel Michael in Jude 9, Virtues in Peter 1, Principalities and Powers in Romans 8:38 and Colossians 2:10, Archangels and Angels in 1 Thessalonians 4:16, and Thrones and Dominions in Colossians 1:16.

Like Judaism and Christianity, Islam also includes angels in its belief system. The Quran mentions Gabriel as the angel of revelation; Michael, the bringer of food; Israfel, the horn blower who signals the end of things; Azrael, the angel of death; Raqib, who writes good doings; Aatid, who writes bad doings; Maalik, the guardian of Hell; and Ridwan, the guardian of Heaven.

According to Islam, angels can take on different forms. The prophet Muhammad, describing the appearance of Gabriel, said that his wings spanned from the eastern to the western horizon. Muhammad was well acquainted with Gabriel, who is believed to have taught the prophet the entire Quran in a single night. But in all of angelology the most spectacular description of an angel is Islam's description of Michael. The great Archangel is depicted robed in red and green, with dazzling emerald wings and a head covered with bright red curls. Each strand of hair is encrusted with millions of tiny faces, all of them crying and asking Michael for his help in the solution of their problems. They represent the millions of prayers uttered every second by human beings in need of the Archangel's help. From Michael's emerald eyes falls an eternal stream of emerald tears that he sheds for the sufferings of humanity.

Most angelic names end in either -el, meaning "son of God," or -on, meaning "great." Thus we have Michael, Gabriel, Raphael, Uriel, Cassiel, Zadkiel, and Hanael as examples of the -el ending, and Metatron and Sandalphon as examples of the -on ending. There are angels with names that do not have these endings, like Tagas, Gedariah, Seehiah, and Huzia, but they are rare.

Although angels are often depicted in human form with wings and halos, these are not their actual appearances but rather images we have created for them across many thousands of years. This is known as anthropomorphism, giving a human form to something that is not human. Because we feel the need to identify with the angels, we have given them human forms, albeit highly idealized ones. We have done this because it is easier to relate to them if we can visualize them as being similar to ourselves. Lovely faces, radiant white tunics, huge alabaster wings, and dazzling halos all add to the celestial illusion. But angels are pure spirit, immense amounts of cosmic energy of unimaginable power extending across entire galaxies. How can we contain such magnitude in a simple human form, even if its wing span extends from the eastern to the western horizon? The answer is that we cannot. It is the angels themselves who have consented to adapt to our vision of them and manifest to us in forms we can easily identify with.

The Bible shows us this amiable disposition of the angels to manifest to us in human form. In this way they appeared to Abraham, Lot, Isaac, Hagar, Moses, Daniel, and Mary. In such guises they may appear to any of us to help us or to test our good will.

My father used to tell me when I was a child never to deny alms to a beggar, for he might be an angel in disguise. In his Letter to the Hebrews (Hebrews 13:12) Paul says: "Let brotherly love continue. Do not neglect to show hospitality to strangers, for thereby some have entertained angels unawares."

CHAPTER 2

Creation

In the beginning there was light,
and plenty of it.

. . . .

GEORGE GAMOW

T hen God said, 'Let there be light,' and there was light. And God saw that the light was good; and God separated the light from the darkness" (Gen. 1:3–4).

Astrophysics tells us that the universe came into being through a great explosion (physicists prefer to call it expansion) known as the Big Bang, a term coined by cosmologist Fred Hoyle. This explosion came from an infinitesimal point of light, known as a singularity, smaller than a millionth of the diameter of the point of a pin. This point of light exploded, outwardly dispersing vast amounts of radiant energy. Before this point there was nothing—there was no space, and there was no time. Time and space were created with the explosion, or expansion. Because there was no time and space at the time of the explosion, there was no sound. This happened approximately fourteen billion years ago.

. . . .

Within seconds of the Big Bang, the elements came into being. The first element created was hydrogen, composed of one electron—a negative charge—and a proton—a positive charge. This determined the universal plan where everything in the cosmos is formed of a combination of positive and negative forces.

Together with the elements were created the various cosmic laws like electromagnetism, which is the source of visible light, and, most importantly, gravitation, which is the force through which elements unite to form gases, stars, galaxies, and planets.

After the Big Bang the universe continued to grow exponentially, and today physicists believe there are billions of billions of galaxies in the visible universe alone, with billions of billions of stars and planets in each galaxy. How many galaxies may exist beyond the visible universe is not something that physicists are willing to speculate about.

But there is something else in the universe, something that has been discovered recently. It is the existence of two opposite forces. One is known as dark matter and the other as dark energy. No one has seen these forces, but their existence has been determined by scientific calculations. Dark matter forms about 24 percent of the universe, while dark energy forms about 72 percent. The remaining 4 percent forms the entire physical, visible universe. That means that the whole universe—its billions of galaxies, stars, and planets—form only 4 percent of the cosmos; the rest is dark matter and dark energy (see Trimble 1987).

Within the dark matter is the law of gravitation, which is the architect of everything that exists. It is the creative force of the universe. Without dark matter there would not be any galaxies, stars, planets, or even ourselves.

Dark energy is dark matter's opposite. It repels the law of gravity. What it does is create more space between galaxies. Until nine billion years ago, dark matter dominated dark energy, giving rise to an ever-growing number of galaxies. But as more galaxies and stars were created, the velocity and power of dark matter began to diminish. This gave a greater impulse and power to dark energy, which began to grow stronger, creating more and more space between galaxies. That is why galaxies are receding. They are not moving or separating themselves from the rest of the universe; there is simply more space being created between them by the dark energy.

There is also space being constantly created between stars and their planets and between planets and their satellites. The moon is moving away from the earth and the earth is moving away from the sun. It is happening very slowly, a millimeter per century, but across billions of years, the distance will be insurmountable.

If dark energy continues to create space between galaxies and stars, the universe will eventually become empty, and all its stars will die in a frozen void. According to actual calculations, that is probably what is going to happen. Scientists believe dark energy will complete its annihilating task in approximately fifty billion years, and the universe will be no more.

Interestingly enough, physics tells us that both dark matter and dark energy are passing, invisible and undetected, throughout all matter, including our bodies, every second (see Jungman 1996). Apparently they do not affect us, but it is disconcerting, to say the least, to know that Life (in the form of dark matter) and Death (in the form of dark energy) are coursing through our bodies every passing second. Several years ago during a meditation, I saw a huge black mass coming toward me. It was blacker than black, yet it had form and purpose. I knew it was Death. I felt I was not ready to die and said in my mind, *No, not yet*. But it continued to move relentlessly forward, and I knew I could not stop it. As it came closer, I surrendered to it and said, *Your will be done*. It coursed through me swiftly and disappeared. I believe that what I saw that day was dark energy.

But how did dark matter and dark energy came into being? Physicists have discovered recently that at the moment of the Big Bang a small bubble emerged, the size of a fraction of an atom. Inside this bubble were the four forces that are the foundation of the universe. These forces are electromagnetism, gravity, the weak nuclear force, and the strong nuclear force. Less than a second after the Big Bang, gravity was separated from the other three forces and became known as dark matter. The other three forces remained united and became dark energy. From the separation of the four forces was emitted a small amount of physical energy, which was the hydrogen element. This happened within three minutes after the explosion of the Big Bang. From the element hydrogen, through atomic aggregation, were formed the other elements. Helium was the second element to come into being, approximately 380,000 years after hydrogen. A billion years later the first stars were formed, producing other elements in their interiors. This resulted in the eventual creation of the universe as we know it with its billions of galaxies, stars, and planets.

This is how physics explains the creation of the universe and predicts its ultimate demise. But where is the Creator in all of this? Many scientists believe there is no Creator, but a growing number of them seem to see an intelligent, creative force at work in the universe. Chief among these scientists is British astrophysicist and best-selling author Paul Davies. In his book *The Mind of God*, Davies expresses his belief that, in all probability, there is an intelligent design in the creation of the universe. In the last paragraph of *The Mind of God*, he says, "Through conscious beings the universe has generated self-awareness. This can be no trivial detail, no minor byproduct of mindless, purposeless forces. We are truly meant to be here." And Stephen Hawking, walking the precarious line between belief and unbelief, asserts that "if we do discover a theory of everything, it would be the ultimate triumph of human reason—for then we would truly know the mind of God."

CHAPTER 3

The Nature of the Creator

In the Divine act of creation
God is unobserved and unwitnessed.

· · · · · · · · · · · · ·

E. A. MILNE

Science tells us that the universe was created as a result of the cataclysmic explosion of a tiny point of light known as the Big Bang. The book of Genesis tells us that God created light and separated it from the darkness. This happened on the first day.

Light is matter; it is the *primum mobile* that gave rise to the universe. This light is sustained by the dark matter and its main characteristic, the law of gravity. When God separated light from darkness, he separated dark matter, which is the source of everything that exists, from dark energy, which creates the growing space between galaxies, stars, and planets. This darkness is responsible for the ultimate fate of the universe. It is clear, then, that God did not create an eternal universe, but rather a universe that would have an eventual end. Why should God want to destroy his own creation? In order to understand this, we must begin by

· · · · · · · · · · · ·

understanding the nature of the Creator, and the best and clearest expla-nation of the Creator is found in the Kabbalah.

Although the Kabbalah's origins are rooted in deep antiquity, from the time of ancient Babylon, its wisdom has remained hidden from human-ity since it appeared more than four thousand years ago. Very few peo-ple know what Kabbalah really is. It is intrinsically Jewish, but you do not have to be Jewish to study it. Essentially it teaches that there is an all-pervasive force, known as the Creator, which controls everything that exists. This Creator is unknowable because his essence is beyond the reach of human perception. Yet Kabbalah reveals subtle insights into the nature of the Creator that make him and his creation easier to under-stand. How Kabbalah acquired this knowledge is unknown. It is believed that it was given to a few select human beings in the form of divine reve-lations. God wanted us to know him and his plan.

The first thing Kabbalah teaches is that God created the universe for the purpose of manifestation. He wanted to manifest his essence in the world of matter. He had to do this in stages because the true nature of God is Nothingness. This does not imply "nothing" in the simple meaning of the word. It means absolute, incomprehensible absence of being. In his true essence God does not think, act, or "exist." He just is. This state of nonexistence is known in Kabbalah as the Ain. God is the Ain.

At some point in the beginning of creation, the Ain began to concen-trate its essence until it emanated a second aspect of its nonbeing. This was the Ain Soph, which is infinity in existence while still not existing. Ain Soph is often described as the waters.

The Ain Soph, in turn, emanated the third aspect of eternal nonbeing, the Ain Soph Aur, which is limitless light. The three aspects of the Cre-ator—Ain, Ain Soph, and Ain Soph Aur—are known as the three veils of Negative Existence. They are seen as abstract infinity, abstract space, and abstract action (movement) where Ain is the Mother, Ain Soph is the Father, and Ain Soph Aur is the Crown.

. . . .

The Ain Soph Aur then emitted a single point of light—a singularity?—and this point of light traversed the Nothingness and became Something. This Something was the creation of the universe. This is the light that God separated from the darkness. It is the light that created the explosion known as the Big Bang.

Genesis says that in the second day of creation God said, "Let there be a dome in the midst of the waters, and let it separate the waters from the waters." And God called the dome sky (Gen. 1:6–8). We know the waters are the Ain Soph; the dome that is called sky is space. On this second day space was created, and together with space there was time. The universe was ready to be populated.

On the third day God said, "Let the waters under the sky be gathered together in one place and let dry land appear." God called the dry land earth, and the waters that were gathered together he called seas (Gen.1:9–10). The dry land described by Genesis is a symbol of solid matter. On this "third day" all the galaxies, stars, and planets came into being through the process of cosmic evolution. Our Earth was part of this evolution, but it was not the only creation.

It is interesting that although Genesis tells us what God did with the "waters" under the "dome," it does not say what he did with the waters that were *above*. The waters above the dome were the Ain Soph, the Father, the true Creator. The waters under the dome were the creation. The dome was the space where the creation came into being.

At this point many readers may be wondering how long a day is to God. We know that science tells us our universe is about fourteen billion years old, yet Genesis says that God only took six days to complete this awesome task. On the seventh, as we know, he rested.

Time is a human concept. The idea of time divided into seconds, hours, days, weeks, months, and years was conceived for our convenience. But is a God-day the same length as ours?

Seven hundred years ago a kabbalist known as Rabbi Isaac of Acco calculated that one of God's days is equal to two billion years. He did this using a hint from Psalm 90 (supposedly written by Moses), where the psalmist says, "For a thousand years in thy sight are but as yesterday" (Psalms 90:4). According to Kabbalah there are seven cycles of creation, each lasting 7,000 years. We are near the end of the fifth cycle. Through kabbalistic calculations a God-year equals fourteen billion of our years, if you take the seven cycles of creation into consideration. If Isaac of Acco was correct in his arithmetic, where one of God's days equals two billion years, the seven days of creation (including the day of rest) totals fourteen billion of our years, which is what science says is the approximate age of the universe. And we must remember that Isaac of Acco did his calculations seven hundred years ago, long before the theory of the Big Bang.

Kabbalah tells us that when the point of light emitted by the Ain Soph Aur traversed space, it created a series of ten concentric circles, or spheres, in descending order. Each sphere emanated the next one, becoming denser and more solid as they descended. These spheres are known as sephiroth, and they form the Tree of Life (see appendix 6, figure 6), which represents the universe and all that exists within it. But something happened as the spheres were formed. The light that emanated from the point of light emitted by the Ain Soph Aur was too strong, and the spheres were shattered by the immense pressure within them. The shards, or splinters, of the shattered sephiroth fell to the bottom of the Tree, where they became embedded and trapped. All of this happened in chapter 1 of Genesis, after the creation of all living things, including plants, animals, and human beings. And it happened during God's day of rest, which is not mentioned in chapter 1.

After the shattering of the spheres, the Ain Soph Aur emitted a second point of light with less power and created a new Tree of Life. This is known kabbalistically as the second creation, and it is the second chapter of the book of Genesis.

In the second chapter Genesis does not speak about the shattered spheres and the need for a new Tree of Life. Instead, it tells us that before

God created any living thing, including humanity, still on the second day, he formed a man from the dust of the ground and breathed life into his nostrils. This man was Adam. He then proceeded to plant the garden in Eden, on the east. And in this garden he placed two trees: the Tree of the Knowledge of Good and Evil and the Tree of Life. He then created Eve from one of Adam's ribs and admonished them not to eat from the Tree of the Knowledge of Good and Evil. He did not mention the Tree of Life, and there was a reason: Adam and Eve were already immortal. It mattered not if they ate of the Tree of Life, which gives life eternal.

What this part of Genesis tells us is that Adam and Eve were a special creation, spiritual archetypes who were supposed to be guides for the human beings that were to be created.

There was another creation on the second day, but this creation is not mentioned in Genesis 1. This was the creation of the angels. According to the book of Enoch, God created the angels from a ray that issued from one of his eyes. From this ray he created lightning, "which is fire and water in perfect balance," and with the lightning he struck a rock and melted it. From this flaming liquid he formed the heavenly host, "ten milliard angels," their garments and armor made of burning flames. He gave angels free will, as he gave it to Adam and all of humanity, but most of the angels returned this free will, preferring to do the will of God. The angels who retained their free will later became the fallen ones.

As we have seen, the Angels of the Presence and the Angels of Sanctification were created on the first day, when God created Heaven and Earth (Gen. 1:1). They are part of the structure of the heavenly realm. The rest of the angels were created on the second day. They are part of the structure of the universe. These angels are equated with the innumerable cosmic laws that maintain the harmonious balance of the universe. Some of these laws are known to us, like electromagnetism, gravity, inertia, momentum, fluidity, conservation of energy, equilibrium, diffraction and refraction, probability, action, and reaction. There is also an infinity of other laws, also represented by angels, which we are not familiar with.

Some of the laws that create disturbances in the universe—like the law of indeterminism, the law of chaos, and the law of entropy—are represented by fallen angels.

The angels as cosmic laws ensure the stability of the universe as designed by God. They also carry out God's plan "till the end of time." For that reason they were created before all living things, including humanity.

Chapter 3 of Genesis says that after they ate from the forbidden fruit, Adam and Eve were dressed in garments of skins made for them by God (Gen. 3:21). These "garments of skin" were actually physical bodies, because before their transgressions Adam and Eve were spiritual beings. Because of their sin they were stripped of their heavenly essence and transformed into ordinary human beings. Genesis goes on to say:

> Then the Lord God said, "See, the man has become like one of us, knowing good and evil; and now, he might reach out his hand and take also from the Tree of Life, and eat, and live forever.' Therefore the Lord God sent him forth from the Garden of Eden, to till the ground from which he was taken. He drove out the man; and at the east of the Garden of Eden he placed the Cherubim, and a sword flaming and turning to guard the way to the Tree of Life (Gen. 3: 22–24).

It is clear from these versicles that before their transgression Adam and Eve could eat from the Tree of Life because they were spiritual beings and could not die. But after they fell from God's grace they were no longer immortal, and therefore the Tree of Life was forbidden to them. As one of the ruling princes of the Cherubim, Raphael was the angel in charge of guarding the Tree of Life. Raphael also represents the law of gravity, which is the source of physical existence; therefore, the Tree of Life is under his direct protection.

As a matrix for the created universe, the Tree of Life embodies God's divine plan. Each sephira, or sphere, is awarded a name of God (with its corresponding meaning), an angelic choir, a ruling angel, a planet, an element, and a vast diversity of attributes such as flowers, plants and herbs, stones, colors, and numbers. But as we have already seen, the Tree of Life is a second creation. The initial spheres, or sephiroth, were broken by the power of the initial ray of light emitted by the Ain Soph Aur. In the form of sparks or shattered vessels this light lies at the bottom of the Tree, and they are mixed with the angels that fell into the Abyss after their rebellion. This area of the Tree of Life is known as the Qlipoth.

Kabbalistic tradition says that there are two trees. One is the actual Tree of Life. The other—which is behind the Tree of Life, back-to-back with it—is the Tree of Evil. It is known as the Qlipothic Tree, and it also has ten spheres, or sephiroth, unbalanced and chaotic, that are the complete opposites of the harmonious forces that form the Tree of Life. It is said that the highest sphere of the Qlipothic Tree is the lowest sphere of the Tree of Life. This lowest sphere is the world we live in, known as Malkuth.

In other words, our Earth is at the top of the Qlipothic Tree. The Qlipoth itself is underneath us in what is known as the kingdom of the shells. That is why there is evil in our world. We are surrounded by the chaotic forces of the Qlipothic Tree and by those of the Qlipoth itself. Most of the evil on Earth is the result of our destructive actions.

The Kabbalah teaches the concept of the *egregore*, which is a thought form or collective group mind, an autonomous psychic entity made of the thoughts of a group of people (see Flowers 1995).

The word *egregore* derives from the Greek and means "watchers." The word appears in Lamentations, Jubilees, and the Book of Enoch. Companies, political parties, religions, and even nations can be said to have egregores, a psychic compilation of the beliefs and ideals of the collective mind of the group. But there are two specific egregores in the astral world that are repositories of all human emotions. One is the white egregore, and the other is the black egregore. Every positive thought that is not materialized as a physical action goes immediately to the white egregor, which serves as inspiration and a good influence on human behavior.

On the other hand, all negative and destructive thoughts, also unrealized physically, are added to the black egregore, which is the source of many terrible and evil actions. If you are filled with hatred toward a specific individual and do something to harm that person, the dark energies that are created as a result of your action are not added to the black egregore because they are manifested in the material world. But your actions were nurtured and influenced by the concentration of destructive energy that forms the black egregor. Likewise, good actions are motivated by the white egregore but not added to it, as they were manifested physically.

Anger, envy, hatred, jealousy, contempt, and bad wishes directed to other people—all are added to the black egregore and will eventually be funneled into another person, who may react to that pernicious influence with a destructive or criminal act. Love, compassion, tenderness, generosity, and good wishes toward others will nurture the white egregore and act as deterrents of evil or the source of positive and laudable actions. It is therefore important to control our thoughts and render them impermeable to negative influences.

Kabbalists teach that the best way to render null and void all destructive thoughts is to express them physically without harming anyone. One of the ways in which this can be accomplished is by banging a table or a wall with a fist as the negative thought comes to the mind. This dispels the destructive energy of the thought and does not allow it to enter the black egregore.

According to Kabbalah, the black egregore is part of the Qlipothic forces, and it is equated with the black holes of astrophysics. Every destructive human action, including wars and world tragedies, has its origin in the black egregore, which is an intrinsic part of the collective unconscious of the human race. Freud called it the Id and Jung called it the Shadow. We are all responsible, in some measure, for all our worldly troubles even as we condemn and regret them.

God gave us free will and a set of laws that we must follow to ensure the balance of the universe and our world. We often use this free will to break the laws instead of observing them. Such actions empower the fallen angels that feed on the shells of the Qlipoth, and the result is further mayhem on Earth. It is the duty and mission of each human being to rescue the sparks that fell into the Qlipoth, because ultimately they must return to their original source in the Ain Soph Aur. We can do this through good actions, prayer, and meditation; this is humanity's most sacred task. The name of this mission is *tikkun*.

CHAPTER 4

And God Created Man in His Own Image

I want to know God's thoughts; the rest are details.

. . . .

ALBERT EINSTEIN

S o God created humankind in his own image; in the image of God
created he them; male and female he created them" (Genesis
1:27). In the first chapter of Genesis, God is Elohim, a plural of
El or possibly Eloah, a female concept of the deity. The plural Elohim is
masculine, but it has the root of a female form as its basis. It suggests the
union of the male and the female as one being. This does not imply an
actual physical androgynous being but rather the *spiritual* essence of God
as male/female in unison. Furthermore, in Genesis 1:26 God (Elohim)
says, "Let us make humankind in our image, according to our likeness,"
and then proceeds to create humanity as male and female (see appendix
6, figure 7).

. . . .

27

The idea of God as both male and female is at the center of both rabbinical and kabbalistic teachings. This does not imply that God is divided into male and female beings. Indeed, the idea of such duality is a sacrilege in Judaism. God, male and female, is still one united force. That is why the Shema, the most important of Jewish prayers, says, "Here, O Israel, the Lord our God is the Eternal. The Eternal is ONE." What it means is that God's essence is feminine and masculine, positive and negative, proton and electron, united as ONE for the purpose of manifestation. Light itself, the structure of the atom, and everything that exists is based on those two basic principles.

In chapter 2 of Genesis, the Creator is not referred to as God but as the Lord God. Indeed, throughout the entire Bible we see references to the deity in different forms: God (Elohim), the Lord God (Jehovah Elohim), the Lord (Adonai), the Lord of Hosts (Jehovah Tzabaoth), and many others. Each name of the Godhead has a special meaning and a specific connotation. It also describes one or more of the deity's powers. We can see this in the Tree of Life, where each sephira has been awarded a different name of the Godhead.

From Genesis 2:4 onwards and throughout all of chapter 3, the deity is referred to as the Lord God, Jehovah Elohim. Jehovah is the holiest of God's names and is known as the Tetragrammaton, or name of four letters. These four letters in Hebrew are Yod Heh Vau Heh, transliterated as YHVH (see appendix 6, figure 3). Because Hebrew does not have vowels, the sounds of the vowels are indicated by dots and dashes under the letters, known as *nekkudot.* Across the centuries, the vowel marks, or *nekkudot,* under the letters of the Tetragrammaton were lost or deliberately erased by Hebrew theologians, who did not want the holy name to be pronounced. Even today devout Jews do not pronounce the holy name and substitute the name Adonai (LORD) instead.

Because of the absence of the *nekkudot* under the Tetragrammaton, we do not know its exact pronunciation. It is most commonly transliterated as Jehovah or Yaweh, but it is doubtful these are correct pronunciations.

Whereas Elohim is the Creator on a spiritual level, Jehovah Elohim is the Elohim manifested in the phenomenal world. It is through Jehovah Elohim that the physical universe came into being. That is why Genesis 2:4 says, "In the day that the Lord God (Jehovah Elohim) made the earth and the heavens," while Genesis 1:1 says, "In the beginning, when God (Elohim) created the heavens and the earth." This means that in chapter 1 God (Elohim) created a spiritual concept of the universe, while in chapter 2—the "second" creation—the Lord God (Jehovah Elohim) manifested that spiritual concept into reality. Notice that in chapter 1 God creates Heaven first and then Earth, while in chapter 2 the Lord God creates Earth first and then Heaven. That is because Heaven is an idea, a belief, that is to become part of humanity after humanity is created as part of the physical world.

The concept that the human soul is both feminine and masculine may be seen in the fact that the Lord God creates Adam (a spiritual being) but not Eve. The female counterpart of Adam is "taken" from him in the form of a "rib." That means that the female and the male aspects of the soul coexist as one, as they do in God himself. But in order to manifest physically, they must be divided, and that is why the Lord God extracts Eve from Adam, separating them. This is the concept behind the term *soul mates*.

Kabbalistic tradition teaches that when a soul is incarnated, it is divided from its counterpart and born as male and female. These two parts of the same soul rarely meet in the material world but are reunited after their physical deaths.

This duality of the human soul is mirrored in the composition of the human body. Although each individual being belongs to a specific gender, male or female, the physical characteristics that identify a person are known biologically as dominant. The human genome is composed of twenty-three pairs of chromosomes; among them are the chromosomes that determine the sex of an individual. The female chromosome is composed of two parts, XX, and its male counterpart also is composed of two parts, XY. Upon conception, each parent contributes half of its sex chromosome to the child. The mother can only send an X, but the father can send either an X or a Y. It is the father who determines the sex of the unborn child. If he sends an X, the child will be a girl. If he sends a Y, the child will be a boy. These combinations of the parents' chromosomes are known as the dominant sexual characteristics of the child. When the child is born, it will be either a male or a female. But deep inside his or her human genome, he or she will also have the sexual characteristics of the opposite sex, because he or she is the result of the union of a mother and a father. These dormant characteristics are said to be latent in all human beings and in all mammals. Therefore, though we may have the outward appearance of one sex, in reality we have the characteristics and tendencies of both. There is a male hidden in every female (her father) and a female hidden in every male (his mother).

There is also another part in the human body—and, indeed, in many animals—that attests to the intrinsic duality of our natures. It is the biological construct known as bilateral symmetry. It can be defined as the symmetrical arrangement of an organism or a body part along its central axis, so that the body is divided into equivalent right and left halves by only one plane. The two halves are mirrors of each other. For example, the right and left sides of the human body are practically identical. We have two arms, two legs, two eyes, two nostrils, two lungs, two kidneys, two testes in the male and two ovaries in the female. These two sides are blended harmoniously along the axis of the spinal cord. In Kabbalah the left side of the body is seen as female and the right, male. These are two of the columns, or pillars, of the Tree of Life. The third, or middle, pillar is equated with the spinal cord. The Elohim resonates in all of us.

As we have seen, the Elohim is the source of the male and female principle. Elohim is the Creator on a spiritual/mental plane. Elohim is God, and Jehovah is his/her name. The name *Jehovah* by itself means Lord, but when it unites with Elohim it means the Lord God—that is, God, whose name is Jehovah. In other words, the first manifestation of

Elohim in the physical world is his/her name, and that name is Jehovah. From that moment onwards, Elohim is known as Jehovah, the Creator on the physical plane. Wherever the Bible mentions the Lord after Genesis 3, it is referring to Jehovah.

As we have seen, Adonai is often used as a substitute for Jehovah. Adonai is the plural of Adon, meaning Lord, master, or owner. To avoid confusion, many modern bibles render Jehovah as LORD in small capital letters and Adonai in all capital letters—LORD. Neither Elohim nor Jehovah demand observance of the commandments or divine law. It is Adonai who demands such obedience. Adonai signifies ownership of everything that exists. Because God (Elohim) possesses every human being, he demands obedience of his statutes. Therefore, it is Adonai who calls us to the service of God. All the prophets who were called to serve the deity received this mandate directly from Adonai. Ezekiel, Isaiah, and Jeremiah describe this call of God as coming from Adonai. As Adonai Jehovah, the LORD LORD, the deity commands all that exists on the earth, the winds, the seasons, the tides, and all of nature.

It is said that Jehovah has eight appellations, which are used to ask specific things from him:

JEHOVAH-JIREH—means "God will provide." It is repeated
   ten times daily to ensure God will provide all of our needs.

JEHOVAH-RAPHA—means "Jehovah heals." *Rapha* is the root
   of the Archangel Raphael's name, who is the divine healer.
   This is the name of God that is spoken during illnesses. It is
   associated with Psalm 103, which is read when a person is ill.
   There is a part in the biblical book of Malachi that connects
   this name of God with the sun's power of healing and with
   Raphael's wings: "For you who revere my name, the sun of
   righteousness shall rise with healing in its wings" (Malachi 4:2).

JEHOVAH-NISSI—means "Jehovah, my banner." It refers to
   the altar that Moses built for God and suggests that an altar

should be erected to God facing the east. It must be made of stone, not of wood. To worship God (Jehovah) and ask for his help, the person must stand—never kneel—at this altar, arms raised to Heaven, and make the petition.

JEHOVAH-M'KADDESH—means "Jehovah sanctifies," as well as dedication to him. It suggests the pursuit of goodness, self-purification, and dedication to God in order to acquire his blessings and protection.

JEHOVAH-SHALOM—means "God is peace," also perfection. It indicates that it is important to pursue perfection in order to obtain God's peace, which is the greatest desire of the human heart. This name is said when a person is in deep anguish and despair. It is said to bring immediate solace.

JEHOVAH-TZIDNEKU—means "Jehovah is our rectitude." It is derived from the word *Tzedek*, or Chesed, which is the name of the fourth sphere of the Tree of Life. It refers to our duties and behavior toward other persons. It implies kindness and beneficence. This name is spoken when we must make an important decision that will affect another person, to ensure the decision will be a fair one. It is also said when we need to ask a favor of someone in power.

JEHOVAH-ROHE—means "Jehovah is my shepherd." It is found in Psalm 23 ("The LORD is my shepherd, I shall not want."). This is one of the most beautiful psalms in the Bible and evokes complete trust in God's love and compassion. This name, repeated daily, will ensure God's constant protection and prosperity.

JEHOVAH-SHAMMAH—means "Jehovah is here." This name indicates that God is always with every human being if that person welcomes him into his or her heart. The name is said ten times daily to ensure the protection of a home and the presence of God in a person's life.

. . . .

Despite the fact that the deity is referred to in a limited number of ways in the Tanakh, or Hebrew Bible, there are many alternate names of the Godhead in Hebrew that are part of the Kabbalah. Three of the most powerful of these names are the name of 22 letters, the name of 42 letters, and the name of 72 letters.

The Book of Raziel (*Sepher Raziel HaMalakh*) describes these names in great detail, as well as other names of the deity. This is a very famous kabbalistic treatise that is said to contain all secret knowledge. The book is very rare and difficult to obtain. I obtained a copy of what is said to be a Hebrew version of the book after many years of searching. I always carry it in my purse as an amulet of good luck. No one knows the human origin of the book.

Raziel is an Archangel whose name means "secrets of God." He is known as Keeper of the Secrets and the Angel of Mysteries. He is a ruling prince of the Second Heaven and belongs to several choirs, including the Cherubim and the *Ophanim*. He is also said to be the chief of the *Erelim* and the ruling angel of Chokmah, the second sphere of the Tree of Life.

Raziel always stands close to God's throne and writes down everything that is discussed during the heavenly councils. After compiling a vast amount of secret celestial knowledge, he created the book that bears his name. He purportedly gave the book to Adam and Eve after their transgression so the two of them could return to Heaven. The other angels were jealous that Adam and Eve should have this secret knowledge and stole the book from them and threw it into the ocean. God was not angry with Raziel but instead instructed the angel Rahab, who rules the depths of the sea, to retrieve the book and return it to Adam and Eve. According to some sources, the book passed on through generations to Enoch (believed to have later become the Archangel Metatron), who may have incorporated his own writings into the book. From Enoch, the Archangel Raphael gave it to Noah, who is said to have used its wisdom to build the ark. Eventually, the secret writings came into the hands of Solomon, which may explain his famous wisdom.

. . . .

The Book of Raziel explains the mysteries of many of the names of God. The name that is most used in the book is composed of four letters like the Tetragrammaton. These letters, HQBH, have been expanded through notarikon as *Hova Quedesh Berek Hova*, meaning "he is holy, holy is he."

Notarikon is a kabbalistic system where an entire word may be formed from an initial or single letter. Raziel also reveals the mysteries of the names of 22 and 42 letters and the 1,500 keys that unlock the mysteries of creation. He also speaks of the name of 72 letters, better known as the Shemamphora, and the 670 mysteries of this name (see appendix 6, figures 4 and 5).

The name of 22 letters (in Hebrew) is pronounced ANAKTAM PASTAM PASPASIM DIONSIN. It is associated with the high priest's blessing and is said to give great protection against all dangers. It is used in many angelic invocations and magic rituals.

The name of 42 letters is abbreviated. The first word is ABGITAZ and the last word is SHAKVASIT. Thus the name of God of 42 letters is ABGITAZ SHAKVASIT. It is associated with the famous prayer Ana Bekoah, which is derived from the first letters of Genesis. It is said that by saying this prayer daily and meditating upon it, a person will receive great illumination from God and his angels. The prayer is said to be written in the language of creation. It is said aloud.

Ana Bekoah

Ana, Bekoah, Gedulah, Yeminka, Tatir, Tserura, Kabel,
Rinat, Amkha, Sagveinu, Tajareinu, Nora, Na, Gibor,
Dorshei, Yejudka, Kevavat, Shamrem, Barkhem,
Tajarem, Rahmei, Tzidkatkha, Tamid, Gamlem, Jasin,
Kadosh, Berov, Tuvka, Najel, Adateka, Yajid, Ge-eh,
Lamka, Pinei, Zokrei, Kedushateka, Shavateinu,
Kabel, Ushma, Tzakateinu, Yodea, Taamulot.

After meditating on the prayer, the person makes a petition to God and his angels. He then reads the following names in silence.

Baruk, Shem, Kevod, Malkuto, Leolam, Vaed.

These last words cause the sacred name of God to manifest in the material world.

When one wishes to ask an angel for a specific favor, one must use either the name of 42 letters or the name of 72 letters, the Shemamphora.

The Shemamphora is derived from the book of Exodus (Exodus 14:19–21). In the Hebrew version, each of these three versicles contains 72 letters. The letters of the three versicles were combined to form the 72 names of God, each of which contains three letters. Thus the Shemamphora is composed of 72 names of three letters each. The names are enclosed in small squares along eight horizontal and nine vertical lines. They are read horizontally from right to left, as is done in the Hebrew language, beginning with the first horizontal line until the entire name is read. Each letter of each name is read individually. In order to do this, the person must purify himself very thoroughly. According to the Talmud, reading the Shemamphora without proper purification can cause a person grave disturbances in his life—even death. Proper purification means abstaining from sexual relations for at least twenty-four hours before the ritual and avoiding alcohol, meat, and drugs of any kind, including coffee, tea, or tobacco. The person must also bathe thoroughly and be dressed in white.

There are 72 angels associated with the 72 names of the Shemamphora. These angels' names are also placed in the same form as the Shemamphora, each in its own square. Some kabbalists recommend using the angelic names instead of the actual Shemamphora, as they believe they are safer. Angels, after all, are God's words, and they are more accessible to human beings.

Raziel divides the Shemamphora into ten parts. Nine parts are formed of seven groups of three letters each. The tenth part is formed of the last nine names. The name is so powerful that any combination of these ten parts may be used to achieve any objective, no matter how difficult it may seem.

Before using the chosen names, and after careful purification, the person should begin by invoking three of the angels of the Shemamphora—Haniel, Hasdiel, and Zadkiel—in the following form:

> *I ask you, angels Haniel, Hasdiel, and Zadkiel,*
> *through the holy name (here pronounce*
> *the chosen parts of the Shemamphora), to*
> *carry on the task I command you today,*
> *which is (here state what is desired).*

This is repeated three times. This invocation must be said facing east and always within the confines of a magic circle.

Magic rituals must be conducted before the sun comes out, preferably at midnight or on the hour of the angel that rules the day of the ritual. These hours and days will be discussed later in the book.

The words of the ritual should be spoken in low tones, most especially the names of God.

In the third part of the book Raziel reminds Adam and Eve that all the pure of heart will be blessed and favored by God; the impure will not achieve the gift of wisdom. He also tells them that in order to earn God's favor they must serve the Shekinah—the Holy Spirit, *Ruach Hakadesh*, who is the Cosmic Mother—in perfect purity of mind, body, and soul.

CHAPTER 5

The Tree of Life

Why are there trees I never walk under but large
and melodious thoughts descend upon me?

. . . .

WALT WHITMAN

The Tree of Life, *Etz Hayim*, is composed of ten spheres known as sephiroth (sephira is the singular form); see appendix 6, figure 6. It is a glyph that represents both the Heavenly Man, known as Adam Kadmon (the universe or macrocosm; see appendix 6, figure 7) and man in the material world or microcosm.

The ten sephiroth are emanations from the first point of light that emanated from the Ain Soph Aur. They are divided into three columns, or pillars. The right-hand column, or Pillar of Mercy, is a male-active potency. The left-hand column is the Pillar of Judgment or Severity, which is a female-passive principle. The middle column, or Pillar of Mildness or Equilibrium, is the harmonizing factor that blends and unites the forces of the left- and right-hand pillars.

. . . .

The three pillars are united by lines that are called paths. There are twenty-two paths, which represent the twenty-two letters of the Hebrew alphabet (see appendix 6, figure 1). The ten sephiroth and the twenty-two paths are known collectively as the thirty-two Paths of Wisdom.

From the primordial point of light, the sephiroth were emanated in succession in the following order:

1: Kether—Crown

This first sephira is the source of the other nine. As the result of the initial outpouring of divine light, it is outside of human experience; its essence cannot be comprehended by the human mind. There are no forms in this sphere. It is a concentration of pure being because matter has not yet come into existence.

The name of God in Kether is AHIH (Eheieh, meaning "existence," the name given by God to Moses in the burning bush). Its Archangel is Metatron. The angelical order is *Chayot Ha Qodesh,* or "Holy Living Creatures." Its color is white brilliance. It is identified with the cosmos and with the planet Neptune. Its correspondence in the human body is the skull.

We may conceive of Kether as a formless state of latent existence, the void of interstellar space that nevertheless harbors within it all the potentials of life.

2: Chokmah—Wisdom

This is a masculine-active potency that is also known as Aba, the father image. The name of God in this sphere is Jehovah. Its Archangel is Raziel, and the angelic order is the *Ophanim*, or "Wheels." Its color is pearly or opalescent grey. It is identified with the zodiac and the planet Uranus. Its correspondence in the human body is the right side of the face.

Chokmah is seen as the sphere of thoughts and ideas not yet crystallized. It is the beginning of mind, as God begins to conceive the idea of the creation of the universe.

3: Binah—Understanding

This sephira is a feminine-passive potency, also called Ama (the Mother image) and Aima (the Fertile Mother who is eternally conjoined with the Father, Aba/Chokmah, for the maintenance of the universe in order). Binah is also called Marah, the Great Sea, which is the root for Mary and is known as the Mother of All Living Things. She is the feminine aspect of God, identified with Eloah, the root of the Elohim.

It is from the union of Chokmah and Binah that the physical universe sprang. Before their union, the universe was an idea in the mind of God. These two sephiroth are the primordial blocks of life, proton and electron, that constitute all aspects of creation. They also represent biological opposites and therefore are the keys to human sexuality.

Chokmah and Binah occur both in space and in time. They may be seen in alternating periods of our lives, in the tides of the seas, in our physiological processes, and even in international affairs. To everything there is a season, says Solomon in Ecclesiastes. These alternating currents of activity and passivity, construction and destruction are the result of the interplay between these polarizing spheres.

The name of God in Binah is Jehovah Elohim. Its Archangel is Tzaphkiel and its angelic choir is the *Erelim*, or "Thrones." Its color is black. Its planet is Saturn. Its correspondence in the human body is the left side of the face.

The first three sephiroth—Kether, Chokmah, and Binah—form a triad, the first one of the Tree of Life. Together they are known as the Supernals and are beyond human reach because they are the prime movers—the architects of human reality—and creation only begins after them. Kether, Chokmah, and Binah are equated with the Higher Self, the great unconscious. They are also known as the macroprosopos and the *Arik Anpin* (the "vast countenance").

Daath

Halfway between Chokmah and Binah, in the center of the Tree, there exists another sphere, Daath, known as the hidden sephira. It is not assigned a number or any other attribute. It is defined as "knowledge." According to Kabbalah, it is the gate to the Qlipoth, known as the Abyss, and the Qlipothic Tree. One must pass through Daath in order to reach the three higher spheres, which means leaving the confinement of our conscious personalities to reach the deep unconscious. Daath is placed on the throat.

4: Chesed—Mercy

This sephira is a male potency, and it is the first emanated from the union of Chokmah and Binah. Chesed is also called Gedulah, which means "greatness" or "magnificence." Its quality is mercy or love on a higher, cosmic scale. Thus we see that the first human qualities emanated from God were love and mercy.

Chesed is the first sephira that may be conceived by the human mind. The name of God ascribed to this sphere is El, a root of Elohim.

Its Archangel is Zadkiel. Its angel choir is the *Chasmalim,* or "Brilliant Ones." Its color is bright blue. Its planet is Jupiter. Its correspondence in the human body is the right shoulder or right arm.

5: Geburah—Strength, Severity

Geburah is a female potency emanated from Chesed. Alternate titles of this sphere are Din (Justice) and Pachad (Fear).

Geburah is the most forceful and disciplined of all the sephiroth. Its force is not evil unless its essence overflows from justice into cruelty. It is essentially a conciliatory force, a restriction of the unbounded, merciful love of Chesed that, if unchecked, can lead to folly and cowardice. Likewise, without the loving mercy of Chesed, the severe powers of Geburah can degenerate into cruelty and injustice. That is how the spheres of the left- and right-hand columns of the Tree balance each other.

The name of God in Geburah is Elohim Gebor. Its Archangel is Kamael. The angelic choir is the *Seraphim*, or "Fiery Serpents." Its color is red. Its planet is Mars. Its correspondence in the human body is the left shoulder or left arm.

6: Tiphareth—Beauty

This sphere is placed in the Middle Pillar directly below Daath, the hidden sphere. Tiphareth is an emanation of Chesed and Geburah.

Other titles given to this sphere are Zoar Anpin (the "lesser countenance"), Melekh (the king), the Son, Adam, and the Man. Two of its symbols are a child and a sacrificed god, in which we may see both Jesus and the Egyptian god Osiris.

In Tiphareth we see that beauty (clemency, forgiveness) is obtained from the union of mercy and justice. The spheres of Chesed, Geburah, and Tiphareth form the second triad of the Tree of Life.

Tiphareth is the center of equilibrium in the Tree; it is a link, a point of transition, from where divine energies are poured into the rest of the sephiroth.

The name of God of this sephira is Jehovah Elo ve Daath, which points to the union of Jehovah and Elohim and Daath as the point of union. Its Archangel is Raphael. Its choir of angels is the *Malachim*, or "Kings." Its color is yellow. Its planet is the sun. Its correspondence in the human body is the breast.

7: Netzach—Victory

This sephira is a male potency emanated from Tiphareth.

One of its titles is Firmness. It represents the instincts and human emotions. It is mostly equated with human love. This is a sphere densely populated with the thoughtforms of the collective unconscious or group mind. Thus it is essentially an illusory plane where archetypal ideas have not yet been expressed as forms.

The God name of this sphere is Jehovah Tzabaoth. Its Archangel is Hanael (also spelled Haniel or Anael). Its choir of angels is the *Elohim,* or

"Gods." Its color is emerald green. Its planet is Venus. Its correspondence in the human body is the right hip and right leg.

8: Hod—Glory

This sephira is a female potency emanated from Netzach.

Hod represents the intellectual powers of humanity. It is the sphere where the emotions and instincts of Netzach take form and come into action.

Hod is known as the sphere of magic, where visualizations of things desired are realized.

The name of God of this sephira is Elohim Tzabaoth. Its Archangel is Michael. Its choir of angels is the *Bene Elohim,* or "Sons of God." Its color is orange. Its planet is Mercury. Its correspondence in the human body is the left hip or left leg.

9: Yesod—Foundation

This sephira is located in the Middle Pillar and is a result of the union between Netzach and Hod. It is placed directly under Tiphareth.

Yesod is the seat of intuition. It is the sphere of the Astral Light and a receptacle of the emanations of the other sephiroth. Its function is to correct and purify the emanations to make them accessible to the human mind, which it represents.

The name of God of this sphere is Shaddai El Chai. Its Archangel is Gabriel. Its choir of angels is the *Cherubim,* or "the Strong." Its color is violet. Its planet is the moon. Its correspondence in the human body is the reproductive organs.

Because Yesod is associated with the moon, it controls the lunar tides and fertility, as well as body fluids. It is the realm of the Moon Goddess in all of her aspects. Yesod is the gate that leads to the higher spheres and is also said to be the seat of the First Heaven.

Chesed, Geburah, Tiphareth, Netzach, Hod, and Yesod are known collectively as the Microprosopos and the *Zaur Anpin* (the "lesser countenance"). Microprosopos is sometimes known as *Melekh,* or "King."

10: Malkuth—Kingdom

This sephira is an emanation from Yesod. It represents the earth and the material world. Among its titles are the Queen, the Inferior Mother, the Bride of Microprosopos, and the Shekinah, which is the feminine aspect of God associated with the elohim. The Shekinah is said to be in exile in the material world.

Malkuth is placed in the Middle Pillar directly beneath Yesod.

Because Yesod (moon) lies between Malkuth and Tiphareth (sun), it creates a solar eclipse, and the sun's rays cannot reach the earth. For that reason, the earth is in continuous darkness.

In order to achieve illumination, it is necessary to rise to the sphere of Yesod and therefore receive the life-giving energies of Tiphareth. This can only be done through meditation and rituals.

The name of God in Malkuth is Adonai ha Aretz. Its Archangel is Sandalphon. Its choir of angels is the *Ishim,* or "Souls of the Saints." Its colors are lemon green, olive green, russet, and black. Its planet is Earth. Its correspondence in the human body is the feet. It is also associated with the four elements.

There are three veils in the Tree of Life that separate some of the spheres. First, there is the Veil of the Profane, separating Malkuth from Yesod. Second, there is the Veil of Paroketh, separating Tiphareth from the lower four sephiroth. And third, there is the Veil of the Presence of the Ancient of Days, separating Kether, the first sephira, from the rest of the Tree. These veils represent three different states of consciousness that must be reached and transcended before one can reach the ultimate mysteries of creation and God.

The Tree of Life with its ten sephiroth is classified in five stages or phases. As we saw in the beginning, the first ten sephiroth that emanated from the Infinite Light were too powerful and broke under the pressure. God then emanated ten more sephiroth with lesser light, but the Kabbalah says that this process had to be repeated four times until the light was sufficiently diffused for the material world to perceive it. This resulted in four different worlds, plus the original one.

The original world emanated by the Ain Soph Aur is known as Adam Kadmon, which is beyond human comprehension. The next world to come into existence was the World of Emanation (Atziluth). This was, in reality, the first world.

The second was the World of Creation (Briah). The third was the World of Formation (Yetzirah), and the fourth was the World of Action (Assiah).

The first class of manifested reality is the spiritual plane. This is *Shamaym,* or Heaven—a plane of pure thought and the basis of the various kinds of phenomenal energies. The second class of manifested reality is the phenomenal plane itself, the plane of objective realm. It is called *Aretz,* or Earth, and represents the entire material world.

Shamaym is composed of the first three worlds: Atziluth, Briah, and Yetzirah. Aretz, or Earth, is composed of Assiah, the World of Action.

Shamaym, or Heaven, is God's realm. In Atziluth dwells only his divine essence. In Briah creative patterns begin to emerge. This is the site of God's throne, envisioned by Ezekiel through divine revelation, and the realm of the Archangels. God's crystal palace, criss-crossed by blinding lightning bolts as described in the First Book of Enoch, also belongs to the World of Briah. The celestial councils, the Angels of the Presence, and the Angels of Sanctification all dwell within it. Facing God's throne—made of a single sapphire, as described by Ezekiel—is a great curtain of searing white light where the entire history of the universe, from its beginning to its ultimate end, is inscribed with letters of white fire. A crystal staircase winds down below this curtain, and at the bottom flows eternally the river of fire, Hidekkel, where angels dip their tongues before they can speak. This is God's realm, the Plethora.

God's Presence is hidden behind the curtain of white light, and so blinding is the radiance of his light that angels cannot gaze upon it.

God's throne is held aloft by four of the *Ophanim*, who balance it between two of their fingers. Four of the *Erelim* are beneath the *Ophanim* to sustain them in their task. God's throne is the *Merkabah*, the divine chariot, as envisioned by Ezekiel.

Briah is encompassed by the sephiroth Chokmah and Binah.

Yetzirah, the World of Formation, is where the rest of the angels were created and where the Seraphim reside. It is where we find the patterns, formulas, and paradigms that form the matrix for the material plane. Yetzirah is encompassed by the six sephiroth that follow Chokmah and Binah. They are Chesed, Geburah, Tiphareth, Hod, Netzach, and Yesod.

Below the Shamaym, made of Atziluth, Briah, and Yetzirah, is our world of action, Assiah. This is not just the earthly plane but that of the entire universe. Assiah is physical reality. It is God's plan manifested in the material world. But how do we explain all this in logical terms?

The Multiverse Theory is a new concept in physics that proposes the existence of multiple universes set one upon the other like disks or "soap bubbles" and joined by a common unifying factor (see Guth 1998).

When a large star explodes and collapses upon itself, it forms what is known as a black hole. It is believed that within black holes there is a point called a singularity, similar to the one that started the Big Bang and the one emanated by the Ain Soph to create the universe. Within this singularity all physical laws cease to exist. It has been theorized that beyond each singularity there may be a tunnel that leads to another universe. As there are innumerable black holes in our visible universe, there is the definite possibility that there may be a vast amount of universes beyond our own.

Well-known astrophysicist Martin Rees says that our universe may be just one element, one atom, in an infinite ensemble that he calls a cosmic archipelago. Each universe starts with its own Big Bang, develops its own physical laws, and determines its own cosmic cycle. He adds that the Big Bang that started our own universe is, in this grander perspective, an infinitesimal part of an elaborate structure that extends far beyond the range of any telescope.

There is also the cosmic inflation theory proposed by MIT physicist Alan Guth. According to Guth, the cosmic inflation that was one of the results of the Big Bang is an ongoing process throughout the universe. This inflation is causing different regions of the cosmos to break away, evolving into separate universes.

Around the beginning of the new millennium, science still scoffed at the idea of a multiverse. Then physicists discovered dark energy. What astonished them about the new finding was not that it existed, but that it should exist in such specific quantity that it would allow the universe to continue being.

As we have seen, dark energy is creating space between galaxies, stars, and planets but is not ripping them apart. "If dark energy had been any bigger, there would have been enough repulsion from it to overwhelm the gravity that drew galaxies and stars together, and we wouldn't be here right now to talk about it," says Stanford physicist Leonard Susskind. "It's one of the great mysteries of physics." Nobel laureate Steven Weinberg agrees. "This is the one fine-tuning that seems to be extreme, far beyond what you could imagine just having to accept as a mere accident" (see Folger 2008).

Dark energy makes it impossible to ignore the multiverse theory. Another branch of physics, String Theory, supports it as well. Einstein discovered that our three dimensions of space are linked with a fourth dimension, which is time; thus the concept of space-time was created. Recently, String Theory has begun to study the possibility of additional dimensions beyond ordinary space-time. They calculate that these new dimensions have a range of ten spacial dimensions and one time dimension that links them together. We cannot see these dimensions because we exist in a three-dimensional world and cannot perceive other realities (see Woit 2001).

. . . .

According to String Theory, the ultimate blocks of physical reality are not particles but minuscule vibrating strings whose different oscillations give rise to all the particles and forces in the universe. Many physicists believe that String Theory is another clue that the multiverse is real. Susskind, a leading proponent of this view, thinks that the various versions of String Theory may describe different universes that are all real (see Susskind 2005).

The concepts of the multiverse and the ten dimensions of String Theory are in accordance with the four kabbalistic worlds and the Tree of Life. These four worlds are infinite in scope and, as such, can emanate an infinity of universes. As God is infinite, so must be his creation.

One of the most exacting principles of String Theory is that in order for the strings to work, they must be ten-dimensional. The sephiroth of the Tree of Life, which are vibrating constantly like the strings, are also ten in number. Like the strings in String Theory, they cannot be perceived by us because they exist in another state of being, in another dimension.

These parallels between science and Kabbalah cannot be coincidence. The various theories of physics and the teachings of Kabbalah blend harmoniously together "like large and melodious thoughts." And as Jung said, there are no coincidences, only synchronized events.

CHAPTER 6

The World of Matter

*Some part of the human Self or Soul is not
subject to the laws of space and time.*

CARL GUSTAV JUNG

The world of matter is Assiah. It is composed of the entire universe and of Earth itself. As we have seen, science believes that there may be many universes and at least ten dimensions, which may be identified with the ten sephiroth of the Tree of Life.

In this universe Earth is a rare occurrence for, as far as we know, it is the only one that harbors intelligent life. Many exoplanets—planets orbiting stars other than our sun—have been identified. At last count 463 such planets have been discovered, but none of them has complex life forms. That does not mean there are no planets with intelligent life in the universe; we simply have not found any yet.

Earth is around 4.5 billion years old. It formed, together with the rest of the solar system, from a rotating cloud of interstellar dust and gas called the solar nebula. This nebula was composed of hydrogen and helium (created shortly after the Big Bang) and heavier elements ejected by exploding stars known as supernovas. The nebula rotated around the sun, which had been created around 300 million years earlier, and eventually condensed into the planets of the solar system, including Earth.

Details about the origin of life on Earth are unknown. There are two schools of thoughts about the subject. One is the Panspermia Theory, according to which organic compounds leading to life arrived on Earth from outer space. The other says that life originated on Earth. The best-known proponent of the Panspermia Theory was noted astronomer Sir Fred Hoyle, who coined the term Big Bang.

Despite their different views on the origin of life, both theories agree on several points. In order for intelligent living organisms to exist on a planet, that planet must have water, an atmosphere, and oxygen, and it also must have algae, which produce the oxygen. There must be an interaction between plant and animal life, because animals produce carbon dioxide upon exhaling and plants transform the carbon dioxide into oxygen. This is a continuous cycle that ensures the lives of both plants and animals.

The planet must also have tectonic plates that ensure the creation of continents upon the surface of oceans. It must be at a perfect distance from its central star; in our case, the sun. If it is too near it will boil, vaporize, or burn itself. If it is too far, it will freeze. It must have a satellite, like our moon, to regulate the tides and the liquids of the body. It also must have larger planets beyond it to shield it from severe meteorite bombardment. In our case, the planets Saturn and Jupiter (especially Jupiter) act as such shields.

But even with all these elements in place, it is still impossible to determine how life itself originated on Earth. The idea that there may be other planets like ours in the universe is the subject of much scientific debate.

In an explosive book titled *Rare Earth*, Peter D. Ward, a paleontologist and professor of geological science at Washington University in Seattle, and Donald Brownlee, a professor of astronomy also at Washington University and principal investigator at NASA's Stardust Mission, present the view that Earth is a unique occurrence in the universe and that the likelihood of intelligent life like that of humanity elsewhere in the universe is very unlikely. According to them, there may be life in the form of bacteria or spores in the cosmos, but human intelligence such as ours is highly improbable (see Ward and Brownlee 2003).

People who believe in extraterrestrials and UFOs may find these allegations difficult to accept. But they may find consolation in the fact that such unearthly visitors may be coming from our distant future in the form of time travel or perhaps from one of the ten dimensions described in String Theory.

The concept of a "rare earth," and of humanity as an even rarer occurrence, is in essential agreement with the kabbalistic views of creation. There are other universes (the four kabbalistic worlds and their outpourings) and there are ten dimensions (the ten sephiroth of the Tree of Life), but Earth itself is a very especial creation, and human beings are spiritual and physical prototypes that are meant to evolve exponentially and to eventually disseminate the human race to other worlds and throughout the universe. According to the Kabbalah, hat is why humanity was created.

The concept of life, especially human life, leads inevitably to the concept of death, because life and death are parts of a cycle. But what happens after death? Does the personality survive physical death? If we think of personality as the soul, the answer is yes. This is one of the central tenets of the Kabbalah. Not only does the soul survive the death of the body, but it will return to Earth in another body through the process known as reincarnation. This only happens if the soul has not completed its mission, or *tikkun*. Once it has completed its *tikkun*, it is free from the human coil and can return to God's light.

Several years ago a woman from the Midwest started to speak with a Swedish accent, with Swedish words interspersed in her speech. This happened after an accident where she suffered a brain concussion. Doctors

. . . .

could not explain the phenomenon, but they say it is not a unique case. There are many people who develop the same changes in their speech, which is known scientifically as Foreign Accent Syndrome. In the case of the woman who began to speak with a Swedish accent, it is believed that the brain concussion released an ancestral memory where perhaps one of her ancestors was Swedish (see Gurd 1998).

There are many cases of people who speak in tongues. The Bible refers to this phenomenon in Acts 2, 10:46 and 19:6; Mark 16:17; and I Corinthians 12:14 and 14:14. This is known as *xenoglossia*, a Greek word meaning "foreign tongue." There are African tribes, tribes in Borneo and Indonesia, and sects in Japan that also speak strange tongues. Pentecostals and Charismatics speak in tongues when they fall into trances, and they believe the language they speak is the language of angels. These languages may very well have existed in the ancient past or in the times of the Phoenicians or Babylonians, and their occurence may support the idea of reincarnation.

When a person dies, he or she is said to go in the area known as the astral light or astral plane. This is the same place we go during sleep. That is why sometimes we dream with loved ones who have passed away or with people who are alive. It is the meeting place of souls, both incarnated and disincarnated.

Very often when we dream with a person who has died, we see stars, a sort of strange light, emanating from their eyes. This also may happen when a person is close to death—we see strange lights flowing from their eyes. I have seen this only once, in a nine-month-old baby who was very ill with cancer of the kidneys. One day I was sitting with him and I saw stars in his eyes. Then he put out his tiny hand and bent his small fingers up and down several times as if he were waving goodbye. I was devastated because I knew he was leaving us and he was letting me know. He died later that night. I had lit a candle to Archangel Raphael, asking him to heal the baby, and when I learned he had died I decided to put it out. But just as I reached my hand toward the candle, the flame wavered very gently and went out by itself. I knew this was Raphael's way of telling me this child had completed his *tikkun* and had returned to God's light. In the early hours of the morning, still grieving over the baby's death, I suddenly heard a rush of wings and the sound of kisses blown outside my window. To me, this was his final goodbye.

Survival of death has been the subject of many studies, some of which I discuss in my book *What Happens After Death*. Sometimes people who die may appear in dreams to those who knew them to let them know of their passing. Many years ago I dreamt that my mother's personal physician was lying atop a large white sarcophagus. He was wearing a long white gown. As I approached the sarcophagus, he sat up and started to walk toward me. I was so terrified that I woke up trembling and covered with sweat. When I looked at the clock, I saw that it was 4:30 in the morning. I could not get back to sleep. I told the dream to my mother as soon as she was up and asked her to call the doctor's home to inquire about his health, as he had not been feeling well. The telephone rang for a very long time, and finally the doctor's wife answered it. She then told my mother the doctor had died in the early morning—at exactly 4:30.

There are two spheres that are connected with death and reincarnation. They are Geburah and Chesed. Geburah represents the Shemamphora, the 72 names of God of three letters each. In Geburah the 72 names are multiplied by three, equaling 216. This is Geburah's number. The 72 names are also represented by Chesed but they are not multiplied by three. Thus Chesed's number is 72. When Geburah and Chesed unite, their numbers are added and equal 288, which is the number of sparks that fell to the Qlipoth when the spheres were shattered.

Through the combined work of these two spheres, the sparks can be redeemed so they may return to the Creator. This is also the mystery of death and reincarnation.

As long as there are sparks trapped in the Qlipoth, humanity's mission is not completed. It takes the combined effort of many souls to redeem just one spark. Whenever a human being commits an injustice or an act of cruelty or destruction, he or she drives the sparks deeper into the Qlipoth. This prolongs not only the sufferings of the world of the living but also of those who have died. They must return to Earth in new incarnations to continue the rescue of the sparks. This is the adverse aspect of Geburah. Conversely, each act of kindness and generosity, each word of compassion, helps to elevate the sparks and thus bring greater peace and healing to the world and hope to our souls and the souls of those who have died. This is Chesed in action. That is why human *tikkun* begins in Chesed, which is compassion, and ends in Geburah, which is divine justice.

The zodiac sign that is ruling when a person dies indicates the evolutionary state of that person's soul and what is left of their mission. That is the same sign that person is going to be born under if they have not finished their *tikkun* and have to reincarnate. What the sign rules is what that soul has to perfect in its new incarnation. It also indicates what influenced the person's death and the tests and sufferings they endured during their lifetime. The angel that rules the sign under which a person dies is the angel to whom we must pray to help their soul reach a higher level of evolution.

Following is a list of the zodiac signs and the angels who rule them.

ARIES—Kamael

TAURUS—Anael

GEMINI—Raphael

CANCER—Gabriel

LEO—Michael

VIRGO—Raphael

LIBRA—Hanael

SCORPIO—Azrael

SAGITTARIUS—Zadkiel

CAPRICORN—Cassiel

AQUARIUS—Uriel

PISCES—Asariel

According to certain kabbalistic teachings, the element that rules the sign under which a person dies indicates whether or not that soul will be reincarnated.

SIGNS OF FIRE (ARIES, LEO, SAGITTARIUS)——Very often these people do not return if they are highly evolved. If they reincarnate they suffer greatly, and their new incarnation is usually very short, as they often complete their *tikkun* in that lifetime. If they are not highly evolved, their new incarnation may be long and painful, because they are offered the opportunity to complete their mission so they do not have to return. The souls of very evil or destructive individuals who die under a fire sign may go directly to the Qlipoth or be disintegrated if the soul is beyond redemption. Sometimes these souls are given the possibility of purification through many cycles of very painful incarnations.

SIGNS OF EARTH (TAURUS, VIRGO, CAPRICORN)——Generally people who die under these signs are reincarnated again very quickly. The new incarnation is usually very long and offers many opportunities of purification but also many temptations to test the soul's determination to finish its *tikkun*. The souls of very evil individuals who die under these signs are often without redemption and are sent to the Qlipoth or disintegrated.

SIGNS OF AIR (GEMINI, LIBRA, AQUARIUS)——These souls return very rarely if they are highly evolved. Otherwise they may have to reincarnate many times. The souls of very evil people who die under these signs are either sent to the Qlipoth or allowed to reincarnate in the form of lower species and work their way back to the human state. This is a long process that requires multiple reincarnations.

SIGNS OF WATER (CANCER, SCORPIO, PISCES)——They usually reincarnate with many family complications, especially with their children, in their new lives. If they suffer greatly before dying in

. . . .

a water sign, these souls evolve rapidly and do not reincarnate. If they return they live existences where they can do a lot of good for the world and humanity. Many people who die under a water sign return as great teachers and philanthropists. The souls of very evil people who die in a water sign are sent to the Qlipoth or disintegrated if they are beyond redemption.

People who are born and die in the same sign do not reincarnate if they are highly evolved or did many good actions while on Earth. These souls go directly into God's light. If they led dissolute lives or committed many evil acts during their lives on Earth, they do not reincarnate; they either go to the Qlipoth or are disintegrated. This happens because when they are born and die in the same sign, these souls embrace the twelve zodiac signs. They are fully aware of the importance of their actions, which usually affect all of humanity. This is particularly true of people who were born and died in earth signs. Two examples of people who were born and died under earth signs are Mother Teresa and Adolph Hitler. Mother Teresa was born and died under the sign of Virgo. Hitler was born and died under the sign of Taurus.

Another case of someone who was born and died in the same sign is that of Elizabeth Bathory, the "Blood Countess," who was said to have murdered hundreds of young women for the purpose of bathing in their blood to retain her youth and beauty. It is now an accepted fact that she could not have done this, as the blood of her victims would have coagulated before she could bathe in it. Also, King Mathias of Hungary, who instigated the investigation and subsequent trial of Bathory, was deeply in debt to her and could not repay the moneys he had borrowed. It is therefore possible that the accusations leveled against her were fabricated. There are also proven accounts of the help she extended to many women who were destitute or who were sexually abused. It would have been therefore out of character for her to carry on abuses against women. If Bathory was guilty of the crimes she was accused of, she was indeed a monster. If she was innocent of these accusations, she was a martyr. If guilty, she would have been a candidate for the Qlipoth. If innocent, she would have been received into the light. In either case, she would not reincarnate again. Elizabeth Bathory was born and died in the sign of Leo.

When a person dies in a sign before or after the sign in which they were born, and they were highly evolved or did many good actions for the benefit of humankind, they are deemed great souls and become part of the light of the galactic center. These are souls of such immense power that they help illuminate the entire solar system and are the source of innumerable stars. This is particularly true if they die in the sign of Aries, which is the first sign of the zodiac. Examples of such individuals are Albert Einstein, who was born in Pisces and died in Aries, and Pope John Paul II, who was born in Taurus and died in Aries. Persons who die in the sign before or after they were born and led normal lives are said to reincarnate in that sign for a very short time, as they are given the opportunity to complete their mission, rectify their weaknesses, and return to the light. Those who did a great deal of evil are either sent to the Qlipoth or disintegrated.

The philosophical term for reincarnation is metempsychosis; it is also known as the transmigration of souls. The reincarnation of a soul in another human body or the body of an animal or lower form is known as *gilgul hanefesh* and *gilgul neshamot*. *Gilgul* means "to roll over." The idea is that the soul rolls over from one body to the next through different incarnations. Reincarnation is not discussed in the Bible or the Talmud, but the Zohar, the most important of the kabbalistic treatises, refers to it in several of its passages. According to the great kabbalist Nahmanides, who lived in the twelfth century CE, reincarnation is a great mystery and the principal key to the understanding of many biblical passages.

Kabbalah teaches that many sins are punished through reincarnation. For example, the souls of very evil or cruel people may reincarnate as animals until their sins are rectified. The word *rectification* is very important in this doctrine. The entire process of reincarnation is

. . . .

directed toward rectification—that is, to the correction and purification of errors or sins. On the other hand, highly illuminated or evolved souls may reincarnate as persons equally illuminated or of higher illumination. It is said that Abel, who was killed by his brother Cain, was reincarnated as Moses. Cain, after many cycles of purification, was reincarnated as Jethro, the brother of Moses. The great love and harmony that existed between Moses and Jethro rectified the tragedy of Abel and Cain.

There are three types of reincarnation:

GILGUL—when a soul is reincarnated in a new body

IBBUR—this is known as impregnation, when a soul descends
    from Heaven to assist another soul who is already incarnated;
    this means that two souls are inhabiting the same body,
    and the second soul is always very highly evolved

DYBBUK—in this case, an evil spirit is chased by infernal forces
    and enters or possesses a human body to escape the persecution;
    this destructive spirit has to be cleansed or exorcised

The great medieval kabbalist Isaac Luria discusses reincarnation at length in his treatise *The Gate of Reincarnations*. In this book he teaches that when God created Adam he infused him with a universal soul or spirit (*Neshamah kalit*). This universal soul contained all the aspects of creation. God asked each of the angels and animals he created to give a part of their essence to Adam's spirit, which also contained all the human souls, incarnated or disincarnated. When Adam ate of the forbidden tree, his soul was fragmented into billions of sparks that fell down to the bottom of the Qlipoth and joined the 288 sparks already there. This answers the fundamental question of where souls come from.

There were only a few souls at the beginning of human evolution, then there were thousands, then there were millions, and now there are over six billion souls incarnated on Earth, and millions are incarnated every year. How can a few thousand souls reincarnate into millions, and how can millions reincarnate into billions? What is the source of all these souls? The answer is that they come from the Qlipoth. All of our souls originated in the Qlipoth through the process of *tikkun*, or rectification. They are the sparks that resulted from the fragmentation of Adam's soul.

This is a secret teaching few kabbalists are willing to reveal, but it is the answer to the origin of souls. We do not come from above but from below—a rather disturbing and sobering account of our souls' early beginnings.

This concept explains our physical and spiritual evolution in very clear and logical terms. The first time a soul incarnates, such as in the body of a Neanderthal man, what is born is the darkest, most primitive aspect of Adam's fragmented soul, still reeking with the darkness of the Abyss. As these early souls continued to reincarnate, they evolved both physically and spiritually, growing in intelligence and human perception.

Through successive reincarnations they continued to rectify and purify their essence. Five thousand years ago we had already developed the concepts of agriculture, metal working, writing, and the first swirls of science, mathematics, and religion.

Unfortunately, in every generation are also born abominable souls, capable of terrible crimes and atrocities. Why? Because it is the first time they have incarnated, and they are still in the realm of the animal soul—as yet unaware of the light of love and reason, totally devoid of conscience. In our times and in future times these as-yet unborn and chaotic souls will continue to emerge from the Qlipoth to our anguish and dismay. That is why *tikkun* is so important. Through our own efforts and our own actions we can elevate and purify these souls before they are born. It is in our hands to avoid the emergence of another Hitler or another Attila the Hun. We can still be victimized by our own lower passions, which are part of our Adamic nature, and become a danger to our society and to our own spiritual evolution.

Eventually, if we persevere across thousands of years, all these sparks will be rescued and purified. Because—and this is an important part of this doctrine—there is only a certain amount of sparks in Adam's fragmented soul. Nobody knows how many exist—ten billion, twenty billion, a hundred billion, no one knows for sure. When they are gone, there can be no more births or reincarnations. But if we continue to evolve spiritually and carry on our *tikkun*, one day all these sparks—our own included—will return to their original source, the Ain Soph Aur.

It is interesting that in the Kabbalah the angel of reincarnation is called Duma, who is considered by many kabbalists to be a dark angel. The reason Duma is considered a dark force is that the process of reincarnation entails many sufferings, because there can be no life without affliction and sorrow.

The human body is a vessel known in Kabbalah as the *Guf*. It is an empty shell until it is inhabited by the soul, which has five parts (see appendix 6, figure 8). These parts are:

YESHIDAH——The highest of the soul's divisions, it is archetypal
    in nature and corresponds to the World of Adam Kadmon.

CHAYA——Also archetypal in nature, it corresponds to
    Atziluth, the World of Emanation. Both Yeshidah
    and Chaya are beyond human reach.

The next three divisions are known as the three "elements of the soul."

NESHAMAH——This is the Higher Self and comprises the first three
    sephiroth of the Tree of Life: Kether, Chokmah, and Binah. It can
    only be reached through Binah. *Neshamah* resides in the brain.

RUACH——This is known as "spirit" and comprises the next six
    sephiroth: Chesed, Geburah, Tiphareth, Netzach, Hod, and
    Yesod. It is the seat of human emotions and resides in the heart.

NEPHESH——This the human lower nature, the instincts, and is
    assigned the tenth and last sphere, Malkuth, which it shares
    with the *Guf*, or human body. It resides in the liver.

Neshamah is the source; it represents intelligence or knowledge. *Ruach* is the incentive to action. *Nephesh* is the power of life that gives movement to the parts of the body. Thus every act must begin in the brain (*Neshamah*), transmitted to the heart (*Ruach*), and finally to the organs that bring the act to completion (*Nephesh*), because the body (*Guf*) has no volition or power to move by itself. *Ruach* is also seen as the will, the force that makes every action possible.

Interestingly enough, these three "elements" of the body are very similar to the Jungian concepts of the Self, the Psyche, and the Shadow.

Every human life is a struggle between the lower instincts (represented by the *Nephesh*) and the higher feelings and emotions (represented by the *Ruach*). Only through the control of the *Nephesh* can we evolve and rise to higher states of being. Nephesh is the animal part of our bodies, whose only interest is the satisfaction of its instincts. People with little or no self-control are slaves of the *Nephesh*. It is the *Nephesh* that tempts people to eat and drink in excess, to give in to sexual excesses and immoral behavior, and makes us react irrationally and exhibit antisocial behavior and even commit crimes. For that reason, the first thing we must do to achieve any success in magic or in contacting angelic forces is try to control the *Nephesh*. There are simple exercises that kabbalists teach for this purpose:

1. Prepare your favorite food and then throw it away or let somebody else in your family eat it.

2. Buy a beautiful outfit that you really love and then give it away to a friend or family member.

3. Avoid seeing your favorite television program for several weeks.

4. If you are a coffee drinker and do not like tea, drink tea for a week.

These are only some of the ways through which you can teach the *Nephesh* it must obey you and do what you ask it to do. If you do not control the *Nephesh*, you cannot do angel magic or any kind of magic, which is why so many magic rituals and spells fail. This does not mean that the *Nephesh* is evil; on the contrary, it is the force that keeps us alive. The

Nephesh tells us when we must eat or drink liquids, when we must rest, when we must perform all of our bodily functions. It also regulates the workings of the entire body; it is, therefore, vital for our survival. But it must be carefully trained to do our will. It must never control our minds or our actions. When it does, it supersedes the positive influence of both the *Ruach* and the *Neshamah* and interrupts our spiritual evolution.

It is said that because there is so much suffering and chaos in the world due to the fallen sparks and the presence of so many destructive forces in our midst, God decided to place a highly evolved group of souls on the Earth. They are called the Lamed Vovniks, a term derived from the Hebrew letters Lamed and Vau. Lamed has a value of thirty, and Vau has a value of six; therefore, there are thirty-six Lamed Vovniks in the world. God decreed that as long as there are thirty-six perfectly good people on the planet, the world will continue to exist. If the number falls below thirty-six, even by one, the world will end. The Lamed Vovnik can be anyone—a street cleaner, a pauper, a millionaire, or a movie star. What these people have in common is their intrinsic goodness and their deep empathy with the world's sufferings. Lamed Vovniks seek to ameliorate all suffering, both animal and human. They cry when someone is in pain and rejoice when they see someone happy. Some of these people may be very old and some may still be at their mothers' breast, for God changes them every two years, but together they ensure the safety of our world. No one knows who they are, not even themselves, because they are too good and too humble to count themselves among God's Chosen. But it is their gracious and gentle presence on this planet that sustains us in our daily strife.

CHAPTER 7

God Geometrizes

Plato said God geometrizes continuously.

. . . .

PLUTARCH

T he belief that God created the universe through geometry is traced back to Plato, who had such faith in the divine origins of this branch of mathematics that he placed a sign over the gate to his academy that read, "Only he who is familiar with geometry will be admitted here." To Plato, geometry was sacred.

Sacred geometry is used in the planning and construction of religious structures such as churches, mosques, temples, altars, and other religious structures. Also, in sacred geometry symbolic and divine meanings are given to some geometric shapes and proportions. The basis of sacred geometry is the golden ratio, also known as the God ratio, the golden section, or the golden mean.

The golden ratio is an irrational mathematical constant with a value of approximately 1.6180339887. It is considered an irrational number because the best rational approximations to it are as inaccurate as is

. . . .

mathematically possible. It is often denoted by the Greek letter phi. It is interesting to note that the word philosophy, from the Greek *philosophia*, means "the wisdom of phi."

Euclid (325–265 BCE), in his famous work *Elements*, was the first Greek mathematician to give a definition of the golden ratio, which he called an "extreme and mean ratio." But it was nearly fifteen centuries later that Italian mathematician Leonardo Fibonacci gave the numerical sequence that results in the golden ratio. The Fibonacci sequence is generated by adding the previous two numbers in a consecutive series to form the next number in that series—for example, 1, 1, 2, 3, 5, 8, 13, 21, 34, and so on. If one divides any number in the Fibonacci series by the one preceding it, the answer is always 1.6180339887, which is the golden ratio.

The golden ratio is found in many natural forms, like sunflowers, snowflakes, the chambered nautilus shell, a bee honeycomb, tree branches, DNA base sequences and gene sequences, diamond crystals, and spiral galaxies. It is also found in architecture, such as the Acropolis, including the Parthenon, and the Egyptian pyramids. Many painters, like Leonardo da Vinci in *The Last Supper* and Salvador Dali in *The Sacrament of the Last Supper*, used the golden ratio in the composition of their masterpieces. Many composers, notably Debussy in *La Mer* and Chopin in his nocturnes and etudes, based their music on the golden ratio. No one knows if the composers consciously sought such proportions in their works or if they used them because of their intrinsic harmony. Even in investment strategies, some practitioners of technical analysis use the golden ratio to indicate support of a price level or resistance to price increases of a stock or commodity.

Modern scholars rejected the concept of the golden ratio until professor Robert Moon at the University of Chicago showed that the entire periodic table of elements is based on some of the geometrical forms ruled by the golden ratio. In recent years it has pervaded new concepts such as String Theory and the idea of multiple universes (see Rawles 1997).

One of the geometrical forms that shows a perfect connection to the golden ratio is the pentagram, one of the most popular symbols in occultism. The pentagram includes ten isosceles triangles, five acute and five obtuse (see appendix 6, figure 9). In all of them, the ratio of the longer side to the shorter side is phi, or the golden ratio. The pentagram was the symbol of Pythagoras.

Among the most prevalent traditional geometric forms ascribed to sacred geometry are the sine wave, the sphere, the vesica piscis, the golden spiral, fractals, the five Platonic solids (see appendix 6, figure 11), and the star tetrahedron. This last form is composed of two oppositely oriented and interpenetrating tetrahedrons, which is known as the *Merkabah*, or God's chariot. Therefore we can establish a connection between sacred geometry and Ezekiel's vision. As we saw in the introduction, Ezekiel's vision of the *Merkabah* is the richest and most descriptive of all the encounters and descriptions of angels in the Bible.

The Kabbalah teaches that we can only reach God through the angels. The angels were emanated from God, and only through them can we receive the Glory of God, who is in Atziluth. Every time God speaks, each of his words, each sound, is an angel. This does not mean that God creates a new angel with each word. The angels are in God, and when he speaks, one of his angels is projected outside him and brings us that word or message. Each angel has its own individuality but exists continuously within the Divine Essence. Not only each word, but each act of God takes place through one or more of his angels.

The Bible speaks of various prophets who receive divine visions. The two most exalted of these prophets were Moses and Isaiah, but Moses was the closest to God. The first five books of the Bible are known as the Pentateuch. They are also known as the Torah or the Law and were said to have been written by Moses. Of these, the most important is Deuteronomy because it was the Shekinah herself, God's feminine aspect, who gave this book to Moses.

Deuteronomy is the last book of the Pentateuch. Its last versicle (Deuteronomy 34:10) says, "Never since has there arisen a prophet in Israel like Moses, whom the LORD knew face to face." This name of God, as we saw earlier, refers to Adonai, which signifies ownership of everything that exists. Adonai is one of the names associated with the Shekinah, to whom belongs all that exists. In the tenth sphere of the Tree of Life, Malkuth, the given name of God is Adonai Ha Aretz, or LORD of the Earth. The Shekinah resides in Malkuth. All the prophets who were called to serve God received this call to service directly from Adonai. It was therefore Adonai, the Shekinah, who gave Deuteronomy to Moses, who was the only prophet to speak to God "face to face." The other four books of the Torah—Genesis, Exodus, Leviticus, and Numbers—were given to Moses through the angels.

In Sinai Moses reached the highest level of prophecy among all prophets because he perceived God directly, the Glory of Atziluth, through Briah.

The medium through which prophets receive their visions is called *ispaklaria*. In most of the prophets the ispaklaria is not brilliant but opaque. Only in Moses is the ispaklaria shining and clear. That is because he receives his visions of Atziluth through a crystal, which is Briah. The other prophets see their visions through a mirror, a reflection, which is Yetzirah, the world inhabited by the angels, who bring God's words and visions to them.

Ezekiel prophesied in Babylonia before the destruction of the first temple. The book of Ezekiel has forty-seven chapters, but the only chapter that describes the full vision is the first chapter (Ezekiel 1:1). Ezekiel does not mention the *Merkabah* in this chapter. He only describes the angels or living creatures that form the *Merkabah*.

In the first versicle, Ezekiel refers to himself in the first person: "In the thirtieth year, in the first month, on the fifth day of the month, I was among the exiles by the river Chebar, the heavens were opened and I saw visions of God (Elohim)."

In the second versicle, he refers to himself in the third person: "On the fifth day of the month…the word of the LORD (Adonai) came to the priest Ezekiel…"

This means that in the first versicle Ezekiel is speaking from within himself, in his conscious personality, whereas in the second versicle he has momentarily disconnected from the world of matter and is speaking from outside himself, as if he were another person. He is in Adonai's sphere, which is outside the physical world. In the rest of the chapter he reverses to the first person because Adonai has restored him to his conscious self so he may perceive the vision.

Ezekiel then proceeds to describe three things: a stormy wind that came from the north, a great cloud with brightness around it, and fire flashing forth continuously. In the middle of this fire he sees something like gleaming amber, and it is within the gleaming amber that he sees the four angels, the Chayot, or Living Creatures. Each has four wings, two of which are extended and touch the wings next to them, forming a square. They always move in a straight line forwards, backwards, and to the sides, but they never turn. Each has a different visage: a man's face that always looks to the front, the face of a lion on the right side, the face of an ox on the left side, and the face of an eagle behind. These are Throne angels and represent the four elements (air, fire, earth, and water) and the four seasons, which combined are the basis of the material world.

Beneath each of the Chayot there is something that looks like a wheel within a wheel, all covered with many eyes. These are the *Ophanim* angels that always move with the Chayot. The *Ophanim* are identified with the Cherubim. But Ezekiel mentions something else. In the middle of the Throne angels there are burning coals of fire, like torches moving to and fro among them. The fire is bright, and lightning issues from it. These fire torches are the Seraphim, which have been described as Serpents of fire. They are the highest order of angels and are always near God's throne.

The four Thrones and the four Wheels form a star tetrahedron. A normal tetrahedron is one of the five Platonic solids (see appendix 6, figure

11) and is a three-dimensional triangle with four sides, made of three sides and a bottom. When two tetrahedrons interconnect, they form a star tetrahedron, which is a three-dimensional Star of David (see appendix 6, figure 10). Therefore the geometrical shape of God's chariot, or *Merkabah*, is a Star of David in three-dimensional space. The first tetrahedron is in Yetzirah, the World of Formation, where angels abide. The second tetrahedron is in Assiah, the World of Matter, where Ezekiel exists. It is from the World of Formation that matter comes into being. Thus the three-dimensional Star of David, the *Merkabah*, is the basis for the physical world.

As we saw, the first three things described by Ezekiel are a stormy wind, a great cloud, and a flashing fire. The stormy wind is the air element, the great cloud is the water element, and the flashing fire is the fire element. The earth element is not part of the vision because it is represented by the physical world. These three elements represent the material barriers that prevent us from reaching the spiritual dimension.

In order to enter the prophetic state, it is necessary to meditate. Before meditation the mind is in a state of chaos. It is necessary to calm it down, emptying it of all thought. This is then followed by slowing the breathing. The stormy wind in Ezekiel's vision is the chaotic breathing before the meditative state. As one goes deeper into meditation, the mind is at rest; it does not think any longer. This is the second of Ezekiel's visions, the great cloud. The flashing fire is the third vision. When a person is in a deep meditative state, he or she feels naked in the face of God. All the good actions and the bad actions come rushing out of the unconscious. The good actions fill the person's soul with joy, while the evil acts fill it with shame. This shame burns the soul in a fire of repentance for its sins. The burning shame is the flashing fire in Ezekiel's third vision, which cleanses the soul of its impurities.

At this point the soul sees "the gleaming amber," the *Chasmal*, which is the light of God. It is in the midst of the Chasmal that Ezekiel sees the four Living Creatures—the Chayoth—and the vision of the *Merkabah*.

. . . .

The Chasmal is known as the silence that speaks. It is the Glory of God, Jehovah, and it is called the silence that speaks because Jehovah, who inhabits the silence, speaks to Ezekiel (Ezekiel 1:28), and the words he speaks are angels.

Above the *Merkabah* Ezekiel sees a dome of blinding light, and upon it is the throne of God, made of a single sapphire. The Glory of God is upon the throne, and Ezekiel describes it as shining like brilliant copper, so bright it resembles fire. The Chayot and the Wheels move the *Merkabah*, constantly ascending and descending, forever in motion, while the Seraphim encircle them with their fire and lightning. But it is God (the LORD Jehovah) who is directing the angels' motions. It is his will that determines the movements of the chariot, which represents God's manifestations in the physical world through the four elements and the four seasons.

Ezekiel's vision is a revelation of how God created the four worlds (Atziluth, Briah, Yetzirah, and Assiah) in descending order through the motions of three of the angelic choirs: the Seraphim, the Chayot, and the *Ophanim*. These are the rulers of the first three spheres of the Tree of Life: Kether, Chokmah, and Binah. The sapphire throne refers to the fourth sphere, Chesed, which emanates from the union of Chokmah and Binah. Chesed's attributed color is deep blue, the color of sapphire. The numbers three and four appear repeatedly in the vision because they represent the four sides of the three-dimensional star tetrahedron.

We saw earlier that the tetrahedron is one of the five Platonic solids, which are among the forms of sacred geometry. These are known collectively as polyhedra. The five polyhedra are the tetrahedron (which is the four-sided triangle and the simplest form), the cube with six sides, the octahedron with eight sides, the dodecahedron with twelve sides, and the icosahedron with twenty sides. They are the primal models of crystal patterns that occur throughout the world of minerals in countless variations and in many other natural forms, such as viruses like herpes.

The golden ratio occurs very often in the Platonic solids. Although they bear Plato's name, it is now known that he was not the first to describe the five solids, or polyhedra. That description is now ascribed to another Greek mathematician called Theaetetus, who was a friend of Plato's.

In any case, Plato was very impressed with the five solids because they constitute the only perfectly symmetrical arrangement of a set of points in space. So impressed was he that he expounded a "theory of everything" in his treatise *Timaeus*, which is based explicitly on the five solids. Nearly 2,000 years later, Johannes Kepler was equally fascinated by the five polyhedra and developed his own cosmology based on them.

In *Timaeus*, Plato chose to constitute these solids from right angles, which he equated with the "subatomic particles" in his theory of everything. From this he determined that the tetrahedron, the octahedron, and icosahedron consisted of 24, 48, and 120 triangles, respectively. If the basic triangles were the subatomic particles, he concluded that the polyhedra were the atoms or corpuscles of the various substances in the universe. One of the intriguing aspects of Plato's theory is that he believed that it was possible for the subatomic particles to split and recombine into other kinds of atoms, which is at the core of modern physics.

We can find echoes of Plato's ideas in Isaac Newton's corpuscular theory. Newton's comments about the "sides" of light particles are very reminiscent of Plato's descriptions in *Timaeus*. In Newton's *Principia* he says that "all the diversity of created things, each in its place and time, could only have arisen from the ideas and the will of a necessarily existing being" (see Newton 2007).

Plato associated the cube, octahedron, icosahedron, tetrahedron, and dodecahedron with the elements earth, air, water, fire, and the cosmos (quintessence), respectively. In *Timaeus* he said, "God used the dodecahedron for the whole universe, embroidering figures on it." He also said that "although God did make use of the relevant auxiliary causes, it was he himself who gave their fair design to all that comes to be. That is why we must distinguish two forms of causes, the divine and the necessary."

Timaeus contains a very detailed discussion of virtually all aspects of physical existence, including biology, cosmology, geography, chemistry, physics, and psychological perceptions, all expressed on the four basic elements and their transmutations by means of the constituent triangles of the five Platonic solids. It is strikingly similar in its combinatorial and numerological aspects to some modern speculative theories of every thing, as well as expressing ideas that have obvious counterparts in modern chemistry and the Periodic Table of Elements.

The five Platonic solids and Plato's theory of everything, which is based on them, can be delineated in a mysterious and mystical template known as Metatron's cube. In early kabbalist scriptures, Metatron is said to have formed this cube from his soul. The cube can be later seen in Christian art, where it appears on his chest or floating behind him. It is considered a holy glyph and was often drawn around a person or placed on doors to ward off demons and satanic forces. In alchemy, the cube was seen as a containment or creation circle.

Metatron's cube is made of thirteen circles. There are six circles on the outer rim of the figure, which can be connected to form two triangles, and six circles inside it, with a seventh circle in the middle. Each of the thirteen circles, referred to as nodes, are connected to the other nodes with a single line, creating a total of 78 lines, which are often linked with the 78 cards of the tarot deck. The lines connecting the outside circles form a hexagon. Lines extending inside the cube, connecting the six outer circles, form a clearly defined Star of David (see Orlov 2005).

Metatron's cube also contains two-dimensional images of the five Platonic solids and many other primal forms (see appendix 6, figure 12).

Some occultists believe that Metatron's cube is derived from the Fruit of Life, which is a geometrical figure composed of six outer circles and eight inner circles. This design then develops into the Flower of Life, with circles so evenly spaced that they form a pattern of many six-petalled flowers when the circles converge. The Tree of Life is also said to originate in this figure. The Fruit of Life and the Flower of Life were derived from the Seed of Life, which was formed on the sixth day of creation. On the first day of creation was formed the vesica piscis, two circles intertwined, representing the proton and electron of the hydrogen atom and the cosmic womb. The circles kept multiplying on each successive day until the sixth day, when the Seed of Life was finally formed. Metatron took this seed into his soul, where it produced the Fruit of Life and the Flower of Life. All the various geometrical forms that exist in the universe were then developed in his soul as Metatron's cube. This he presented to the Creator, who used it to create the universe. The final design was the Tree of Life (see appendix 6, figures 13, 14, 15, and 16).

Metatron is said to be the highest of angels, who serves as a celestial scribe and Chancellor of Heaven. He sits next to God in his throne and is often identified with the Shekinah. He is both a Seraph and an Archangel. He is identified as the "Lesser YHVH," or Lesser Tetragrammaton. The word *Metatron* is numerically equivalent to Shaddai, one of God's names, in the kabbalistic system known as gematria. He is said, therefore, to have a "Name Like His Master."

It is said of Metatron that he is the prince of the Divine Countenance, angel of the covenant, the logos, chief of the ministering angels, and the Supreme Angel of Death, to whom God gives daily instructions as to the souls he must take that day. He is also the teacher of prematurely dead children in paradise.

Metatron is the angel who led the children of Israel through the wilderness after the Exodus. He is the twin brother of Sandalphon and the tallest angel in Heaven after Anafiel. The twin angel brothers rule the first sphere of the Tree of Life (Kether—Metatron) and the tenth sphere (Malkuth—Sandalphon); therefore, they can be said to rule Heaven and Earth.

In Enoch 3, Enoch is brought to Heaven by Metatron. Enoch was later transformed into the great Archangel, equipped with thirty-six pairs of wings and innumerable eyes.

When he is invoked, Metatron appears as a pillar of fire, his face more dazzling than the sun. He is said to be the author of Psalm 37:25 and at least part of Isaiah 24:16.

According to Talmudic tradition, Metatron is an emanation of the "Cause of Causes," specifically the tenth and the last emanation, identified with the Earthly Divine Presence, or Shekinah. In earlier traditions, Metatron is said to have been created by God at the same time he created the universe. As soon as he was created as the Lesser Jehovah, Metatron formed his famed Cube from the depths of his soul and presented it to God. This became the matrix of Creation and that is why the geometric forms known as the Platonic solids are the foundation of all that exists.

Some kabbalists believe that Metatron was the seed of creation and that all the other angels emanated from him.

About a year ago I received a letter from one of my readers from Texas. This woman had read my book *Dreams and What They Mean to You* and wanted me to help her interpret a very disturbing dream she had had two years earlier.

In the dream she saw an immense angel with huge wings who floated high above the ground from the left to the right and up and down with terrifying speed. He was dressed in a short grey tunic with a longer white tunic underneath. He was barefoot. He did not speak to her, but she heard his voice in her mind. The voice sounded like rushing waters. It was not a human voice, and the name she heard sounded like Megatron.

Suddenly she saw three graves in a row in front of her. The grave on her right had a higher headstone than the other two. The angel moved forward and hovered over that grave for several minutes. Then he disappeared.

The dream impressed her badly and remained on her mind for several weeks, but after a while she forgot about it. Several months later, her oldest son, who was forty-four years old, died of renal failure. She then remembered the dream and understood its meaning. She had three children, the one who died and two others. She knew the three graves were her children's graves. The angel floated over the grave with the higher stone because it represented her oldest child. Now she feared for the lives of her two other children, whose graves she had also seen in the dream. After she read my book, she decided to write to me and ask me to interpret the dream and tell her if her two other children were in danger of dying.

I wrote her back and told her the angel in her dream was Metatron, who is known as the Supreme Angel of Death. He showed her three graves because she had three children, and he hovered over the one on the right with the larger headstone to tell her that the oldest of her three children was going to die. The other two were safe because Metatron did not approach their graves.

This woman had never heard of Metatron and does not know anything about the Kabbalah. Yet the angel revealed his name to her, even though she did not understand it correctly. He appeared to her dressed in a white tunic with a shorter grey one on top. White is the color of Kether, ruled by Metatron; grey is the color of Chokmah, the higher of the lower spheres through which Metatron could manifest. The name of God in Chokmah is Jehovah, and Metatron is known as the Lesser Jehovah; that is why he was dressed in white and grey. He floated rapidly from right to left and up and down because he belongs to the order of the Seraphim, who are the fire that fuels the *Merkabah*, whose angels move unceasingly.

God indeed geometrizes.

CHAPTER 8

Time and Space

I shall exist till the end of time,
for my being has no end.

. . . .

KAHLIL GIBRAN

Time and space were created simultaneously during the explosion of the Big Bang. As we have seen, the first element that was created as a result of this primordial explosion was hydrogen, which is composed of a proton (positive charge) and an electron (negative charge). The chemical symbol for hydrogen is H. This letter appears twice in the holy name of four letters, the Tetragrammaton, commonly spelled out as Jehovah. These four letters, transliterated from the Hebrew, are YHVH (Yod Heh Vau Heh).

The two Hs that are part of the Tetragrammaton can be equated with the proton and electron that form the hydrogen element. Yod is the point of light that started the process, and Vau is the cosmic "glue" that joined the other three creative principles. The meaning of Vau in Hebrew is "nail," something that unites and binds together.

. . . .

We can then see that Yod is the point of light emanated by God to create the universe, and the two Hs are the element hydrogen from which the universe evolved. Vau made this possible by binding the two Hs, proton and electron, together.

Time and space can be seen as two intersecting lines, vertical and horizontal, which also represent the proton and electron of the original hydrogen element. When these two lines meet, they form a cosmic cross.

The point where they intersect is the present. To the right of that point is the past, and to the left is the future. Because the universe is in constant motion, so is time. For that reason, the vertical line, time, that intersects the horizontal line, space, is always moving, which is why the present is a fleeting transition between past and future. It really does not exist. It vanishes like a wreath of smoke even as we are living it. We can try to measure it as a minute, a second, or an instant, but it does not have any substance except in our memories. Time is linear and moves inexorably forward along the space line, and we are hapless witnesses to its continuous motion, unable to capture it or detain it. The lines of time and space are so inextricably linked that modern science considers them a whole and calls them the space-time continuum (see appendix 6, figure 18). Time represents the electron that moves continuously around the proton in the nucleus of the hydrogen atom. The proton can be equated with space.

It is interesting to note that the gravitational force in a solar system that keeps planets revolving around their sun has the same mathematical equivalent as the electrical force between the positively charged proton in the nucleus of the hydrogen atom and the negatively charged electron that revolves around it. This is true of all atoms and shows that the universe follows an identical plan, from the tiny atom—which is the foundation of matter—to the solar systems, the galaxies, and the entire universe.

Electromagnetism is the force responsible for practically all the phenomena we encounter in our daily lives, with the exception of gravity.

. . . .

Electromagnetism is also the force that holds protons and electrons together inside atoms. As we have seen, it is the Vau in the YHVH (Yod Heh Vau Heh) formula of Creation, where the two Hs are the proton and electron of the hydrogen atom and Y, or Yod, is the initial point of light that gave birth to the universe.

Electromagnetic energy is expressed in the form of waves known as radiation. This radiation, or rays, is known as the electromagnetic spectrum, which is classified according to the frequency of its waves. These include—in order of increasing frequency and decreasing wavelength—radio waves, microwaves, infrared radiation, visible light, ultraviolet light, x-rays, and gamma rays. We only perceive the visible light that comes from the sun and that is known as the solar spectrum (see appendix 6, figure 17).

The line of time that intersects the line of space forms the whole range of electromagnetic radiation, with visible light located at the point where time and space intersect. This point, which we identify as the present, reflects white light from the sun. This white light immediately refracts into the seven colors of the spectrum. Yellow is in the center. To its right is orange, followed by red and the invisible rays of infrared radiation, microwave and radio waves. To the left of yellow is green, followed by light blue, dark blue, and violet. Beyond violet are the invisible and higher electromagnetic rays, which are ultraviolet, x-rays, and gamma rays.

Therefore white light contains all the colors of the solar spectrum. We can see a specific color when all the other colors are absorbed by an object. The color we see is the one reflected on the surface of the object. We cannot see a color when it is absorbed by an object. Leaves reflect green and yellow and absorb all other colors. That is why we can only see green or yellow leaves. When we see a white object, we perceive all the colors of the spectrum at the same time.

On the other hand, black is the absence of color. Black absorbs all light. It is the denial of light and all the colors within it. It does not reflect light and totally annihilates it. Black is the color associated with

Binah, the third sphere of the Tree of Life, and symbolizes the Shekinah's sorrow because of the sins of the world. That is why one of the titles of this sephira is Marah, signifying the bitter waters.

Time and space, through the electromagnetic force, give us the white light of the Ain Soph Aur. From the lower wavelengths of radio waves, microwaves, and infrared radiation, through the visible light of the solar spectrum to the higher wavelengths of ultraviolet light, x-rays, and gamma rays, this supernal light expresses itself in the created universe.

Radio waves, microwaves, and infrared rays are the radiations associated with the lower wavelengths and the lesser aspects of matter. They are necessary but must be carefully controlled because they are linked to the Qlipoth and the fallen sparks. Beyond the radio waves is the black void that absorbs all light.

Ultraviolet light, x-rays, and gamma rays are both the highest waves and the highest expressions of the divine light. Because of their powerful energies they must also be controlled, but they open gates to spiritual dimensions that lead us deep into the angelic realms. Specifically, gamma rays are connected directly to God and are very useful during visualizations and angel magic.

Between the lower and the higher wavelengths of electromagnetic radiation is our link to the divine in the form of visible light, refracted in the seven colors of the solar spectrum. It is our reality, the world we live in, made possible to us by the space-time continuum.

The seven colors of the spectrum are also reflected in the Tree of Life, the human aura, and the seven chakras. As in the spectrum, the colors of the chakras are, in ascending order, red, orange, yellow, green, light blue, dark blue, and violet. Appropriately enough, the yellow or solar chakra is associated with the sun and is located at the solar plexus, the site of Tiphareth in the Tree of Life, whose color is also yellow.

The four points of the cosmic cross formed by time and space also represent the four elements, the four directions, and the four seasons upon which our world is based. They also represent four states of matter: solid, liquid, gas, and plasma.

Most people think of matter as solid, liquid, or gas, but there is a fourth state, known in physics as plasma, which consists of a mix of electrons, ions, and neutral atoms. It responds strongly to electromagnetic fields. Like gas, plasma does not have a specific shape or a definite volume unless enclosed in a container. In space, we can see examples of plasma in the sun and other stars, the solar wind, the space between planets, between star systems and galaxies, as well as the interstellar nebulae. Plasma can be artificially produced, as in plasma televisions, neon signs, and the popular plasma balls. In nature, we can see examples of plasma in lightning, the ionosphere, the aurora borealis, and in most flames, which is why it is identified with the fire element.

Therefore, we can see that the four states of matter can also be equated with the four elements. Solid is the earth element, liquid is the water element, gas is the air element, and plasma is the fire element.

The four elements can also be associated with the four basic forces in the universe, which are electromagnetism (earth), gravity (liquid), the strong force (fire), and the weak force (air).

There are four great Archangels associated with the four elements. They are known as the elemental angels.

AIR——Raphael

FIRE——Michael

WATER——Gabriel

EARTH——Uriel

The four elements and their ruling Archangels are located in the four points of the compass and represent the solar wheel, the four seasons, and the four divisions of the day. Each Archangel dresses in complementary colors, and their appearance suggests the path of the sun from morning till evening.

AIR/EAST/SPRING—Raphael, the element's ruler, is
visualized as a blue-eyed adolescent with golden curls
close to his head, dressed in a yellow mantle with
violet facings. He represents the rising of the sun.

FIRE/SOUTH/SUMMER—Michael, who rules the element, is
visualized as a young man in his early twenties with green eyes
and bright red curls reaching to his shoulders. He is dressed
in a red mantle with green facings. He represents noon.

WATER/WEST/AUTUMN—Gabriel, who rules this element,
is visualized as a man in his thirties with hazel eyes and dark
brown hair reaching below his shoulders. He is dressed in a blue
mantle with orange facings. He represents the afternoon.

EARTH/NORTH/WINTER—Uriel, the ruler of this element, is
visualized as a man in his late forties with long black hair and
dark brown eyes. His skin is also dark, and he has a long black
beard. He is dressed in the colors of the earth—russet, olive
green, brown, and black. He represents the setting of the sun.

From the description of the Archangels, we can see how the day is
progressing from sunrise to sunset, each Archangel looking older and
darker in complexion from the one preceding him, to symbolize the four
divisions of the day.

These four Archangels also rule the four zodiac triplicities. The twelve
signs are divided into four groups of three signs, known as triplicities,
each of which falls within the aegis of one of the four elements and one
of the four Archangels.

FIRE—Aries, Leo, and Sagittarius, ruled by Michael

EARTH—Taurus, Virgo, and Capricorn, ruled by Uriel

AIR—Gemini, Libra, and Aquarius, ruled by Raphael

WATER—Cancer, Scorpio, and Pisces, ruled by Gabriel

Each sign also has a zodiac or planetary angel, as well as the elemental angel.

Sign	Zodiac or Planetary Angel	Planet
Aries—fire	Kamael	Mars
Taurus—earth	Hanael	Venus
Gemini—air	Raphael	Mercury
Cancer—water	Gabriel	Moon
Leo—fire	Michael	Sun
Virgo—earth	Raphael	Mercury
Libra —air	Hanael	Venus
Scorpio—water	Azrael	Pluto
Sagittarius—fire	Zadkiel	Jupiter
Capricorn—earth	Cassiel	Saturn
Aquarius—air	Uriel	Uranus
Pisces—water	Asariel	Neptune

You will notice that the twelve signs are also divided into three groups of four signs, following the same elemental order: fire, earth, air, and water. Raphael and Hanael are the only two angels that rule more than one sign. They each rule an earth and an air sign, but only one planet.

The four elements belong to the sephira known as Malkuth in the Tree of Life, which is represented by the planet Earth and physical existence. Malkuth is also known as *Olam Yesodoth*, the sphere of the elements. Each element is ascribed a divine name, an Archangel, an angel, a ruler, and an elemental kingdom with its king.

	Fire	Water	Air	Earth
Divine Name	YHVH Tzabaoth	Elohim	Shaddai El Chai	Adonai ha Aretz
Archangel	Michael	Gabriel	Raphael	Uriel
Angel	Aral	Taliahad	Chassan	Phorlak
Ruler	Seraph	Tharsis	Ariel	Kerub
Kingdom	Salamanders	Undines	Sylphs	Gnomes
King	Djinn	Nixsa	Paralda	Ghob

The concept of the four elemental kingdoms and their kings can be traced to Paracelsus, who was an alchemist, physician, astrologer, and occultist of the Renaissance. Paracelsus pioneered the use of chemicals and minerals in medicine. Astrology was a very important part of his medical practices, and he created astrological talismans for curing illnesses and for all the signs of the zodiac. He also invented the Alphabet of the Magi for engraving angelic names on talismans (see appendix 6, figure 2, for other examples of angelic alphabets).

Paracelsus based his esoteric and medical practices on the four elements, which he identified as mystical beings. He coined the term *sylph* to identify the elementals of air, and he attributed magical powers to gnomes as the elementals of earth, the salamanders as the elementals of fire, and the undines as the elementals of water.

The elemental kingdoms and their kings are the embodiment of their elements. They concentrate their collective energies to actually produce the element they represent. Each king acts as the point of fusion that gathers the energies of his mind group to create his element. The elemental kings work with the angels and Archangels of the elements, who command and guide them.

Sylphs were described by Paracelsus as invisible beings of the air that controlled the air element. They rule the winds, hurricanes, and everything that moves or flies, including thought and mind. They also rule the clouds in the sky and the sky itself. They are a symbol of change and transition and make motion possible. Paralda is their king, who commands their every action. He is an ethereal being made of air itself, whose tenuous shape is transformed continuously. Paralda follows the instructions of the angel Chassan and the Archangel Raphael in the workings of the air element. His ruler is Ariel, and he has a subtle connection to the moon because the moon rules the mental processes in human beings. This connection can be seen in the fact that the divine name for the air element is Shaddai el Chai, which is also the divine name of Yesod, whose planet is the moon. Ariel, the ruler of the sylphs and the air element, is the chief sylph in Alexander Pope's *Rape of the Lock*. He also appears as Prospero's servant in Shakespeare's *The Tempest*, where winds are of the utmost importance.

The real salamander is an amphibian, lizardlike in form. The elemental salamander is depicted very much like the amphibian from which it borrowed its name but with a strong affinity to fire. This connection probably originates from a behavior typical to many species of salamanders: hibernating in and under rotting logs. When wood was brought indoors and put on the fire, the salamanders mysteriously appeared from the flames. In his autobiography, Benvenuto Cellini describes how, as a child, he saw salamanders cavorting among the flames in a fireplace.

The Talmud describes the salamander as a creature that is a product of fire. Anyone who is smeared with its blood is said to be immune to harm from fire. Rashi, the chief commentator of the Talmud, said the salamander can be produced by burning a fire in the same place for seven years. And Leonardo da Vinci believed that salamanders fed from fire in which they constantly renewed their skin.

Salamanders as fire elementals create fire itself through the concentration of their combined energies. This action is commanded by their king, Djinn, under the orders of the angel and Archangel of the fire element, Aral and Michael.

Although identified as a king, Djinn is envisioned as a female entity made entirely of fire, her body covered with flaming scales and her hair as rivulets of lava. Her eyes are burning charcoals emitting blinding, fiery rays.

Salamanders rule all forms of combustion and life itself. They work in the heart and in the blood and provide the essential energy of the cosmos. They create the magma beneath the earth's crust, and their blood is the lava of the volcanoes. Seraph, their ruler, is one of the angels of the Seraphim choir. He is the angel who seared Isaiah's lips with a live coal to enable him to speak with God (Isaiah 6:6). Salamanders provide the energy of every magic ritual and every human action.

According to Paracelsus, undines are water nymphs, or water spirits, and are identified as the elementals of water. They are usually found in forest pools and waterfalls. They love to sing and have beautiful voices, which can sometimes be heard above the sound of water. They are often compared to sirens and mermaids, but they are different entities.

Like sylphs and salamanders, undines create their element by concentrating their collective energies through the command of their king.

The undines' king is Nixsa, also a female entity, who is visualized as made of water, her rippling blue skin wreathed with pearls and tiny seashells. Her hair is described as a rushing waterfall, and her garments are made of dazzling mother-of-pearl. Nixsa follows the orders of the angel and Archangel of the water element, Taliahad and Gabriel. Her ruler, Tharsis, is an angel governing the element of water in rabbinical literature.

Undines create all liquids and rule their flow, including the ocean tides and the course of blood and all bodily fluids. They oversee the birth and growth of all things, including nations. They also rule lunar phases, families, maternity, and the milk that flows from a mother's breast. As they rule the flow of things, they also rule their stagnation, including the creative process in the human mind and the course of progress in individual and world economies. Their work impacts mightily on the history of nature and of the human race.

The word *gnome* comes from the Latin *gnomus*, which means "knowledge." It first appeared in the alchemy works of Paracelsus. The word literally means "an earth dweller." Paracelsus described gnomes as eighteen inches high, of wide girth, and with rough features. He claimed gnomes were very reluctant to interact with humans and were able to move through earth as easily as humans can move through air. To Paracelsus, the gnome became the embodiment of elemental earth.

Gnomes do not create the earth element, they simply rule it. They do it by following the commands of their king, Ghob, who gets his orders from the angel and the Archangel of the earth element, Phorlak and Uriel. His ruler is Kerub, whom the Zohar names as chief of the choir of the Cherubim and who was made the guardian of paradise, armed with a sword of flame.

Gnomes and the earth element belong specifically to Malkuth, the tenth sephira of the Tree of Life. This connection can be seen in the fact that the divine name of the earth element, *Adonai ha Aretz*, is the same as that of the Malkuth sphere.

Ghob is the origin of the word *goblin*, a creature physically similar to the gnome but evilly inclined. Ghob is visualized as an old man, greyhaired, dressed in dark robes, with a magical sword in his hand. Some people envision him wearing clothes made from ferns woven together with cobwebs. He is said to announce his presence with a cold blast of air.

Gnomes are shy and avoid contact with human beings. Their work is to protect and heal the earth. They rule all natural resources and all the earth's riches. They often work in underground mines, creating mineral deposits and lodes of gold, copper, silver, and precious stones. They protect mountains and valleys and ensure the stability of the tectonic plates to minimize natural disasters like earthquakes and volcanic eruptions. These earthly rumbles are subject to inscrutable cycles that are ruled by the gnomes. Our continued abuse of the earth and its ecology are affecting those cycles, increasing their occurrence and complicating the task of the earth elementals. Yet they continue to keep the earth fertile so it can produce the grains, fruits, and vegetables that feed us and the flowers that delight us. They are indeed the guardians of treasures without number.

Gnomes are immensely generous and can give us financial stability and triumph in all earthly endeavors, but we must first gain their trust and friendship by caring for nature and all its creatures. I had a dream once that illustrates the gnomes' generosity. In the dream, I was in the company of several gnomes. We were standing around a long wooden table darkened with age. One of the gnomes was getting ready to cut off a slice from a huge bar of golden butter for me. He started to cut about a foot of the bar of butter. He placed the knife over the bar, hesitated, and then he smiled and moved the knife forward and cut off twice the amount of butter he had originally intended to give me. I can still see the rich, golden butter and the smile on the gnome's face.

Gnomes are particularly fond of trees, flowers, rocks, gems, and crystals, which they protect zealously. Because of their stability and earthiness, gnomes can help keep us grounded. Whenever you feel out of sorts, depressed, or out of touch with reality, ask the gnomes and Ghob to help you regain your inner balance. You will be astounded by the results.

The four elemental forces—air, fire, water, and earth—are joined by a fifth, which is spirit, or akasha. This fifth force is the divine spark that illuminates and empowers the other four. Together, the five elemental forces form a pentagram. The lower-right point represents fire, courage, and daring; the lower-left point represents earth and stability; the upper-right point represents water, emotions, and intuition; the upper-left point represents air, intellect, and art; and the uppermost point represents spirit and the Divine (see appendix 6, figure 24).

When the pentagram is inverted, it is a symbol of chaos and destruction (see appendix 6, figure 20). The famed occultist Eliphas Levi said that "a reversed pentagram, with two points projecting upward, is a symbol of evil and attracts sinister forces because it overturns the proper order of things and demonstrates the triumph of matter over spirit" (see Levi 1923).

From the preceding text we can see that the elements and the elemental forces are the foundations of nature that ensure the survival of our planet and everything that inhabits it, including us. It is vital that we learn to identify with nature and natural forces and the elements that sustain them if we wish to survive. All of nature is alive—it is intelligent, sentient, and aware—and it is eager to connect with us. Trees, plants, flowers, and all the creatures around us will respond if we reach out to them. They cannot speak, but they can show us their love in their own special way.

Many years ago I moved to a house in a section of New York known as Fresh Meadows. Nesting close to the house was a peach tree that had long been abused. Most of its branches had been cut off to make room for additions to the house. Its trunk was cracked in several places, and its remaining branches were mostly bare, with a few leaves struggling to survive. It was clear that the tree was dying. I was strongly moved by the tree. It seemed to be crying out to me. I started to water it regularly; I spread special tree food around its roots and spoke to it constantly, rubbing its old trunk and encouraging it to survive. This was in late fall. Winter came and went, and when spring arrived, the old peach tree covered itself with a giant canopy of leaves and a most glorious show of flowers. But the big surprise was the summer. The tree exploded in a huge display of peaches—large, luscious red and purple peaches as big as grapefruits. There were so many peaches I had to climb on a ladder to gather them all. Everyone ate from the peaches—my family, my neighbors, my friends, and people who worked for me. They were the sweetest, juiciest peaches we had ever eaten.

. . . .

I knew it was the tree's way of expressing its gratitude and its love. Those were the last peaches the tree gave. It died that year, but I will never forget it.

I had another experience with a tree that happened recently. Next to my present house there is a large tree with a beautiful leafy frond. In spring it is covered with beautiful pink flowers. Whenever I come home I stop by the tree and speak to it, as I usually do with plants. Last year I was working extremely hard and often came home exhausted and with very little energy. I would rest my forehead on the tree and mentally ask it to give me some of its energy. Immediately afterward I felt refreshed and energized. Several months later I noticed that the tree's leaves were drying out and the branches were sagging badly. I called a tree expert to come and find out what was wrong. The man examined the tree carefully and told me he could not find the reason for its condition, but in his opinion the tree was probably dying of some type of infestation and I should consider cutting it down. I was aghast at the suggestion, and I immediately sensed what had happened. I had been asking the tree for energy, and it had given it to me in such quantities that it had none left for itself. That was the reason it was dying. I was overwhelmed with guilt, and I started to meditate on the tree, sending it vast amounts of gamma light every night. During the winter the tree lost all of its leaves and I waited with baited breath for spring to come to see if the tree would renew its foliage—and it did. The flowers were beautiful and plentiful, and the tree looked happy and healthy again.

Nature is alive. Try talking to plants, feed the birds and the squirrels, embrace nature in all its forms. It will respond. The birds in my yard come flying to me when I go out to feed them—pigeons, blue jays, cardinals, finches, and tiny sparrows. They know me and trust me. We are friends.

And if you want to try something special to test how nature responds when you approach it, go to the beach and stand about four feet away from the water mark, where the waves wash on shore. Close your eyes and mentally greet the sea—send it your love and ask it to come to you and give you its blessing. And the sea will rise above its mark and kiss your feet. Try it. It always works.

CHAPTER 9

The Angelic Realms

If we were all like angels
the world would be a heavenly place.

. . . .

ANONYMOUS

The universe is controlled by immutable cosmic laws, and those laws are angels. We only know some of the cosmic laws because there are many that have yet to be discovered. Among the known laws, there are ten that are directly responsible for the maintenance and the working of the universe. Those ten laws are identified with the ruling angels of the ten sephiroth of the Tree of Life.

These ten laws are of great importance in the practice of angel magic because they tell us what the angels control and which angel should be invoked to attain a specific goal.

. . . .

Sephira	Angel	Cosmic Law
1. Kether	Metatron	Law of Electromagnetism
2. Chokmah	Raziel	Law of Inertia
3. Binah	Tzaphkiel	Law of Probability
4. Chesed	Zadkiel	Law of Cause and Effect
5. Geburah	Kamael	Law of Momentum
6. Tiphareth	Raphael	Law of Gravity
7. Netzach	Hanael	Law of Change and Stability
8. Hod	Michael	Law of Equilibrium
9. Yesod	Gabriel	Law of Fluids
10. Malkuth	Sandalphon	Law of Conservation of Energy

1. THE LAW OF ELECTROMAGNETISM is one of the four basic
forces of the universe. The other three are gravity, the strong
force, and the weak force. As we have seen, electromagnetism is
responsible for practically everything that exists. It was created
at the time of the Big Bang, together with time and space. It is
the beginning of creation. That is why it is associated with Kether
and the Archangel Metatron, upon whose cube the universe was
created. Electromagnetism is expressed in the form of all radiation, including visible light. It is the first point of light of the Ain
Soph Aur manifested as the beginning of the created universe.

2. THE LAW OF INERTIA basically says that an object will keep moving—or stay still—unless something else influences it to do otherwise. As a basic example, when a car is moving at a certain speed, all the objects in the car, including the driver and passengers, are moving at that speed. When the car stops, the objects inside continue to move forward unless an outside force, like a seat belt, acts upon them. Understanding the basic principle of inertia helps us comprehend the way many objects in the universe behave. In many ways inertia is nonaction capable of action when compelled by an outside force. That is why it is identified with Chokmah, the second sephira of the Tree of Life and the Archangel Raziel. Chokmah is the sphere of ideas that have not yet been manifested in the material world. Raziel holds the key to its mysteries, which he revealed in the famous book that bears his name.

3. THE LAW OF PROBABILITY is the chance that something will happen. In math the definition of probability is a numerical measure of the likelihood of an event. For example, if you want to take a blue marble out of a bag containing one blue marble and five red marbles, the probability you pick the blue marble is one in five, or 20 percent. Referring to everyday occurrences, Aristotle said that the probable is what usually happens. Everything is possible, but not everything is probable. Probability sustains the logic of the universe, where anything can happen, but what generally happens is based on established laws. That is why we can send probes into outer space. We are relying on the law of probability. It is the basis of our technologies and every human decision. The law of probability is identified with Binah, the third sephira of the Tree of Life, and the Archangel Tzaphkiel. In this sphere, the law of inertia and nonaction, we find Chokmah is changed into "probable action." Everything is possible in Binah, but only the probable will happen. Nothing has happened yet in the material world, but the seeds of probability have been planted.

· · · · · · · · · · · · ·

4. THE LAW OF CAUSE AND EFFECT is the relationship between an event (cause) and a second event (effect) that is the result or consequence of the first. Everything in the universe is based upon this law. "Be-cause" is the explanation of every effect. Everything happens for a reason. When we consider the law of cause and effect, the first thought that comes into mind is a first cause. This is known as the cosmological argument, which attempts to explain the origins of the universe as the work of an "unconditional" or supreme being usually identified as God. The basic premise is that something caused the universe to exist and this first cause must be God. This argument has been presented by many theologians and philosophers over the centuries, including Plato, Aristotle, and Saint Thomas Aquinas (see Aquinas 1941).

In modern times, the cosmological argument has been expressed in three axioms: (a) whatever begins to exist has a cause; (b) the universe began to exist; and (c) therefore, the universe has a cause. This first cause is at the core of the law of cause and effect, because it is with this law that the universe came into existence. The law of cause and effect is identified with Chesed, the fourth sphere of the Tree of Life, and the Archangel Zadkiel. It is in Chesed that the material world is first manifested. The material world, the universe, is the result of the progressive evolution of electromagnetic radiation, the light of the Ain Soph Aur, into the first swirlings of thoughts and ideas still in a state of inertia, which are finally expressed as a cosmic plan and based on the logic of probability. These three laws or three spheres are the matrix of the created universe, which is first manifested in the fourth sphere, also seen as the world of cause and effect. They are the cause. It is in Chesed that the cosmic plan first comes into effect and things begin to happen. Stars, planets, and galaxies are formed. Our own world comes into being. Zadkiel is the Archangel that rules this causal sphere and all it contains. He rules potentates, people in power, abundance, and prosperity.

5. THE LAW OF MOMENTUM refers to moving things. It is a product of the mass of an object and its velocity. Momentum is why the driver of a car applies the brake to reduce the velocity of the car or to stop it. The car has gathered momentum and will continue to move forward even after the driver stops accelerating. The greater the mass of an object, the more the momentum. It is harder to stop a large tractor-trailer than a small compact car. The law of momentum is identified with Geburah, the fifth sephira of the Tree of Life, and the Archangel Kamael. Once the law of cause and effect, represented by Chesed, has started its cosmic motion, it gathers power and continuation through the law of momentum, exemplified by Geburah. Kamael, who rules this sphere, is the personification of divine justice and great power. He rules legal matters, violence, and war.

6. THE LAW OF GRAVITY is the force that pulls together all matter. The more the matter, the greater the gravity, which is why stars and planets have such great gravitational pull. As we walk on the surface of the earth, it pulls on us and we pull back, but because the earth is more massive than we are, we stay on the ground instead of floating out into space. Gravity also depends on the distance between objects. That is why we are stuck on the surface of the earth instead of being pulled away into the sun, which has many more times the gravity of the earth but is too far away to affect us. Gravity is not just the attraction between objects and the earth. It is an attraction that exists between all objects everywhere in the universe. It is the sun's gravity that keeps the earth in orbit. It is the pull of lunar gravity that controls the ocean tides and the flow of blood in our veins. Gravity is the result of the union of the law of cause and effect and the law of momentum. It keeps the universe in motion, and it also

works with dark matter to maintain stars, planets, and galaxies in harmonious balance. For that reason it is equated with Tiphareth, the sixth sphere of the Tree of Life, which is in the center of the Tree beneath Kether, the first sphere. Tiphareth is identified with the sun, which is at the center of the solar system and keeps its planets in steady orbits through gravitation. Raphael is the ruling Archangel of this sphere. He is a solar angel who is said to stand in the sun. He rules worldly riches, fame, and good health.

7. THE LAW OF CHANGE AND STABILITY is expressed as dual complements of the fundamental unit of energy. Change and stability are total opposites but are inseparably interlocked; they coexist simultaneously and are relative to each other like the two halves of the yin-yang symbol. They are the essential driving forces of the existence and nature of our universe and all it contains. Stability, the factor that generates the continuous existence of the universe, is the primary force of this duo. Change is the second-ary force. Without stability, nothing could exist for more than a split second, and without change, things would forever remain the same. But when the two are joined together, everything is not only possible but probable. The law of change and stability is identified with Netzach, the seventh sphere of the Tree of Life, which is the victory of matter, energy, through the unifying force of gravity. Through Netzach things change, and their changes are stabilized to maintain the order of the universe. The ruling Arch-angel is Hanael, a mediating force who brings harmony to the world. He rules love, friendship, and the arts in angel magic.

8. THE LAW OF EQUILIBRIUM is a state in which no change is taking place. Something in a state of equilibrium would be con-sidered to be stable, balanced, or unchanging. This concept is very important in all the sciences, influencing everything from mathematics, biology, and chemistry to the study of the universe. This law maintains the principles governing the law of change and

stability, which is why it is identified with Hod, the eighth sephira of the Tree of Life, and the Archangel Michael, who holds a scale in his hand to symbolize the balance of this sephira. Hod is the sphere of practical magic, contracts, studies, and all paperwork.

9. THE LAW OF FLUIDS refers to any substance that continuously flows under an applied shear stress—that is, anything that presses on it or presses it forward. Rivers flow to the sea because of gravity, and because their origins are higher, like waterfalls, and provide the shear stress that make the water flow slightly downhill. Fluid is often used as a synonym for liquid. The fluidity of a liquid, how fast it moves, depends upon its viscosity or density. For example, water flows faster than honey, and honey faster than lava.

The law of fluids is identified with Yesod, the ninth sephira of the Tree of Life, and the Archangel Gabriel. Yesod is in the middle of the Tree and is the result of the union of the law of change and stability and the law of equilibrium. Yesod rules the moon, which in turn rules all liquids. Gabriel is the ruler of the water element. River waters flow through gravity, which is directly over Yesod. This sphere and Gabriel rule the mind, dreams, travels, the mother, and the family.

10. THE LAW OF CONSERVATION OF ENERGY states that the amount of energy in any given system remains constant over time. A consequence of this law is that energy can change its form but can neither be created nor destroyed. This is also known as the first law of thermodynamics. As mass and energy are the same thing, according to Einstein, this means that matter particles, such as atoms, can be converted into nonmatter forms of energy, such as light or heat, without affecting the total mass of the systems. This means that all the energy created at the time of the Big Bang still exists, albeit in multiple, diverse forms. That is why the law of conservation of energy is identified with Malkuth, the tenth sephira of the Tree of Life, and the Archangel Sandalphon. The

energy that poured out through the initial point or singularity at the time of the Big Bang, equated with Kether and Metatron, has been preserved and manifested through the outpouring of the other spheres and into the receiving sephira, Malkuth, the physical earth. It is here that the initial energies of Kether are finally expressed and manifested as the material world and all its wonders. Sandalphon, the ruler of the last and tenth sphere, is the twin brother of Metatron, the ruler of the first. This sephira rules all material things. It is here that magic is created and realized.

From the ten laws and the ten sephiroth and angels with which they are identified, we can readily see that the first three spheres are outside the physical realm. Matter had not yet been created at those exalted levels, where the radiation of electromagnetism, the law of inertia, and the law of probability had not yet yielded a physical manifestation.

It is only when we reach the law of cause and effect with its first probable cause in the sphere of Chesed that the world of matter began to reach physical reality. The law of momentum in Geburah gave impulse to the law of cause and effect and the creation of matter. The law of gravity in Tiphareth held matter together, and the law of change and stability in Netzach created a stable diversity in the universe and nature. The law of equilibrium in Hod reasserted the stability and balance of the law of change and stability. The world of matter was then both diverse and stable. The law of fluids made the created forms flow downward, preserving them in the actual physical world through the law of conservation of energy. The Creator's cosmic plan had finally been realized in all its glory. And it was through the angels, which are the sentient, intelligent cosmic laws, that the plan was realized. All of this happened within the framework of the space-time continuum because space and time were created together with the universe.

Whereas space is where the universe was formed, time is the measurement of its existence. Time may be an illusion, but it is necessary to regulate and to record cosmic and earthly events. We have designated specific measurements of time that permit us to do that. We measure time in seconds, minutes, hours, days, months, years, decades, centuries, millennia, and eons. We speak of eras, centennials, bicentennials, and jubilees, all within a time frame. We also have seasons and seasonal festivals and observances, among which are the solstices and equinoxes. All of these are ruled by angels (see appendix 6, figure 21).

The days of the week are ruled by seven of the great Archangels. All the great Archangels are also known as archons.

SUNDAY—Michael (Sun)

MONDAY—Gabriel (Moon)

TUESDAY—Kamael (Mars)

WEDNESDAY—Raphael (Mercury)

THURSDAY—Zadkiel (Jupiter)

FRIDAY—Hanael (Venus)

SATURDAY—Cassiel (Saturn)

The hours of the day are also ruled by angels in the following order, starting on Sunday:

1 AM—Michael

2 AM—Hanael

3 AM—Raphael

4 AM—Gabriel

5 AM—Cassiel

6 AM—Zadkiel

7 AM—Kamael

The angels are then repeated:

8 AM—Michael

9 AM—Hanael

10 AM——Raphael

11 AM——Gabriel

12 PM——Cassiel

1 PM——Zadkiel

2 PM——Kamael

3 PM——Michael

4 PM——Hanael

5 PM——Raphael

6 PM——Gabriel

7 PM——Cassiel

8 PM——Zadkiel

9 PM——Kamael

10 PM——Michael

11 PM——Hanael

12 AM——Raphael

The angelic hour cycle begins at 1 AM on each day of the week and ends at midnight. The hours from 1 AM to 12 PM are considered day hours, while the hours from 1 PM to midnight are considered night hours.

Each of the seven angels rules his day at 1 AM, 8 AM, 3 PM, and 10 PM. Thus Michael rules Sundays at 1 AM, 8 AM, 3 PM, and 10 PM; Gabriel rules Mondays at 1 AM, 8 AM, 3 PM, and 10 PM; Kamael rules Tuesdays at 1 AM, 8 AM, 3 PM, and 10 PM; and so on.

In order to establish a strong connection with these powerful Archangels, a simple ritual is recommended by kabbalists. Choose one of the four hours ruled by each Archangel, and every day at the same hour invoke the Archangel of the day, asking him to grant you his protection and your desires. After the invocation eat a small piece of bread and drink

. . . .

a small glass of sweet wine. Bread and wine are offered and consumed in all magic rituals to earth the ceremony and bring it to fruition. This custom goes back to Melchizedek, king of Salem and priest of God Most High, who blessed Abraham and gave him bread and wine after winning a battle (Genesis 14:18–20). Psalm 110:4 also mentions Melchizedek, "where the victorious ruler is declared to be a priest after the order of Melchizedek." This is also the main reason why bread and wine are offered during Catholic masses and during the ceremonies of Orthodox churches, not only as symbols of the body and blood of Jesus Christ.

Angels also rule the four seasons:

SPRING——Spugliguel

SUMMER——Tubiel

AUTUMN——Torquaret

WINTER——Attarib

And the twelve months of the year:

JANUARY——Gabriel

FEBRUARY——Barchiel

MARCH——Machidiel

APRIL——Asmodel

MAY——Ambriel

JUNE——Muriel

JULY——Verchiel

AUGUST——Hamaliel

SEPTEMBER——Uriel

OCTOBER——Barbiel

NOVEMBER——Adnachiel

DECEMBER——Hanael

In the practice of angel magic, one begins each day invoking the names of the angel of the season, the angel of the ruling sign of the zodiac, the name of the angel of the month, the name of the angel of the day, and the name of the angel of the hour. For example, on a July 4 that falls on a Sunday, at 9 AM one begins by invoking Tubiel (angel of summer), Gabriel (angel of Cancer), Verchiel (angel of July), Michael (angel of Sunday), and Hanael (who rules at 9 AM on Sundays). These angels are petitioned to protect the person and guide him or her throughout the day.

The equinoxes and solstices are very important in the practice of angel magic and all kinds of magic, because they start the four seasons and create natural changes that result in the release of immense quantities of energies. These energies are of vital importance in the practice of angel magic, which channels and transforms them through the powers of the angels to achieve the things we desire.

The spring or vernal equinox takes place on March 20 in the Northern Hemisphere, and on that day the sun enters into the sign of Aries. Day and night are of the same approximate length. In the Southern Hemisphere, the spring equinox happens on September 22.

The summer solstice takes place on June 21 in the Northern Hemisphere, and on that day the sun enters into the sign of Cancer. This is the longest day of the year and the shortest night. In the Southern Hemisphere, the summer solstice happens on December 21.

The autumn equinox takes place on September 22 in the Northern Hemisphere, and on that day the sun enters into the sign of Libra. The day and night are of the same approximate length. In the Southern Hemisphere, the autumn equinox happens on March 20.

The winter solstice takes place on December 21 in the Northern Hemisphere, and the sun enters into the sign of Capricorn. This is the shortest day of the year and the longest night. In the Southern Hemisphere, the winter solstice happens on June 20.

The equinoxes and solstices are ruled by the four elements and their four Archangels:

Spring Equinox	Aries	Fire	Michael
Summer Solstice	Cancer	Water	Gabriel
Autumn Equinox	Libra	Air	Raphael
Winter Solstice	Capricorn	Earth	Uriel

During spring the earth awakens from its long winter sleep, and through the fire element it warms itself and renews all life on the planet. The Archangel Michael rules the earth's awakening with the blossoming of flowers and the welcome sound of bird's songs. It is a time of hope and new beginnings. Angel magic done during spring concerns new things, new plans, new enterprises, and especially love.

During summer the water element and the Archangel Gabriel refresh the earth and bring us the seasonal fruits. New crops ripen and get ready to be harvested. It is a time for the achievement of many goals and the realization of the hopes promised by the spring season. Angel magic during the summer especially concerns travels, communications, loans, contracts, and anything one may desire, because the solstices are very powerful.

During autumn the air element and the Archangel Raphael bring us the gathering of the harvests and begin to cool the earth. Leaves change into vibrant colors, and temperatures begin to fall. It is a time for reconciliation and gathering the fruits of all magic rituals. Angel magic during this season concerns health issues, asking for raises and promotions, and asking for special favors.

During winter the earth element and the Archangel Uriel bring rest and solace to the earth. Leaves fall from the trees, birds fold their wings, all nature's creatures curl in their secret lairs, and the earth sleeps and recovers its strength in preparation for the next spring. It is a time for meditation and quiet repose. Angel magic during the winter concerns all money matters, business transactions, selling and buying real state, settling court cases, and generally improving one's fortunes. The winter solstice gives special power and stability to whatever is desired.

The angel rituals conducted during the equinoxes and solstices should take place at midnight on the eve of the festival. Sample rituals for the equinoxes and solstices will be given in appendix 4.

As we have seen, cosmic laws are identified with angels who carried out God's plan for the creation of the universe. The divisions of time as days, hours, months, equinoxes, solstices, and seasons are also ruled by angels. But according to Kabbalah there are other divisions of time that go beyond the ones we are familiar with. They are known as cosmic days and cosmic nights. A cosmic day is followed by a cosmic night, and each lasts thirty-six years. The last cosmic day ended in 2007. It was followed by a cosmic night that began in 2008 and will last until 2045. Cosmic nights are marked by strife and disturbances on the earth, both natural and human, because the negative forces of the Qlipoth are particularly strong during these cosmic periods. This happens because Qlipothic entities function better in the darkness of the night. This cosmic night is ruled by the feminine aspect of God known as the Shekinah, and the angel that works with her during this dark period is Metatron, with whom she is identified.

According to the Talmud, Metatron is the direct link between God and humanity, and he is charged with the sustenance of the world. This is the angel that will help sustain the earth during the cosmic night that just started, and it is he whom we have to invoke as our principal guide and protector.

CHAPTER 10

The Power of Ten

Not only does God play dice, but he sometimes
throws them where they cannot be seen.

. . . .

STEPHEN HAWKING

The binary system revolves around two ciphers, 1 and 0. The electronic circuits used in this technology are known as two-state or bistable. This means that only two states of electromagnetic energy are possible, as exemplified by the On and Off switches of electrical outlets. "On" means that electricity is pulsating through the system and the circuit is open. "Off" means that the electricity is not flowing and the circuit is closed. The On in the electric system corresponds to the 1 in the binary system; the Off corresponds to the 0. Every computer program is recognized only as combinations of ones and zeroes by digital computers.

The numbers that we commonly know—1, 2, 3, 4, 5, 6, 7, 8, 9, and 0—are found in the decimal system. Any number in the decimal system

. . . .

may be transformed into the binary system by dividing it by two until nothing remains.

Hebrew letters are ascribed numbers from one to nine. After nine, zeroes are added to each of the nine numbers that correspond to the rest of the letters. There are twenty-two letters, which are placed in three rows. The first row has nine letters with numbers one to nine. The second row has nine letters with numbers ten to ninety. The third row has nine letters, including five final letters, with numbers one hundred to nine hundred (see appendix 6, figure 1). The name of God known as the Tetragrammaton, which is sometimes pronounced as Jehovah or Yaweh, is made of four letters in the original Hebrew. These letters are transliterated as Yod Heh Vau Heh. Yod, the first letter, has a value of ten, one, and zero, the ciphers of the binary system. Heh has a value of five, and Vau has a value of six. This means that the numerical value of Yod Heh Vau Heh is twenty-six. To change this decimal number into the binary system, we must divide it by two until it no longer can be reduced.

26 divided by 2 = 13 and the remnant is 0
13 divided by 2 = 6 and the remnant is 1
6 divided by 2 = 3 and the remnant is 0
3 divided by 2 = 1 and the remnant is 1
1 divided by 2 = 0 and the remnant is 1

The remnants are the binary number of twenty-six. This binary number is 01011. But there is an interesting fact about binary numbers. Like the Hebrew language, they must be read from right to left. That means that the correct binary number for Yod Heh Vau Heh is 11010. This number begins with 1 and ends with 0. These two ciphers form the number 10, which corresponds to Yod, the first letter of God's name.

The binary number for Yod Heh Vau Heh, 11010, represents the process of creation. In the beginning, God sent the first ray of light, represented by the first 1 of the binary number. But, as we have seen, the spheres where the light was contained broke through the force of the divine power; therefore, God sent another ray of light, the second 1, and creation was established. God then withdrew, symbolized by the 0, the third cipher in the binary number. What remained were the last 1 and 0—that is, 10—which represents the ten sephiroth of the Tree of Life and the created universe.

If we look at the table of Hebrew letters, we see that the first letter, Aleph, has been ascribed the number 1. Directly under Aleph is the letter Yod, number 10, and underneath Yod is Qoph, number 100. If we put these numbers together, we get 110100, which is the binary number of Yod Heh Vau Heh with another 0 added. The last 0 represents God's state of nonbeing. It means that creation, symbolized by number 10, will eventually return to God.

It is no coincidence that all of our modern technology is based on the binary system, the 1 and the 0, number 10. It is our number. We have just discovered it.

The zero is a state of nonbeing but with infinite powers. The one is the manifestation of matter; it is the beginning of all things. The zero by itself is literally nothing—but if we add it to the one, it multiplies its power and its worth. Add six zeroes to a one and we have a million, which can certainly make a difference if we are speaking about dollars. The more zeroes we add, the more powerful the one becomes. Thus we can create billions and trillions, which brings us to the national debt. That is the power of the zero, but only when it is added after the one, never before.

It is of transcendental importance that we understand the meaning and the power of the binary system, because upon the number ten hinges everything that exists and everything that we may desire to accomplish.

The other numbers, two to nine, exist within the frame of the one and the zero. The sum total of our human experience is expressed as 010.

The first zero represents our soul before its incarnation; the one symbolizes our physical life; and the last zero is our return to the spiritual world where we initially came from. But in reality we are born and we die in the same fraction of an instant. Our physical life, the one, is an illusion. We think it is real because we are trapped in the myth of time, but time does not exist. That is why we cannot hold on to it. Before we know it our life is over, and the transient "one" is absorbed by the eternal "zero," and we return to our true state of infinite existence. Ten is the last part of the human equation 010 because it represents both our physical and our spiritual essence.

Ten is also the number of creation. In Genesis 1, the words "God said" appear ten times. God creates through speech. Each time he creates something, he expresses it vocally. Thus, Genesis tells us:

1. "God said, Let there be light."

2. "God said, Let there be a dome in the midst of the waters, and let it separate the waters from the waters."

3. "God said, Let the waters under the sky be gathered together into one place and let the dry land appear."

4. "Then God said, Let the earth put forth vegetation…"

5. "And God said, Let there be lights in the dome of the sky to separate the day from the night…"

6. "And God said, Let the waters bring forth swarms of living creatures and let birds fly above the earth across the dome of the sky."

7. "And God said, Let the earth bring forth living creatures of every kind…"

8. "Then God said, Let us make humankind in our image, according to our likeness…"

9. "And God said to them, Be fruitful and multiply and fill the earth and subdue it and have dominion …over every living thing that moves upon the earth."

10. "God said, See, I have given you every plant yielding seed that is upon the face of all the earth, and every tree with seed in its fruit; you shall have them for food."

Food for Thought

You will notice that God gave humankind plants and fruit-bearing trees as food. He did not tell them that they could eat any living animal, bird, or fish. It is in Genesis 9 that he tells Noah and his sons, "Every moving thing that lives shall be food for you...Only, you shall not eat flesh with its life, that is, its blood." This permission to eat flesh comes with a prohibitory admonition: flesh—meat— cannot be eaten with its blood. But it is impossible to take the blood out of meat, no matter how carefully and thoroughly you wash it. The blood is in the meat fiber; that is why meat is always red. Even fish and fowl meat will retain some traces of blood in its tissue after washing it. Therefore, this was God's test for Noah and his descendants. They could eat the meat, but in so doing they would be breaking God's commandment not to eat its blood. God wanted Noah and the rest of humankind to know that only plants and fruit-bearing trees were to be their food.

The Creation of Adam

When God created humankind, Adam was not part of that creation. Adam was created in chapter 2 of Genesis, and he was not a physical being but a spiritual being. The Garden of Eden was not on earth but in Heaven. When Adam and Eve ate of the forbidden fruit, they were dressed in skins by God and banished from Eden. The "skins" were physical bodies, and the place to which they were banished was the material world. Thus they became part of humankind, which was already living and multiplying on earth. That is why Cain, after he killed his brother Abel, found a wife in the land of Nod.

As we have seen, God created the universe and the earth with ten "sayings." These ten sayings are represented by the ten spheres of the Tree of Life. The first saying, "God said, Let there be light," is Kether. The fourth, when he created the first signs of life as vegetation, is Chesed. He created humankind in the eighth sphere, Hod. In the tenth, Malkuth, he told them what they should eat as food.

As we have seen, angels are God's words. Therefore, the ten sayings were the emanations of the ten Archangels of the Tree of Life.

The Fingers of God

Creation by speech was followed by the physical act of creation. God not only spoke but actually *made* his creation. And he made it with the fingers of his hands. That is why David, in Psalm 8:3, says: "When I look at your heavens, the work of your fingers…"

Genesis tells us that after God said, "Let there be light," he separated the light from the darkness. And when he said, "Let there be lights to separate the day from the night," he made the two lights that separate the day and the night and the stars. This is when he created the universe. The words in Genesis imply direct action. He made the sun, he made the moon, and he made the stars (Genesis 1).

But does God—an immense, indefinable, and unknowable force that transcends the created universe—have fingers? The fingers that David refers to in Psalm 8:3 and with which God separated the light from the darkness and made the sun, the moon, and the stars are the ten principal cosmic laws that we discussed earlier. And those laws are his angels.

God made humankind after his own image. Humans have two hands and ten fingers. This does not imply that God has physical hands and fingers. Human beings are material beings; God is not. He creates through physical laws. We create through physical action. That is the meaning of the ten fingers. These ten fingers are equated with the ten cosmic laws, the ten angels, and the ten spheres of the Tree of Life:

Left Hand	Right Hand
Thumb—Binah	Thumb—Kether
Index finger—Geburah	Index finger—Chokmah
Middle finger—Hod	Middle finger—Chesed
Ring finger—Yesod	Ring finger—Tiphareth
Little finger—Malkuth	Little finger—Netzach

The five fingers of the left hand and the corresponding sephiroth are considered feminine and are known as the five forces. The five fingers of the right hand and the corresponding sephiroth are considered masculine and are known as the five loves.

The ten fingers and their sephiroth divided between the two hands also represent the two tablets of the Ten Commandments, where each commandment is equated with a sephira. The space that separates the two tablets is known as the covenant of unification and is the focus of great spiritual tension and power. The same is true of the ten sephiroth when they are divided into two columns. When the two hands are placed facing each other and are moved back and forth repeatedly, a great energy field is created between them that can be felt as a soft ball of air. This energy can be impregnated with a specific intention or thought and sent mentally anywhere or to anyone in the world. It is especially useful in healings at a distance. During the Catholic mass, the priest always places his hands on the sides of his face as he reads from the scriptures. This position of the hands is recommended during all prayers and meditations.

Like the mudras, or finger positions, used in yoga, Kabbalah teaches that the fingers of the two hands can be used to make changes in the material world according to our desires. For example, to improve health, the two ring fingers are hooked together and then they are forcefully pulled in opposite directions to create a strong tension between them. This pressure is prolonged while one concentrates on health improvement. The same procedure is used with the little fingers of both hands to attract love and harmony. For money, the little finger of the left hand is hooked with the ring finger of the right hand.

A brain research paper published in the *National Academy of Sciences* in November 2009 demonstrated that hand gestures stimulate the same region of the brain as language.

The physical world is expressed in five dimensions, which contain ten directions. The five dimensions are equated with the five fingers of each hand. There are two opposite directions in each dimension, and these directions are also identified with the ten sephiroth and the ten fingers:

First Dimension

1. Beginning—Chokmah—right index finger

2. End—Binah—left thumb

Second Dimension

3. Good—Kether—right thumb

4. Evil—Malkuth—left little finger

Third Dimension

5. Up—Netzach—right little finger

6. Down—Hod—left middle finger

Fourth Dimension

7. North—Geburah—left index finger

8. South—Chesed—right middle finger

Fifth Dimension

9. East—Tiphareth—right ring finger

10. West—Yesod—left ring finger

Everything that exists is circumscribed by the east (front), the west (back), the south (right), the north (left), up (above), and down (below). It has a beginning (Chokmah) and an end (Binah), and is influenced by good (Kether) and evil (Malkuth, the physical world).

These ten directions are known as the depths. David refers to them in Psalm 130, which is one of the fifteen psalms known as Songs of Ascents (Psalms 120–134). Psalm 130 is a psalm of divine redemption and is the only one of the fifteen Songs of Ascents that mentions the depths. The psalm begins, "Out of the depths I cry to you, O Lord." The depths are the restrictions of the world of matter. David calls out to God from these depths hoping for divine redemption, and as he calls out he ascends from the world of matter (Malkuth) to the world of spirit (Kether) and is redeemed from his iniquities.

There is a kabbalistic exercise that is used to explore the depths of the ten directions in their totality. The exercise helps the soul understand the true meaning of the depths.

1. THE BEGINNING——Bring your mind back one minute, then an hour, then one day, then one year, ten years, twenty years, as far as you can remember, reliving each moment of your life. Then think back one hundred years, five hundred years, a thousand, two thousand, to the beginning of civilization, thinking of what was accomplished in those early days. Then go back a million years, back to the time of the Neanderthal man, and back twenty million years, four billion years—when the earth was created through aggregated gas—then fourteen billion years and the time of the Big Bang, and then further back when there was nothing, because time had not yet been created.

2. THE END——Move your mind forward to tomorrow and what it may bring, to next week, next month, next year, ten years or more, what you may be doing and what may be happening on the earth. Keep going forward twenty years, a hundred years, when you no longer exist, and continue to move forward, imagining what may happen to the earth—will a meteor hit it, will humanity destroy the planet, how far will it evolve, will it populate other planets and the galaxy; then move forward until the sun dies out and becomes a white dwarf, until the earth is turned to ice, and until dark energy continues to create space between galaxies and the universe is empty and creation ends.

3. EVIL——Imagine evil acts and events, each one progressively worse, until you reach the most malefic act you can imagine. Start with small bad actions like a lie that causes harm

to someone and continue with acts of increasing moral degradation until you are faced with the worst possible acts.

4. GOOD——Imagine good actions and good happenings. Start with a flowering shrub, the smell of a rose, the songs of birds in the morning, the gentle and loving pressure of your cat or your dog against your leg, and continue with the tenderness of a kiss, an act of selfless kindness, the love of parents for their children, total peace on earth, the cessation of crime and hatred, and follow this trend of thought with greater and more soul-enriching experiences of good until you reach what to you is the greatest good of all.

5. THE SIX PHYSICAL DIRECTIONS (UP, DOWN, EAST, WEST, SOUTH, NORTH)——Imagine the limits of spatial dimension. Start with the directions around you, and those around other people and things, move on to the directions around earth, the sun, the solar system, the Milky Way galaxy, and further into the outer rims of the universe until you cannot imagine anything else. Then imagine that you descend to the earth, through its crust, through the interior magma and the tectonic plates, deep within the core of the earth until you can go no further. When you reach this point, you have plumbed the ten directions and the depths.

After this exercise the person proceeds to ascend through visualization from the tenth to the first sphere of the Tree of Life. This is done by visualizing the images associated with each sephira:

MALKUTH——a young woman, crowned, sitting on a throne

YESOD——a beautiful naked man

HOD——a hermaphrodite, a being half male and half female

NETZACH——a beautiful naked woman

TIPHARETH——a beautiful young child, surrounded by golden light

GEBURAH——a warrior in armor, standing in a chariot

CHESED——a king, crowned, sitting on a throne

BINAH——a matron, a mature woman, majestic and imperious

CHOKMAH——a bearded man, very stern and impressive

KETHER——an ancient king with a long white beard, sitting in profile

Through the visualization of these images, one after the other, the soul ascends from the depths to the greatest heights where God and the angels dwell. This is the meaning of Psalm 130. If these two meditations are done at least once a week, the soul is greatly purified and attains illumination.

It is important to know that when the images of Chokmah and Kether are visualized, the soul has not reached these exalted spheres because thought is not possible in them. These visualizations are done through Binah because this is as high as the human soul can reach.

There is only one way to ascend to Chokmah and Kether, and that is through a divine edict or commandment. In higher meditations, the sephiroth can be perceived as bolts of lightning that go up and down repeatedly through the Tree. When there is a commandment present, the sephiroth follow it like a rushing wind. That is why kabbalist masters recommend meditation on one of the Ten Commandments, because this is an edict from God and the sephiroth are energized when they perceive it. This acts like the *Merkabah*, God's chariot of fire, and elevates the soul to very high levels.

There are ten names of God, ten choirs of angels, ten great Archangels, and ten planets associated with the ten spheres of the Tree of Life. They can be used during these meditations.

Name of God	Choir	Archangel	Planet
1. Eheieh	Chayot ha Qodesh	Metatron	Neptune
2. Jehovah	Ophanim	Raziel	Uranus
3. Jehovah Elohim	Aralim	Tzaphkiel	Saturn
4. El	Chasmalim	Zadkiel	Jupiter
5. Elohim Gebor	Seraphim	Kamael	Mars
6. Jehovah elo ve Daath	Malachim	Raphael	Sun
7. Jehovah Tzabaoth	Elohim	Hanael	Venus
8. Elohim Tzabaoth	Beni Elohim	Michael	Mercury
9. Shaddai el Chai	Cherubim	Gabriel	Moon
10. Adonai ha Aretz	Ishim	Sandalphon	Earth

The angels belong to Yetzirah, the World of Formation. There are two classes of angels: messengers, or *mal'akh*, made from the divine breath; and ministers made of fire who always remain in one universe. The messengers move continuously, according to divine mandates. They are the superior angels. Guardian angels are the angel ministers.

As we have seen, each angel has a mission or missions. Two angels cannot have the same mission. An angel has no way of knowing anything that does not pertain to his mission. The angel of love knows nothing about money, and the angel of money knows nothing about love. Angels received an immense amount of knowledge and powers pertaining to their missions when they were created, but they cannot learn anything new. For this reason we, as human beings, have an advantage over the angels. We can learn anything and do anything we want within our limitations. But, unlike the angels, our knowledge, though broad, is confined, while theirs is limited but infinite. Also, angels are assigned special stations, which are the heavens they inhabit. They belong to specific levels. They can descend to the lower heavens but cannot ascend to those higher than their own. An angel of the Third Heaven can descend to the second or the first but cannot ascend to the fourth or beyond. The only angels that can ascend to all the heavens are the angelic princes of the Divine Presence.

Unlike angels, human beings can ascend to all the heavens, depending on their evolution. But in order to do that we must remain a part of the material world, which we can transcend through observance of God's laws, good actions, and the aspiration to union with God. When these lofty goals are achieved, the soul can rise above its human level but must always remain an active member of the human race, for it is not possible to live only in the world of spirit and ignore the world of matter. It is necessary to live and act in the physical world, to enjoy and at the same time control it, and act in the most perfect way possible in order to evolve spiritually. It is therefore important to live fully in the world of matter while striving to achieve the world of spirit. That is the meaning of the human equation, 010, where 0 is the state of nonbeing before birth, 1 is the state of physical reality, and the last 0 is the return to the original state of nonbeing.

CHAPTER 11

The Heavenly Hierarchy

*I would rather live my life as if there is a God
and die to find out there isn't, than live my life
as if there isn't and die to find out there is.*

. . . .

ALBERT CAMUS

T he Zohar, the most important of the kabbalistic texts, says that "when the Concealed of the Concealed wished to reveal Himself He first made a single point: the Infinite was entirely unknown, and diffused no light before this luminous point violently broke through into vision." The Concealed of the Concealed is the Ain Soph, and the single point is the Ain Soph Aur, or Kether.

The name of this point is "I am," Eheieh, and it is known as the Crown, the first sphere of the Tree of Life, Kether. From Kether were emitted the other nine spheres. Together they became known as the first system of sephiroth.

These initial ten spheres were called the shining sapphires. Many kabbalists believe that the word *sapphire* is the basis for the word *sephira*,

. . . .

which is the singular of sephiroth. This belief is rooted in the fact that the four worlds, the intelligences or angels, and their hierarchies were established according to the vision of Ezekiel, who described God's throne as a huge sapphire.

The area below the single point manifested as Kether, and the first Tree of Life was then filled by four worlds, or spheres, in descending order. These worlds, as we have seen, are Atziluth, Briah, Yetzirah, and Assiah.

The light of the ten original sephiroth formed from the Ain Soph was reflected down through each of these four worlds in increasingly diffused form. This resulted in four additional Trees, each with ten spheres and each reflecting the light of its world. Thus there were forty sephiroth, or spheres of creation, emitted by the Ain Soph, plus the original nine sephiroth and Kether, the Ain Soph Aur. Between each of these emanated spheres there is a gate. These are the fifty gates of the Trees of Life through which we all must travel to reach God.

As the four worlds unfold, the last sephira of the superior Tree of Life emanates the first sephira of the inferior one following it. Thus the tenth, or Malkuth, sphere of the world of Atziluth emanates the first, or Kether, sphere of the world of Briah. The Malkuth sphere of Briah emanates the Kether sphere of Yetzirah, and the Malkuth sphere of Yetzirah emanates the Kether sphere of Assiah.

The four Trees of Life of the four worlds and their forty spheres are expressed into the four worlds:

ATZILUTH——the boundless world of divine names

BRIAH——the Archangelic world of creation

YETZIRAH——the hierarchal world of formation

ASSIAH——the elemental world of substance

In the world of Atziluth, the ten sephiroth are known as the Rings of the Sacred Names. These first ten spheres and their names were emitted as follows:

- From Ain Soph Aur was emitted the First Crown (Kether) and the name of the first power of God, Eheieh, which means "I am."

- From the First Crown was emitted the First Wisdom (Chokmah) and the name of the second power of God, Jehovah, which means "essence of being."

- From the First Wisdom was emitted the First Understanding (Binah) and the name of the third power of God, Jehovah Elohim, which means "god of gods."

- From the First Understanding was emitted the First Mercy (Chesed) and the name of the fourth power of God, El, which means "God the Creator."

- From the First Mercy was emitted the First Severity (Geburah) and the name of the fifth power of God, Elohim Gebor, which means "God the Potent."

- From the First Severity was emitted the First Beauty (Tiphareth) and the name of the sixth power of God, Jehovah elo ve Daath, which means "God the Strong."

- From the First Beauty was emitted the First Victory (Netzach) and the name of the seventh power of God, Jehovah Tzabaoth, which means "God of Hosts."

- From the First Victory was emitted the First Glory (Hod) and the name of the eighth power of God, Elohim Tzabaoth, which means "Lord God of Hosts."

- From the First Glory was emitted the First Foundation (Yesod) and the name of the ninth power of God, Shaddai el Chai, which means "omnipotent."

- From the First Foundation was emitted the First Kingdom (Malkuth) and the name of the tenth power of God, Adonai ha Aretz, which means "God of the Earth."

This completed the Tree of Life in the world of Atziluth, the boundless World of Divine Names. These spheres are known as the ten roots of the Tree of Life. They are arranged in the form of a human figure known as Adam Kadmon, the universal man, a symbol of the created universe (see appendix 6, figure 7).

In the second world of Briah, the sephiroth are known as the great spirits or divine creatures that assist God in the establishment of order and intelligence in the universe. These are the ten great Archangels of Briah. Their order and powers are as follows:

- From the First Kingdom of Atziluth was emanated the Second Crown of the world of Briah. This is Metatron, Angel of the Presence.

- From the Second Crown was emanated the Second Wisdom. This is Ratziel, the angelic herald who revealed the sacred mysteries to Adam.

- From the Second Wisdom was emanated the Second Understanding. This is Tzaphkiel, the Contemplation of God.

- From the Second Understanding was emanated the Second Mercy. This is Zadkiel, the Mercy of God.

- From the Second Mercy was emanated the Second Severity. This is Kamael, the Justice of God.

- From the Second Severity was emanated the Second Beauty. This is Michael, He Who Is Like God.

- From the Second Beauty was emanated the Second Victory. This is Hanael, the Grace of God.

- From the Second Victory was emanated the Second Glory. This is Raphael, the Divine Physician.

- From the Second Glory was emanated the Second Foundation. This is Gabriel, the Man-God.

- From the Second Foundation was emanated the Second Kingdom. This is Sandalphon, the Messiah.

The duty of these ten great Archangels is to manifest the ten powers of the great names of God existing in the world of Atziluth, which permeates the entire world of creation, Briah.

In the third world of Yetzirah the sephiroth become hierarchies of angels, known as the ten choirs of Yetzirah. They are emanated from the last sphere of the Briatic world as follows:

- From the Second Kingdom of Briah was emanated the Third Crown. The hierarchy is that of the *Chayoth Ha Qodesh*, the "Holy Beings."

- From the Third Crown was emanated the Third Wisdom. The hierarchy is that of the *Ophanim*, the "Wheels."

- From the Third Wisdom was emanated the Third Understanding. The hierarchy is that of the *Erelim*, the "Mighty Ones."

- From the Third Understanding was emanated the Third Mercy. The hierarchy is that of the *Chasmalim*, the "Brilliant Ones."

- From the Third Mercy was emanated the Third Severity. The hierarchy is that of the *Seraphim*, the "Fiery Serpents."

- From the Third Severity was emanated the Third Beauty. The hierarchy is that of the *Malachim*, the "Kings."

- From the Third Beauty was emanated the Third Victory. The hierarchy is that of the *Elohim*, the "Gods."

- From the Third Victory was emanated the Third Glory. The hierarchy is that of the *Beni Elohim*, the "Sons of God."

- From the Third Glory was emanated the Third Foundation. The hierarchy is that of the *Cherubim*, the "Seat of the Sons."

- From the Third Foundation was emanated the Third Kingdom. The hierarchy is that of the *Ishim*, the "Souls of the Saints, or just human beings."

The last world, or Assiah, is emanated from the world of Yetzirah. Assiah is the elemental world of substance and represents the universe and all solar systems.

The ten spheres of Assiah were emanated from Yetzirah as follows:

- From the Third Kingdom of Yetzirah was emanated the Fourth Crown. This is Rashith ha-Galagalum, the primum mobile, the swirling gases of the early universe.

- From the Fourth Crown was emanated the Fourth Wisdom, Masloth, the zodiac, the firmament of fixed stars.

- From the Fourth Wisdom was emanated the Fourth Understanding, Shabbathai, the sphere of Saturn.

- From the Fourth Understanding was emanated the Fourth Mercy, Tzedek, the sphere of Jupiter.

- From the Fourth Mercy was emanated the Fourth Severity, Madim, the sphere of Mars.

- From the Fourth Severity was emanated the Fourth Beauty, Shemesh, the sphere of the sun.

- From the Fourth Beauty was emanated the Fourth Victory, Nogah, the sphere of Venus.

- From the Fourth Victory was emanated the Fourth Glory, Kokab, the sphere of Mercury.

- From the Fourth Glory was emanated the Fourth Foundation, Levanah, the sphere of the moon.

- From the Fourth Foundation was emanated the Fourth Kingdom, Cholom Yosodoth, the sphere of the four elements.

Thus were the ten sephiroth of the world of Assiah emanated and the four worlds completed. In Ezekiel's vision, the man on the throne represents the world of Atziluth, the throne upon which he sits represents Briah, the firmament is the world of Yetzirah, and the living creatures are the world of Assiah.

The human body is also identified with the ten spheres of the world of Assiah. That is why the human being is known as the microcosm, a lesser reflection of the macrocosm, or universe. Although the entire universe, in the form of the ten sephiroth, is part of every human being, most people are unaware of this symbiosis.

Yet these higher spheres exercise a powerful control over each of us, and without them we would cease to exist. The human soul is, in reality, a concentration of this great host of intelligences that are focused upon our substance through a point called the ego. We are supposed to climb through the various worlds and their Trees, using the energies of these same intelligences to help us in our upward journey to the Infinite. The process through which this can be accomplished is called the Fifty Gates of Light, where each gate is an entrance to one of the fifty sephiroth of the five Trees. These portals, also known as the Fifty Gates of Intelligence, emanate from Binah, which represents the first three sephiroth of the original Tree of Life in this work and leads to the Ain Soph. These gates are associated with the created universe and earth. For that reason, only the lower seven spheres in the four worlds form forty-nine of the fifty Gates, with Binah—representing the three higher sephiroth—making the fiftieth gate. The seven spheres, or sephiroth, encompassing the four worlds start with Malkuth in the fourth world and ascend all the way to Chesed in the first world and then to Binah. This is expressed kabbalistically as follows:

First Stage

1. Malkuth within Malkuth

2. Yesod within Malkuth

3. Hod within Malkuth

4. Netzach within Malkuth

5. Tiphereth within Malkuth

6. Geburah within Malkuth

7. Chesed within Malkuth

Second Stage

8. Malkuth within Yesod

9. Yesod within Yesod

10. Hod within Yesod

11. Netzach within Yesod

12. Tiphareth within Yesod

13. Geburah within Yesod

14. Chesed within Yesod

Third Stage

15. Malkuth within Hod

16. Yesod within Hod

17. Hod within Hod

18. Netzach within Hod

19. Tiphareth within Hod

20. Geburah within Hod

21. Chesed within Hod

Fourth Stage

22. Malkuth within Netzach

23. Yesod within Netzach

24. Hod within Netzach

25. Netzach within Netzach

26. Tiphareth within Netzach

27. Geburah within Netzach

28. Chesed within Netzach

Fifth Stage

29. Malkuth within Tiphareth

30. Yesod within Tiphareth

31. Hod within Tiphareth

32. Netzach within Tiphareth

33. Tiphareth within Tiphareth

34. Geburah within Tiphareth

35. Chesed within Tiphareth

Sixth Stage

36. Malkuth within Geburah

37. Yesod within Geburah

38. Hod within Geburah

39. Netzach within Geburah

40. Tiphareth within Geburah

41. Geburah within Geburah

42. Chesed within Geburah

Seventh Stage

43. Malkuth within Chesed

44. Yesod within Chesed

45. Hod within Chesed

46. Netzach within Chesed

47. Tiphareth within Chesed

48. Geburah within Chesed

49. Chesed within Chesed

50. Binah and the Ain Soph

There are seven stages in this ascent from Malkuth within Malkuth in the world of Assiah to Chesed within Chesed in the world of Atziluth. These seven stages are the seven heavens, which are below the higher three:

1. Shamaym, ruled by Gabriel. It is in Yesod and corresponds to the Moon.

2. Raquie, ruled by Raphael. It is in Hod and corresponds to Mercury.

3. Sagun, ruled by Hanael. It is in Netzach and corresponds to Venus.

4. Machonon, ruled by Michael. It is in Tiphareth and corresponds to the sun.

5. Mathey, ruled by Kamael. It is in Geburah and corresponds to Mars.

6. Zebul, ruled by Zadkiel. It is in Chesed and corresponds to Jupiter.

7. Araboth, ruled by Cassiel. It is in Binah and corresponds to Saturn.

The Seventh Heaven is the highest of the lower heavens and connects with Binah, which is the sphere that represents the three upper sephiroth in the ascent through the fifty gates.

In the ascent through these fifty gates and seven heavens, we must rend the three veils that separate the sephiroth in each Tree of Life. We must start by tearing the Veil of the Profane, which separates Malkuth from Yesod. This reveals to us that we are more than our ego and our physical body. At this point, the ego, beginning to stir, aspires to reach higher levels of awareness and a higher consciousness. It ascends further until it reaches the Veil of Paroketh, the Veil of Illusion. Paroketh (PRKT) refers to the four elements, symbolized by four of the Hebrew letters:

Peh, water; Resh, air; Kaph, fire; and Tav, earth. These represent the world of matter, Assiah, which is a mirage, a false reality.

Paroketh is called the Veil of Illusion because what we see below it is illusory. Reality is on the other side of the veil. Our soul resides in the true reality. Our ego and persona reside in the illusion of reality. When the ego begins to discern this truth, the Veil of Paroketh is torn, and the ego meets face to face with the soul. What must be accomplished then is ascent to the Veil of the Ancient of Days, which separates Kether from the rest of the sephiroth, and to tear that veil to come face to face with God.

But in order to reach this last veil, the soul must first pass through the sphere of Daath, the invisible sephira that lies midway between Tiphareth and Kether in the Middle Pillar of the Tree of Life. Daath is a dangerous sphere identified with the Abyss. There are many temptations lurking in its depths because it is a portal to the Qlipoth. And often many souls, unaware of its perils, fall for its allurements and fail in their quest. When a soul undergoes this experience, it is known as Babe of the Abyss. It is indeed the dark night of the soul, and much torment is suffered at such times.

If the soul can overcome the dangers of Daath, it can ascend safely to the Veil of the Ancient of Days. But when this happens in Assiah, the soul has not yet reached the Ain Soph Aur in Kether, but only its fourth reflection. The soul, now burning with the divine desire to unite with God, continues to climb through each of the fifty gates, rending the three veils in each Tree until it reaches the last veil. But even then, it cannot achieve its goal, for this veil can only be torn after death.

It is the soul's mission, its *tikkun*, to ascend these fifty gates and rend the three veils in each of the Trees until it can reach and tear the final veil and become one with God. This lofty goal requires many lives and many incarnations, and the souls hover perilously over the edge of the Qlipoth during their search. It is the work of the angels to help us in this quest.

CHAPTER 12

The Ten Celestial Choirs

Human beings must be known to be loved;
But divine beings must be loved to be known.

. . . .

BLAISE PASCAL

From Revelation 4:2–8:

"And there in Heaven stood a throne, with one seated on the throne! And the one seated there looks like jasper and carnelian, and around the throne is a rainbow that looks like an emerald. Around the throne are twenty-four thrones. And seated on the thrones are twenty-four elders, dressed in white robes, with golden crowns on their heads. Coming from the throne are flashes of lightning, and rumblings and peals of thunder, and in front of the throne burn seven flaming torches, which are the seven spirits of God; and in front of the throne there is something like a sea of glass, like crystal.

"Around the throne, and on each side of the throne, are four living creatures, full of eyes in front and behind: the first living creature like a lion, the second living creature like an ox, the third living creature with

. . . .

a face like a human face, and the fourth living creature like a flying eagle. And the four living creatures, each of them with six wings, are full of eyes all around and inside. Day and night without ceasing they sing: Holy, Holy, Holy, the Lord God the Almighty, who was and is and is to come."

This is part of the vision of John, the youngest disciple of Jesus, in the last book of the Bible, known as Revelation. It is immediately obvious that John's vision is strikingly similar to Ezekiel's, but there are some important differences.

In John's vision the living creatures have six wings, while in Ezekiel's vision they only have four. Ezekiel describes wheels (the *Ophanim*) under God's throne, but these wheels are not present in John's vision.

The reason why the two visions differ is that Ezekiel is looking at the chariot, or *Merkabah*, with God's throne while it is in motion. The living creatures (*Chayot Ha Qadosh*) that hold the chariot with the throne are in continuous movement. He only sees four wings because two wings were folded behind the living creatures. With two wings they held the chariot, and with two wings they covered their feet. The other two wings were not used because they were not flying, they were moving together in one single motion. Ezekiel is seeing his vision from the Third Heaven, which is in Binah. But John is seeing his vision from the First Heaven, which is in Kether. He is in the Plethora, God's realm. The throne is not moving. It is firmly set on the sea of glass, like crystal. And there are lightning bolts and peals of thunder coming from the throne, which are the *Erelim*, or Angels of the Throne. John does not see the Wheels, the *Ophanim*, because they are no longer carrying the chariot with the throne.

Isaiah also sees the living creatures in his own vision, and he describes them very much like John does. He identifies them as Seraphim: "In the year that King Uzziah died, I saw the Lord sitting on a throne, high and lofty, and the hem of his robe filled the temple. Seraphs were in attendance above him; each had six wings: with two they covered their faces, and with two they covered their feet, and with two they flew. And one called another and said: Holy, Holy, Holy is the Lord of Hosts; the whole earth is full of his glory" (Isaiah 6:1–3).

Isaiah is also in the First Heaven in his vision because God's throne is not moving. He does not perceive any of the other angels, the twenty-four elders, or the glass expanse in front of God's throne because the hem of his robe covered the temple. Thus God hid the other holy creatures from Isaiah's view. Of these three prophets, John is the only one who has the full vision of God's realm.

The twenty-four elders in John's vision are both witnesses to God's judgments and the praises of the holy creatures. Thus John says: "And whenever the living creatures give glory and honor and thanks to the one who is seated on the throne, who lives forever and ever, the twenty-four elders fall before the one who is seated on the throne and worship the one who lives forever and ever; they cast their crowns before the throne, singing: 'You are worthy, our Lord and God, to receive glory and honor and power, for you created all things, and by your will they existed and were created'" (Rev. 4:9).

John also sees seven flaming torches in front of God's throne, which he identifies as the seven spirits of God. Ezekiel describes torches moving to and fro among the living creatures. They are like burning coals of fire; the fire is bright and lightning issues from the fire. These are the Seraphim, often described as flaming serpents, and which are always close to God, burning with love for their creator. The seven spirits of God can also be equated with the seven angelic princes of the Divine Presence.

From the visions of these three prophets we can see that while the *Chayot Ha Qadosh*, or "Holy Living Creatures"; the *Ophanim*, or "Wheels"; and the *Erelim*, or "Thrones" are the angelic choirs that are in charge of the *Merkabah* and God's throne while it is in motion, it is the Seraphim (who surround the *Merkabah* in Ezekiel's vision) who are in attendance of God in his throne when the *Merkabah* is at rest. Therefore, the Seraphim are the first of the choirs in the hierarchy of the angels attending to God. That is the reason why they are the First Choir of Angels in Pseudo-Dionysius.

. . . .

The ten angelic choirs can then be described in the Pseudo-Dionysius system as follows :

1. The Seraphim

The etymology of Seraphim comes from the word *saraph*, which is used to connote a burning, fiery state. It is composed of *ser*, which denotes a higher being, and *rapha*, which means "he who heals." Therefore, a Seraph is a higher spirit who heals. The name of Raphael, who is known as the divine physician, is composed of *Rapha* and the suffix *el*, meaning "son of God." Raphael's name means "the son of God who heals." In spite of his name, Raphael does not belong to the choir of the Seraphim.

The Seraphim are described as shining beings, perfect and incorruptible. Their light is so blinding that none of the other choirs can look at them. Human beings would be instantly disintegrated if they were to come face-to-face with a Seraph in its true form.

The mission of the Seraphim is to control and direct the divine energies that flow from the throne of God and to purify and inflame the human heart with love for its creator. For that reason they are known as the angels of love.

In his work *Celestial Hierarchy*, Pseudo-Dionysius says that the name Seraphim "clearly indicates their ceaseless and eternal revolution about Divine Principles, their heat and keenness, the exuberance of their intense, perpetual, tireless activity, and their energetic assimilation of those below, kindling them with their own heat, and wholly purifying them by a burning and all-consuming flame; and by their unhidden, radiant and enlightening power, dispelling and destroying the shadows of darkness" (see Heil 1991).

Thomas of Aquinas, in his *Summa Theologiae*, describes the nature of the Seraphim in terms of fire: "First, the movement is upwards and continuous. This signifies that they are borne inflexibly toward God. Secondly, the active force which is heat signifies the actions of these angels, which are exercised powerfully upon those who are subject to them, rousing them to fervor and cleansing them thoroughly by their heat. Thirdly, we consider in fire the quality of clarity, or brightness, which signifies these angels have in themselves an inextinguishable light, and that they also perfectly enlighten and purify others" (see Kars 2003).

The regent princes of the Seraphim are Seraphiel (who rules them), Metatron, Michael, Uriel, Shemuel, Jehoel, and Natanael.

There is a simple ritual that can be used to contact the Seraphim in order to ascend to God through the ten sephiroth.

One begins by lighting a short white candle. The wick is identified with the material world. The blue of the flame represents Malkuth. The heart of the flame encompasses the sephiroth Yesod to Chesed. The upper yellow of the flame represents the upper three sephiroth: Binah, Chokmah, and Kether. One then empties the mind and concentrates on the various parts of the flame. In this way, the ten sephiroth are united and the soul ascends to the realm of the Seraphim, who then bring it closer to God. This ritual is recommended by kabbalist masters as a sure way to evolve spiritually and unite with God. It is said to help in the development of great psychic powers if done every night before sleep.

2. The Cherubim

The idea of a Cherub as an adorable baby angel with fluffy wings and an ethereal smile is completely erroneous. These "Cherubs" are in reality known as *putti,* and their idealized concept comes to us from the artists of the Middle Ages. Cherubim are fierce warrior angels. After the expulsion of Adam and Eve from paradise, God placed Cherubim at the east of the Garden of Eden and a flaming and turning sword to guard the way to the Tree of Life.

The word *Cherubim* comes from the Assyrian *karibu* and means "he who prays and intercedes." Among the Assyrians, the Cherubs were winged creatures with the face of a man or a lion and the body of a sphinx, an eagle, or an ox. As we have seen, the man, the lion, the eagle, and the ox are symbols of the four elements, the four winds, the four cardinal points and the astrological signs of Aquarius (Air), Leo (Fire), Scorpio

(Water), and Taurus (Earth), respectively. The sphinx is a composite of all four creatures, as it has the face of a man, the feet of a lion, the body of an ox, and the wings of an eagle. The four Holy Living Creatures of Ezekiel's vision are Cherubim, which exemplifies the Assyrian influence in Hebraic religious thought.

Muslims, on the other hand, believe that the Cherubim were formed from Michael's tears, shed for the sins of the faithful. Their name in Arabic is *Al-karubiyan*, which means "those who are closer to Allah."

It is said that from the Cherubim, who are the personification of wisdom, flows a subtle essence of knowledge that they receive directly from God.

Cherubim are mentioned in Genesis, the book of Ezekiel, the book of Isaiah, 1 Kings, 2 Kings, 1 Chronicles, and 2 Chronicles. And in the book of Exodus, God orders Moses to place the image of a Cherub with widespread wings on each side of the Ark of the Covenant.

Cherubs are discussed in the Midrash literature, which deals with the interpretation of biblical scriptures. According to one of the Midrash, when a man sleeps, the body tells the nephesch what it has done during the day, the *Nephesh* tells the *Neshamah*, the *Neshamah* tells the guardian angel, the guardian angel tells a Cherub, and the Cherub tells a Seraph, who then brings it before God. Another Midrash says that "when Pharaoh pursued Israel at the red sea, God took a Cherub from the wheels of his throne and flew to the spot, for God inspects the heavenly worlds while sitting on a Cherub. The Cherub, however, is something not material, and is carried by God, not vice versa."

According to this Midrash, God was very much in charge of the movements of the *Merkabah*, as seen by Ezekiel in his vision.

Rabbi Moshe ben Maimon, better known as Maimonides, had a neo-Aristotelian interpretation of the Bible. In his *Guide to the Perplexed*, he writes that angels are actually symbols of the various laws of nature. To Maimonides, "all forms produced by the active intellect are angels and God created the world and the universe through perfectly natural laws, identified as angels. The imaginative faculty is also called an angel and the mind is called a Cherub."

The regent princes of the Cherubim are Cherubiel (who rules them), Gabriel, Ophaniel, Raphael, Uriel, and Zophiel.

As the choir associated with the second sphere, Chokmah, which represents wisdom, the Cherubim nurture human intelligence and the human mind. It is the Cherubim we must contact when we need lucidity of mind, when we are confused or undecided about a special situation, when we need clarity of intellect and the sharp edge of perspicacity. Cherubim are the patrons of genius and superior intelligence.

A simple ritual to connect with the Cherubim and ask them for clarity of mind or the wisdom to make a right decision requires four short candles in the colors red, yellow, green, and blue. These candles represent the four elements and the four cardinal points associated with the Cherubim. Sit facing the east. Place the yellow candle in front of you, the red to your right, the blue behind you, and the green to your left. Light the candles, and empty your mind; relax, and breathe deeply and evenly. Have a dictionary in front of you. Then ask the Cherubim to give you guidance in your problem. Close your eyes, and open the dictionary. Put a finger on one of the open pages, open your eyes, and read the word or words that are underneath your finger. Interpret the word or words in the light of your situation. You will be astonished at the wisdom of the message you receive.

3. The Thrones

This choir is identified as the *Erelim* in Maimonides's angelic hierarchy. The Thrones are living symbols of God's justice and authority, and are related directly to God's throne, which they hold with the tips of their fingers. They are mentioned in Daniel with other angelic choirs: "As I watched, Thrones were set in place, and an Ancient One took his Throne. His clothing was white as snow, and the hair of his head like pure wool; his Throne was fiery flames, and its Wheels were burning fire. A stream of fire issued and flowed from his presence. A thousand thousands served him, and ten thousand times ten thousand stood attending him. The court sat in judgment and the books were opened" (Daniel 7: 9–10).

Daniel is describing the Thrones as "set in place." He also describes the *Ophanim* as Wheels that were "burning fire," and the Seraphim as a "stream of fire that issued and flowed" from God's presence. He perceives the entire heavenly court with myriad angels in attendance, all serving God's Divine Presence. This happens as the books are opened and God is ready to render his judgment.

It is highly significant that Daniel's vision is strikingly similar to those of Ezekiel, Isaiah, and John. All these prophets are seeing the same scene from different angles, which seems to suggest that there are places in the human collective unconscious where minds converge and share the same or similar images. These experiences take place in altered states of consciousness that are beyond the space-time continuum, and their origin is beyond human comprehension.

Thrones are angels of the Third Order and are beings of tremendous power and movement. They are the keepers of higher, more expanded energies who ensure that these energies flow down through the various angelic realms. In many ways they act as conduits of the physical world and tend to be more stationary in their own existence. God's spirit is shown in a mysterious way to these angels, who in turn pass on the message to humanity and the lower angels.

Thrones are bringers of justice, but their status is often confused with that of the *Ophanim*, or Wheels. Sometimes they are placed above the Seraphim and sometimes they are placed at the same level as the Cherubim. They are nevertheless among the most powerful angels in God's service, as they have the task of pondering the disposition of divine judgment, which they carry out. They also inspire faith in the power of the Creator, which is at the center of all miracles.

Thrones create, channel, and collect incoming and outgoing positive energies. They dispense justice and at the same time send healing energies to victims of injustice, which they reveal through their radiant light. Like the Seraphim and Cherubim, the Thrones are the closest of all angels to spiritual perfection, and they emanate God's light with mirrorlike goodness. Yet, despite their greatness, they are intensely humble, an attribute that allows them to dispense justice with perfect objectivity devoid of pride or ambition.

The prince regents of the Thrones are Oriphiel, Tzaphkiel, Jophiel, and Ratziel.

The Thrones are invoked when we are in need of divine justice in our human affairs or when we need positive energies to help us carry on with our daily lives. They are invaluable during court cases or when one is faced with an injustice.

A very simple but highly effective ritual to invoke the powers of the Thrones on our behalf starts by writing a petition to these angels on parchment paper or a white, unlined paper. Kabbalists suggest writing the petition on parchment with a white quill pen and magic ink, as the Thrones are very exalted and pure entities, but if these are not available, a regular pen will do. Frankincense and myrrh should be burned on a piece of burning charcoal. Relax, empty your mind, and breathe deeply and evenly for a few minutes. Then pass the paper through the incense three times and finally place it on the burning charcoal until it burns to ashes. During this time, the Thrones are invoked to grant the petition. As the paper burns, the Thrones gather the Petition and bring it to God's Presence. If the paper burns completely, the petition is granted. If it does not, the petition is denied. There are reasons why petitions are denied, which are known only to God and his angels. But the ritual can be performed every day during three days if it fails the first time. If the paper does not burn the third time, the ritual cannot be repeated and the denial is final.

The Seraphim, the Cherubim, and the Thrones are the three choirs belonging to the first angelic order.

4. The Dominions

These angels are known as the Lords. They assign their duties and missions to the angels of the lower choirs. God's majesty is revealed through them. These angels are seldom in contact with human beings, as part of their duties is to maintain the cosmic order. In Maimonides's hierarchy they are identified with the *Chasmalim* and connected with the sphere of Chesed.

Among the symbols of authority of the Dominions are the orb and the scepter, which represent the world. They often carry swords as symbols of their power over other creatures. They are said to dress in tunics of green and gold.

This choir receives its instructions from the Cherubim and the Thrones. Paul mentions them in Colossians 1:16 together with the Thrones, the Powers, and the Principalities. The Second Book of Enoch says the Dominions are part of the angelic armies. They are said to be channels of mercy.

Because their work does not bring them in direct contact with human beings, the Dominions are not invoked as a choir for special help. Angels belonging to this choir can be invoked in special ceremonies dedicated to them.

The prince regents of the Dominions are Zadkiel, Chashmal, Zarakiel, and Muriel.

5. The Virtues

As their name indicates, the Virtues are the angels in charge of conferring the quality of virtue to humankind. They also confer grace and valor. The Virtues preside over the elements and rule the process of celestial life. They are also in charge of the motion of the planets, the stars, and the galaxies, as they control the cosmic laws. This choir also rules astronomy and astrophysics.

The Virtues are in charge of nature and natural laws. According to Thomas Aquinas, the Virtues are in charge of all miracles and are connected with all the saints and the heroes who do battle against evil. It is said that the Virtues gave David the strength to overcome the giant Goliath. They are identified with the *Malachim* or *Tarshashim*.

Their regent princes are Michael, Gabriel, Uzziel, Peliel, Hanael, Hamaliel, Barbiel, Sabriel, and Tarshish.

A simple ritual used to invoke the Virtues and obtain a miracle through their help requires a single red rose placed in a flower vase with water and a teaspoon of sugar. Because the Virtues rule natural laws and the motion of the planets, the moon should be waxing to gather its positive energies. At exactly 10 PM on a Sunday, sit toward the east with the red rose facing you and light a short red candle. Relax, empty the mind, and breathe deeply and evenly for a few minutes. Then ask the Virtues for the miracle you desire. The candle is snuffed out without blowing on it. This ritual is repeated every day for seven days at the same time. If the rose does not die or droop during this period, the miracle will be granted.

6. The Powers

The principal mission of this choir is to maintain order in Heaven and to restrain the fallen angels from destroying the world. They are said to be in charge of the history of humanity and are present at the birth or death of human beings. According to some theologians, they preside over all world religions and provide them with the celestial energy to carry on their work.

Powers function primarily through intuition and warn human beings through dreams or premonitions when danger is near. This choir has the divine authority to punish, to forgive, and also to create through divine will, carrying out God's decrees. This gift was bestowed upon the Powers because they were created to be completely loyal to God. Some authorities say that no angel belonging to the Powers has ever fallen from grace, while others contend that most of the rebellious angels belonged to this choir before the Fall. Satan is said to have belonged to the Powers; he was also a Seraph, a Cherub, and an Archangel. One of the fallen angels, called Crocell, told King Solomon that he still hoped to make peace with God and return to the Powers.

. . . .

Part of the mission of the Powers is to help human beings avoid temptation and inspire us to follow God's laws. They also act as guides to lost souls, but their principal mission is the distribution of power among humankind, hence their name.

Powers are said to reside between the First and the Second Heaven and guard the path to the celestial realms. They are also known as Potentates, Dynamis, and Authorities. They collaborate with the Principalities.

The prince regents of the powers are Gabriel, Verchiel, and Kamael.

The Powers are invoked to resist temptation by burning an apple in a fire grill. The apple is used as a symbol for Eve's temptation.

The Dominions, the Virtues, and the Powers belong to the second angelic order.

7. The Principalities

The principal mission of this choir is to guard and protect kings, princes, judges, presidents, governors, and all world leaders, granting them the illumination to rule with wisdom and justice. They also protect the nations of the world, world organizations, and all religious leaders. Their symbols are the cross, the scepter, and the sword. These angels are also known as Princes because of their association with heads of state. In the Kabbalah they are identified as *Sarim*. Their regent princes are Hanael, Cerviel, and Rekiel.

This choir is invoked to protect heads of state. The name of the individual who needs their protection is inscribed on a white pillar candle, which is then anointed with oil of mint. The Principalities are invoked to illuminate that person in their work. The candle is lit thirteen minutes daily until the candle is finished.

8. The Archangels

The main duty of this choir is to intercede on behalf of humanity and their sins so that they may be forgiven by God. The Archangels are constantly at war with Satan and his hordes to protect the world against their continuous assault.

According to the Kabbalah, the Archangels are closely associated with the planets. Other authorities claim that they rule the signs of the zodiac. Pseudo-Dionysius described them as bearers of God's decrees.

Archangels are mentioned in both the Old and the New Testaments. According to the Epistle of Judah, when Michael was battling Satan over the body of Moses after the Lawgiver's death, he did not pass judgment over the prince of Hell. Instead he told him, "The Lord rebukes you."

There is a great confusion about the Archangels and the angels that do not belong to this choir but are addressed as such. The confusion started because in the beginning of angelology there were only two classes of angels: Archangels and Angels. It was through the scholarly efforts of Thomas Aquinas, Saint Augustine, and Pseudo-Dionysius that the various angelic orders were classified. During those early times the most exalted angels were called Archangels, a custom that persists in modern times. But not all the high-ranking angels are Archangels. Zadkiel, Kamael, Cassiel, Azrael, and Asariel, who are among the regents of the signs of the zodiac and wield great power in the celestial hierarchy, are not Archangels but are often referred to by this title. All of these angels belong to choirs superior to that of the Archangels.

The prince regents of the Archangels are Metatron, Michael, Raphael, Gabriel, Barbiel, Barachiel, and Jehudiel.

There is a very poignant ritual that is used to invoke the Archangels and ask for their intercession in the forgiveness of sins.

The person mixes ordinary dirt from a garden or a park with ashes and dust that have been swept from the floor of the house. This mixture is placed on a small dish on the floor. The person then kneels on a white sheet that has been folded four times and placed on the floor next to the mixture of dust, dirt, and ashes. The person should wear only a simple white shirt. Two small cuts should be made on the shirt near its collar. The person relaxes, clears the mind, and breathes deeply and evenly for a few minutes, then proceeds to describe the sin or sins that are troubling his or her soul, asking the Archangels to intercede with God for

. . . .

their forgiveness. The person then proceeds to tear his or her garment until he or she is naked. The mixture is then rubbed all over the body and the person begs forgiveness, saying, "I repent in dust and ashes." This ritual is very cathartic for the individual, who is always moved to tears by the experience. The remnants of the mixture, the sheet, and the shirt are thrown away. A ritual bath is then taken with new white soap, which is also thrown away after the cleansing.

9. The Angels

The principal mission of this choir is to act as intermediaries between God and humanity. Although the entire heavenly host are known as angels, this is a specific choir. Among them are found the guardian angels.

The Angels are the celestial choir who are closest to human beings, and they labor incessantly to guide and protect the human race. According to the First Book of Enoch, there is a school of angels in the Sixth Heaven where this choir is instructed by the Archangels. Enoch claimed to have visited this celestial school during his apocalyptic vision of Heaven. All the Angels Enoch saw had the same faces and were identically dressed.

The regent princes of the Angels are Gabriel, Chayyiel, Adbakiel, and Faleg. As these Angels also belong to higher choirs, it is to be assumed that they do not have to attend the angel school in the Sixth Heaven.

The Principalities, the Archangels, and the Angels belong to the third angelic order.

10. The Ishim

This choir does not appear in the angelic hierarchy of Pseudo-Dionysius and therefore does not belong to any of the three angelic orders. They do, however, appear in Maimonides's hierarchy of angels and are part of the angel choirs that rule the ten sephiroth of the Tree of Life. They are associated with the sphere of Malkuth and are identified as the souls of the saints or as sparks of heavenly fire.

The *Ishim* are said to be made of fire and snow and are often equated with the *Beni Elohim*, or Sons of God. They are the guardian angels of nature and of nature's creatures; thus, they are said to protect vegetation and all animal life, including insects, birds, and earth and sea creatures.

The *Ishim* do not have angel wings but are said instead to have unsubstantial human figures with butterfly wings in rainbow colors. Some authorities compare the *Ishim* with fairies or elves.

The prince regent of the *Ishim* is Sandalphon, who is also the ruler of Malkuth and the protector of the earth.

The *Ishim* may be invoked to protect the home by spreading white rose petals around the perimeters of the house.

The various angelic choirs are of great importance in the practice of angel magic, because everything in creation is ruled by angels, including life and death.

In the film *City of Angels,* we are introduced to a charming angel of death who becomes fascinated with human life and ends up falling in love with a woman. Every day all the angels gather by the seashore and listen intently to a sound only they can hear. This sound is the Holy Trisagion sung by the angelic Ephemeras in Heaven. It is difficult not to empathize with the plight of this angel who wishes so much to be human that he is willing to sacrifice his eternal life as a celestial being. But what the film does not tell us is that upon his human death, this fallen angel would be condemned to become one of the Silent Watchers, imprisoned forever in one of the darkest halls of the Third Heaven. This is the same place where the original fallen angels, the ones described in Genesis who fell in love with the daughters of men, spend all eternity.

CHAPTER 13

The Fallen Angels

If a man is not rising upwards to be an angel,
depend upon it, he is sinking downwards to be a devil.

· · · · · · · · · · · ·

SAMUEL TAYLOR COLERIDGE

Before Creation, there was only the infinite Ain Soph. When the Ain Soph—God, the Creator—wished to manifest his essence in physical form, he contracted himself in the very center of his light. This process is known in Kabbalah as *tzimtzum* and resulted in the Ain Soph Aur, a single point of concentrated light. There remained a void—a hollow, empty space—away from the central point, which was the Ain Soph Aur. A single straight line proceeded downward from the Ain Soph Aur through the void, and it descended in the space of that void, emanating, creating, and forming the four worlds and their sephiroth.

As we have seen, the Ain Soph Aur, wishing to contain and modify his light in this descent, created a series of vessels, or *ha-kelim*, in the empty space. But the vessels were unable to contain God's light and were shattered. This is known in Kabbalah as *shevirat ha-kelim,* or breaking of the

· · · · · · · · · · · ·

vessels. As a result of this cosmic catastrophe, the sephiroth, which are the archetypal values through which the universe was created, were broken and fell into the Abyss in the form of shards or sparks of light. This abyss is the Qlipoth. It is up to humanity to repair and return the fallen sparks to the infinite light through the process known as *tikkun*.

Fortunately, only six of the vessels, or sephiroth, were shattered, from the fourth to the ninth: Chesed, Geburah, Tiphareth, Netzach, Hod, and Yesod. Malkuth, the tenth sephira—which is the physical universe and our world—was only partially broken. The first three sephira—Kether, Chokmah, and Binah—were left intact. As these sephiroth represent will, wisdom, and understanding, if they had been shattered, the universe would have reverted to a state of complete annihilation, the *tohu wa-bohu* that existed prior to Creation. *Tohu wa-bohu* is a Hebrew description that appears in Genesis 1:2. It means waste and void, which describes the state of things before God created the universe. But all other values, particularly those embodied in the cultural and symbolic order of humanity, were shattered. This created chaos at the core of our spiritual, conceptual, moral, and psychological structures and brought discontinuity, imbalance, and evil into the world.

From the preceding we can see that the two sephiroth where the shattering of the vessels initially occurred were Chesed and Geburah, the fourth and fifth spheres of the Tree of Life. As we know, the value of Chesed is 72, while the value of Geburah is 216. When these two numbers are added, the result is 288, which is the number of sparks that fell into the Qlipoth. This cosmic upheaval took place in all the four worlds and the forty sephiroth that existed in them.

After the breaking down of the original vessels, the *shevirat ha-kelim*, the Ain Soph Aur sent another ray of light into the void and emanated four new worlds with their sephiroth, and the universe was finally in place. But what happened in the Qlipoth?

As we have seen, there is a Qlipothic Tree that is the opposite of the Tree of Life. When the four worlds were shaken by the shattering of the vessels, the lowest world of Assiah descended into the world of shells, or fallen sparks. The tenth sphere of the Tree of Life in Assiah, which is Malkuth, became the first sphere, Kether, of the Qlipoth.

Within the Qlipoth tree in Assiah we find ten spheres, known as the Adverse Sephiroth. These are the ten hierarchies of demons that correlate with the ten hierarchies of the good spirits that compose the world of Yetzirah. There are also ten archdemons corresponding to the Archangels of Briah. The ten hierarchies of demons and their archdemons in the world of Assiah are as follows:

1. Thamiel—Duality in God

Where Kether, the first sephira, represents the unity of God, *Thamiel*, as duality, represents a division of the Godhead. The cortex or outer form of the *Thamiel* is called *Cathariel*, the broken or fearful light of God. The main archdemon is Satan, adversary and king. To further stress the duality of the sphere, Satan unites with Moloch, an archdemon associated with child sacrifice and the month of December.

2. Chaigidel—Confusion of the Power of God

This represents the confusion of the great power of Chokmah, the second sphere, which is the concept of creation and relates to God's plan of the universe. The cortex of the *Chaigidel* is called *Goghiel*, "those who go forth into the place empty of God." The main archdemons are Beelzebub, lord of the flies, and Adam Belial, wicked man. Satan is also attributed to this sphere.

3. Sathariel—Concealment of God

Binah, the third sphere, is the revealing sephira who passes on the complete plan of creation to the next sphere, which is Chesed. Its opposite is *Sathariel*, "that which conceals the nature of the Perfect." The cortex of the *Sathariel* is called the order of *Sheireil*, "the hairy ones of God." The archdemon is Lucifuge, "one who flees light." This name is probably a substitute for Lucifer, the light bearer. He is also known as Lucifuge Rofocale and is considered one of the most powerful of the demonic entities, among which he acts as prime minister. He is said to have control over all the riches and treasures of the world.

4. Gamchicoth—Devourers

Chesed, the fourth sphere, is the true beginning of physical creation through God's mercy. Gamchicoth is the order of devourers who seek to destroy the impulse of creation. The cortex or outer form is the order of *Azariel*, "the binding ones of God." The ruler is Astaroth, whose title is One of the Flock. This name is a derivation of the Semitic Astarte or Ishtar, the love goddess of the Assyrians and Babylonians. Astaroth, once a prince of the order of the Seraphim, is now a great duke in the infernal regions where he serves as treasurer. According to the *Grimorium Verum*, one of the best known of the medieval grimoires, he has taken up residence in America.

5. Golachab—Burning Bodies

Geburah, the fifth sephira, is the sphere of severity. It is also known as Din, judgment. It symbolizes God's strength and his perfect sense of justice. Between Mercy, which is Chesed, and Justice, which is Geburah, the universe is perfectly poised and balanced. As the opposite to Geburah, Golachab is composed of those who burn with the desire to destroy, even themselves. The cortex or outer form is the order *Usiel*, "the ruins of God." The archdemon is Asmodeus, the creature of judgment. His name can also be translated as "the one adorned with fire." This demonic entity is of Persian origin but was later incorporated into Jewish lore. He is the demon of impurity, one of the vessels of wrath, and is in charge of all gambling houses in Hell. Some demonologists credit him with being the inventor of music, drama, dancing, and all the latest French fashions.

6. Thagirion—Those Who Bellow Grief and Tears

Tiphareth, the sixth sephira, is identified as beauty and as the joyous, life-giving powers of the sun. The *Thagirion* conjure a world of ugliness and grief, the complete opposite of Tiphareth. The cortex or outer form is the order of *Zomiel*, "the revolt of God." Its archdemon is Belphegor, lord of the dead and lord of opening. Among the Moabites Belphegor was a god of lust and licentiousness who was later incorporated into Jewish lore. He is said to have once belonged to the order of Principalities. According to de Plancy's *Dictionnaire Infernal*, he resides in France.

7. Harab Serapel—Ravens of the Burning of God

Netzach, the seventh sphere, represents the power and victory of love. The *Harab Serapel* are the ravens of death who reject even their own. The cortex or outer form is the order of *Theumiel*, "the fouled substance of God." The archdemons are Baal, lord of darkness, and Tubal-Cain, the maker of sharp weapons. Baal is said to be a great king in the nether regions, assisted by sixty or seventy legions of demons. Tubal-Cain is a descendant of Cain and the first metal worker. It is unclear how he became demonized.

8. Samael—The Desolation of God, or the Left Hand

Hod, the eighth sephira, is identified as the Glory of God, the place of the intellect and of action in the physical world. Samael, as its total opposite, represents the desolation of a failed creation. Samael is not only the name of this adverse sephira but also one of the alternate names of Satan. His name means "angel of poison." He is described as a great serpent with twelve wings that, in his fall, draws after him the entire solar system. Samael is chief of the satans in rabbinic lore and one of the angels of death. He is one of the regents of Hell, served by two million fallen angels. Some demonologists say Samael once belonged to the order of the Seraphim and is credited as the first of the art critics. The cortex or outer form of Samael is *Theuniel*, "the filthy wailing ones of God." The archdemon of Samael (as the eighth hierarchy of the adverse Tree) is Adrammelech, king of fire.

9. Gamaliel—Polluted of God

Yesod, the ninth sephira, is known as the Foundation, where all the energies that flow from the upper spheres take their final form before becoming matter in Malkuth. The *Gamaliel*, as opposites of Yesod, are the misshapen and polluted images that produce vile results. The cortex or outer form is the order of *Ogiel*, "those who flee from God." Gamaliel has a dual personality in angelic lore. In Kabbalah he is one of the great luminaries and is associated with Gabriel, whose mission is to draw the elect up to Heaven. But other authorities, notably Eliphas Levi in his *Occult Philosophy*, describe him as an adversary of the Cherubim, serving under Lilith, the demon of debauchery. In Qlipothic literature Gamaliel is the ninth sphere of the adverse Tree. The archdemon of Gamaliel is Lilith, the bride of Samael (Satan) and the destroyer of children, whom she constantly attacks and kills. Lilith is said to predate Eve, being Adam's first wife. This archdemon is derived from Mesopotamian demonology, where female demons were known as *Ardat Lili*. She is said to be the woman who comes to men in their dreams, and as such she is the embodiment of the succubus.

10. Nehemoth—Whisperers or Night Specters

Malkuth, the tenth sephira, is identified as the Kingdom and the created universe, as well as the earth. The *Nehemoth* are responsible for frightening sounds in strange places. They unsettle the mind and create unspeakable desires in the hearts of humans. There is no cortex or outer form in this adverse sephira. Its archdemon is Nehema, "groaning," who is said to be the sister of Lilith. Some authorities identify Nehema with Naamah, the sister of Tubal-Cain. Naamah is considered to be a powerful female demon.

In addition to the ten adverse sephiroth, there are also the seven infernal habitations or hells. The Book of Raziel lists them as follows:

GIHENAM OR GEHENNA——the entire abode of Hell

SHA'ARIMATH——the portals of Hell

TZALEMOTH——the shadow of death

BARASCHECATH——the Abyss of perdition

TITHIHOZ——the mud of death

ABBADON——perdition

SHAHOL——the deepest and triple Hell

In the Kabbalah these terrible places are known as the seven palaces of the ten hells, which are the ten spheres of the Qlipoth on the reverse of the Tree of Life.

The Kabbalah also recognizes twelve Qlipothic orders of demons, three powers before Satan, and twenty-two demons that correspond to the twenty-two letters of the Hebrew alphabet.

There is also a classification of demons based on the seven deadly sins that originated in the sixteenth century CE. According to this list, the demons associated with these sins were the following:

LUCIFER——pride

MAMMON——greed

ASMODEUS——lust

LEVIATHAN——envy

BEELZEBUB——gluttony

SATAN——wrath

BELPHEGOR——sloth

The *Compendium Maleficarum*, from the seventeenth century CE, is a witch hunter's manual that lists six classes of demons, including:

- demons of the superior layers of the air, which never contact human beings

- demons of the inferior layers of the air, which are responsible for storms

- demons of earth, which dwell in fields, caves, and forests

- demons of water, which are female demons and destroy sea life

- demons of the underground, which cause earthquakes and the crumbling of houses

. . . .

- demons of the night, which are black and evil and cause mayhem in human lives

During the Middle Ages it was believed that certain demons had more power to accomplish their evil deeds during special months of the year:

JANUARY—Belial

FEBRUARY—Leviathan

MARCH—Satan

APRIL—Belphegor

MAY—Lucifer

JUNE—Berith

JULY—Beelzebub

AUGUST—Astaroth

SEPTEMBER—Thammuz

OCTOBER—Baal

NOVEMBER—Asmodai

DECEMBER—Moloch

There are several medieval grimoires, such as *The Lesser Key of Solomon*, *The Arbatel of Magic*, *The Grand Grimoire,* and the *Grimorium Verum*, which not only provide lists of demons but also offer instructions on how to invoke them through the use of seals and incantations.

But in spite of the vast quantity of fallen angels described in the kabbalistic literature and other innumerable sources, the principal character in the demonic hierarchies and the instigator behind the Fall is Satan—or, as he is commonly referred to, the Devil.

Behind the word *satan* stands the Hebrew term *ha-satan*. In Hebrew, *ha* means "the," so a translation of *ha-satan* is "the satan." Therefore, the word *ha-satan* is not a name but a title, a description.

The term in Hebrew means "adversary" or "opponent." Everywhere in the Tanakh, or Old Testament, from Job 1 to I Kings 22, the word used to describe this entity is *ha-satan*, never Satan. The *ha-satan* is an adversary—not God's adversary but humanity's. God is too powerful to be opposed. Human beings are the subject of the *ha-satan*'s malice. Furthermore, there are many *ha-satans* and they are all agents of God, who uses them to test human faith and strengthen our resolve to cling to God (*devekkut*), in spite of all misfortunes. This is Job's story, where the *ha-satan* tells God the only reason Job is faithful to the Godhead is because he has blessed Job with great wealth and a large, happy family. God then gives the *ha-satan* permission to test Job, taking away his family and all his possessions. But in spite of all his suffering, Job still remains faithful to God, proving the *ha-satan* was wrong. God then returns all his wealth to Job and gives him a new family. Therefore, in the Jewish religious tradition, the *ha-satan* is not really evil, but merely God's instrument.

It is in the New Testament that Satan is identified as a demonic force, commonly known as the Devil, which is a derivative of the Latin word *diabolus*. This in turn was borrowed from the Greek *diabolos*, which means "slanderer." Satan is also identified as the serpent that tempted Eve to eat the forbidden fruit. In Revelation Satan is called the deceiver, the dragon, and the old serpent. In Islam he is equated with Shaitan or Iblis, who is formed of smokeless fire along with other *jinn,* or demonic entities.

Satan is also identified as Lucifer, the light giver or light bearer, a misreading of the passage in Isaiah 14:12: "How are you fallen from Heaven, O Lucifer, son of the morning! How you are cut down to the ground, you who weakened the nations!" In reality, this passage refers both to the king of Babylon and to Samael, a cosmic being and the Seraph of purity before the Fall.

The Isaiah passage is actually a lament for the "son of the dawn," the brightest light from Heaven, who descends from his former position as a Seraph to rule over Hell and punish human sinners.

In Christian theology Satan was a ruling prince of several of the celestial orders, specifically the Seraphim, the Cherubim, the Powers, and the Archangels. Instead of six wings, he is usually depicted with twelve. For most Christians he is the chief of the fallen angels who rebelled against God. But how did the *ha-satan*, the adversary of humanity, evolve into Satan, the deceiver and chief of the fallen angels? The answer to this question is found in the First Book of Enoch.

According to Enoch, God created the angels on the second day of Creation from molten rock, fire, and lightning, and established them in nine angelic choirs. But superior to the angelic choirs and their ruling princes, the Creator made the Guardians of the Watchtowers, which are the walls of the seven palaces that are on the Seventh Heaven. These celestial watchers were given immense power by the Creator. Among them he chose seventy, called the Princes of the Kingdoms, who were superior to the other watchers. And he chose still others, who were superior to the seventy. These are the ones who stand in front of the Creator's throne and serve him continuously. Among these, the most beautiful and powerful, with powers almost equal to the Creator, is the Seraph, Cherub, Power, and Archangel Beqa, whose name signifies "he who is good."

But Beqa's spirit was filled with the desire to be like the Creator, and he conspired to overthrow his maker. He tried to induce Michael to join in the conspiracy, but Michael rebuked him and renamed him Kasbel, which means "he who betrays his creator." Kasbel, undeterred by Michael's refusal to join him, gathered one-third of the heavenly host and led them in revolt against God. This was the heavenly war that resulted in the defeat of the rebellious angels, who were then cast into the Abyss. As Michael threw Kasbel into the depths of the Qlipoth, the reprobate angel was renamed again. This time the name he was given was Satanail, which is the origin of Satan, whose real name is Samael.

All of this happened on the second day of Creation. On the first day of Creation, the Creator as the Ain Soph had contracted his light into the infinite point that is the Ain Soph Aur. Genesis tells us this when it says, "Then God said Let there be light...And there was evening and there was morning, the first day." This was Kether. But as the ray of light descended and God separated the waters from the waters and the sky (Heaven) appeared on the second day, Kasbel and his traitorous hordes rebelled. This happened in Chokmah. The light then condensed in Binah, and the vessels broke under the strain of the angelic war, shattering the remaining sephiroth, which fell into the Abyss with the rebel angels. That is why the original Tree of Life was shattered and God had to start Creation anew. This was how Beqa/Kasbel/Satanail/Satan/Samael betrayed his creator.

One third of the heavenly host fell in that cataclysm, and among them were many of the Watchers. These angels are also known as the *Grigori*, from the Greek *egregoroi*. They are similar to men in appearance, but they are said to be taller than giants and are eternally silent. According to Enoch there were two hundred Watchers, but only their leaders are named. These are:

- Semyasa
- Arakiba
- Rameel
- Kokabiel
- Tamiel
- Ramiel
- Danel
- Ezequeel
- Baraquijal
- Asael
- Armaros
- Batarel
- Ananel

- Zaqiel

- Samsapeel

- Satarel

- Turel

- Jomjael

- Sariel

Of the Watcher leaders, some compounded their sin of rebellion by mating with women and teaching them forbidden knowledge. These were:

- Arakiel, who taught humans the signs of the earth

- Armarros, who taught humans the arts of enchantments

- Azazel, who taught humans how to make swords, knives, and shields, and how to devise ornaments

- Gadriel, who taught humans the art of cosmetics

- Baraqijal, who taught humans astrology

- Ezekeel, who taught humans meteorology

- Kokabiel, who also taught humans astrology

- Penemue, who taught humans the art of writing with ink and paper

- Sariel, who taught humans the motions of the moon

- Semyasa, the principal leader of the Watchers

- Shamsiel, who taught humans the motions of the sun

All of these watchers mated with the daughters of men, a most grievous sin in the eyes of the Creator, as angels are never supposed to have sexual knowledge of women. From the forbidden union of the Watchers with women were born the *Nephillim*, fearsome giants "who were the heroes of old, warriors of renown" (Genesis 6:4). In Enoch's tale, it was Satanail/Satan/Samael who tempted the Watchers and told them to cohabit with the daughters of men as part of his revenge for his expulsion from Heaven.

Although most of the *Nephillim* were destroyed during the flood, some remained, and many are believed to be still living on earth under the guise of ordinary humans. Samael, who still roams the earth after his Fall, is said to continue mating with women, and his resulting offspring are now comely and seductive half-breeds with many angelic powers. Other fallen angels are also following Samael's example, creating an ever-growing number of *Nephillim*, most of whom are unaware of the true identity of their fathers. Some Kabbalists believe that Samael and his cohorts are amassing an army of these *Nephillim* with the hope of taking over the earth in a not too distant future. At a precise moment these demons will reveal their true parentage to their children. In this way, they hope to enlist their help in their nefarious plans.

Enoch also tells us that in the beginning of Creation God sent a legion of Watchers to be earthly shepherds to the first humans. They served humanity as vast reservoirs of information, as it was their mission to observe human beings, helping them when they needed help but never interfering with the course of human evolution. These were part of the good Watchers and reside in the Fifth Heaven. The fallen Watchers inhabit a separate section of the Third Heaven, where they are hanging eternally in space, blindfolded and bound through seventy generations. Only their leaders remain free, and chief among them is Samael, the Satan.

The Catholic Church has always been a firm believer in Satan and his determination to destroy the church and create havoc around the world. A medieval Catholic formula for exorcism, recorded in a 1415 manuscript, was found in a Benedictine abbey in Germany. In current Catholic tradition, the formula is given as *Vade Retro Satanas*, meaning "Get thee behind me, Satan." These words, which were spoken to Satan by Jesus after he was tempted by the Devil in the desert (Matthew 4:10), are used as a "spoken amulet" to repel any possible evil thing or happening.

The initials of the formula, rendered *VRS:NSMV:SMQL:IVB*, are often engraved around crucifixes or Saint Benedict medals (see appendix 6, figure 22). The phrase *Vade Retro Satanas* is common in modern usage, dissociated from its religious implications, to express strong rejection of an unacceptable but possibly tempting proposal.

In 1886 a special prayer to Archangel Michael (Saint Michael in the Catholic Church) was added to the famous Leonine prayers that Pope Leo XIII had ordered for the protection of the Holy See (see the Catholic *Encyclical Qui Nuper* of 18 June 1859). The prayer was added after a vision that the pope had during a celebration of High Mass. In one version of the story, the pope was climbing the steps to the altar when he suddenly stopped, stared fixedly at something in the air, and, with a terrible look on his face, collapsed on the floor. After he recovered from the fainting spell, he was asked what had happened. He explained that as he was about to leave the foot of the altar, he suddenly heard two voices that seemed to come from the tabernacle. One of the voices was guttural and harsh, and the other was soft and gentle. As he listened, he heard the following conversation:

The guttural voice, which the Pope ascribed to Satan, said to God: "I can destroy your church."

God answered: "You can? Then go ahead and do so."

Satan: "To do so, I need more time and more power."

God: "How much time? How much power?"

Satan: "Seventy-five to one hundred years, and a greater power over those who will give themselves over into my service."

God: "You have the time, you will have the power. Do with them as you will."

After describing the vision, Leo XIII said, "What a horrible picture I was permitted to see. God gave Satan the choice of one century in which to do his worst work against the church. The devil chose the twentieth century."

The pope was so disturbed by this vision that he composed the prayer to Archangel Michael, which is one of the most famous prayers in the Catholic Church and is still prayed by Catholics daily around the world (see Christopher 2003). The prayer is said to be a strong protection against the powers of Satan. This is the most accepted form of the prayer:

> Saint Michael, the Archangel, defend us in
> battle; be our protection against the wickedness
> and snares of the devil. May God rebuke him,
> we humbly pray; and do thou, O Prince of the
> Heavenly Host, by the power of God, thrust into
> Hell Satan and all the evil spirits who prowl
> about the world seeking the ruin of souls. Amen.

The vision where Leo XIII heard God give power to Satan to try and destroy the church brings to mind the book of Job, where God gives Satan similar power to tempt and destroy Job. It is interesting to note that the twentieth century has brought increasing difficulties and turmoil to the Catholic Church, with scandals surrounding priests and a significant reduction in congregations around the world and in the attendance of Mass and other Catholic rites.

Human belief in Satan as the Devil is very strong. As we saw in the introduction, 70 percent of all Americans believe in the Devil. In 1971 a man called Gerald Mayo filed a lawsuit against Satan and his servants in the United States District Court for the Western District of Pennsylvania. In his lawsuit, Mayo complained that "Satan has on numerous occasions caused plaintiff misery and unwarranted threats, against the will of plaintiff, that Satan has placed deliberate obstacles in his path and has caused plaintiff's downfall" and had therefore "deprived him of his constitutional rights." This is prohibited under several sections of the United States code. Mayo also filed *in forma pauperis*, which meant he could not afford the cost of the litigation and that therefore he should be exempt from paying them.

In his decision, US District Court Judge Gerald J. Weber first noted that the jurisdictional situation was unclear. While no previous cases had been brought by or against Satan, and so no official precedence existed, there was an unofficial account of a trial in New Hampshire where the defendant (Satan) filed an action of mortgage foreclosure as plaintiff (a tongue-in-cheek reference to the short story "The Devil and Daniel Webster" by Stephen Vincent Benet). Judge Weber suggested that Satan, the defendant (who had claimed in the story to be an American), should he appear, might have been therefore stopped from arguing a lack of personal jurisdiction. The judge also noted that the case was certainly appropriate for class action status, and it was not then clear that Mayo could properly represent the interests of the entire (immense) class. The court also refused the request to allow Mayo to file the lawsuit without paying for the litigation on the grounds that the plaintiff had not included instructions on how the US marshal could serve process on Satan (see US District Court, W.D. Pennsylvania, US ex rel. Gerald Mayo vs. Satan and his staff, Misc. No. 5357, December 3, 1971).

Not even the Almighty himself has been spared the indignity of a lawsuit. In 2007, State Senator Ernie Chambers filed a lawsuit against the Creator in the US State Court of Nebraska. Chambers was seeking an injunction as an effort to publicize the issue of public access to the court system. The judge dismissed the case on the grounds that the Almighty was not properly served due to his unlisted home address. Chambers remained unfazed and fired back at the judge, saying, "The court itself acknowledges the existence of God. A consequence of that acknowledgment is recognition of God's omniscience. Since God knows everything, he also knows about this lawsuit." He then charged on with an appeal to the Nebraska Supreme Court of Appeals. The justices were unimpressed by Chambers' accusations against the Eternal and dismissed the appeal on the grounds that the court did not address or dispose of abstract questions or hypothetical issues (see Associated Press, "God Gets an Attorney in Lawsuit," September 21, 2007).

. . . .

Human fascination with our origins is unbounded. The search for clues to our beginnings and the possible existence of God and his angels, the faithful and the unfaithful, is constantly growing. An increasing number of scientists in all the various scientific disciplines is actively looking for these answers. In the meantime, while we wait for the result of these investigations, we continue to live in a world fraught with miracles and unexplainable events, hapless witnesses to the continuous struggle between good and evil, personified as the angels of light and the fallen angels.

CHAPTER 14

Doing the Magic

Magic is believing in yourself. If you can do
that, you can make anything happen.

. . . .

JOHANN WOLFGANG VON GOETHE

M agic has been defined as the power of transforming our environment by means of willpower. These transformations are possible because we live in an impermanent world that is subject to constant change. It is up to each individual either to learn to adapt to the changes around him or to make the changes himself. And these changes are made through the power of mind and will.

There is a subtle clue in the word *impermanent*. It begins with the prefix *imp*. In the preceding chapter we discussed the fallen angels and the belief that they continuously interact with humanity, leaving chaos and mayhem in their wake. One of the meanings of the word *imp* is a devil or a small demon. Most of the words that begin with imp have powerfully negative connotations, such as imperfect, impure, impossible, impotent, impenitent, impatient, improper, imprudent, improbable, impediment,

. . . .

impiety, and of course, impermanent. These words seem to imply that there is a negative supernatural agency at work in the world, influencing human behavior and creating disruptive situations that impede our success and our general well-being. Impermanency means not only change but also instability, and while change can sometimes be a welcome occurrence in a human life, instability is not. Therefore, in the practice of magic it is vital that the changes we make in our lives are not only positive and dynamic but that they also bring added stability and well-being.

In contrast with the negativity of most of the words that begin with *imp*, there are some that start with the same prefix but which are of a very positive nature. Among these words are important, impartial, impeccable, improvement, and, most especially, imparadise, an old and relatively unknown word that means "to enrapture, to make blissfully happy, and to connect with the Divine." These words tell us that the same imps that make us impatient, impenitent, imprudent, and impotent—and place impediments in our lives making our goals seem not only improbable but impossible to attain—are hiding from us important clues for our improvement, which we can achieve through impartial and impeccable actions that will eventually help us imparadise, reaching blissful happiness and a connection with the Divine.

"The Imp of the Perverse" is the title of a short story by Edgar Allan Poe that is commonly used as a metaphor for the perverse tendency, particularly among children and miscreants, to do exactly the opposite thing that is expected of them in a given situation. This impulse is compared to an imp who leads an otherwise decent person into mischief and self-destruction. Recognizing the presence of the imp in our lives and overcoming its malignant influence, using instead those positive aspects of our personalities it hides from our conscious awareness, is what magic is all about.

Ultimately, magic is worked through the mind. The will is the conscious power we use to establish in our deep unconscious the changes we wish to make in order to reach our goals. The first key to accomplish things with the power of the mind is self-knowledge. This is the beginning of personal integrity and is a prerequisite for dealing with any kind of change. That is why one of the oldest tenets of magic is "Man, know thyself," which was inscribed in the Temple of Apollo at Delphi.

In order to achieve self-knowledge, the first thing you must do in the practice of magic is prepare a white and a black "mirror." Find a large notebook with blank pages and an attractive cover with magical symbolism. This will be your magical manual where you will write down all your meditations, visualizations, and rituals. Write your birth and magical names on the first page (you will be instructed on how to receive your magical name later on in this chapter). Below your names write down your zodiac sign and the sign of your ascendant, if you know it. Follow this with the name of the angel that rules your zodiac and ascendant signs.

On the next two pages, which should be facing each other, you will prepare your white and black mirrors. On the top of the left hand page write "white mirror." On the top of the right-hand page write "black mirror."

Under the words "white mirror," make a list of all your good traits and positive qualities. Under the words "black mirror," make a list of all your negative traits and personal faults. It is of great importance that you are completely honest in the preparation of these mirrors. This is the first step to self-knowledge, and if you lie to yourself you will never be able to evolve spiritually or practice magic successfully. No one but you will read this manual. Be true to yourself and reveal to your conscious awareness all those faults that are hidden in the depths of your soul and that you have never confessed to yourself. The more brutally honest you are, the greater your eventual success will be. This is what is meant by "know thyself."

If you do this correctly, you will notice that the black mirror has a longer list than your white mirror. That is because you are human, and by nature human beings are weak and prone to temptations.

Once you have prepared the two mirrors, your spiritual journey has just begun. From that moment onward, your aim will be to reduce the list of faults in your black mirror and increase the good qualities in your white mirror. You will accomplish this by concentrating on one fault at a time and trying to erase it by replacing it with its opposite good quality. This is how you will evolve, grow spiritually, and defeat your personal Imp of the Perverse.

As we have already seen, everything in the universe is made of energy in different forms or manifestations. At the core of all matter lies the heart of the atom, and the atom itself is made of smaller particles still. This is the realm of quantum mechanics, which deals with the infinitesimal—units of energy so small they cannot be properly classified. Everything that exists, from stars to a grain of sand, is made of this unknown, unfathomable energy, which can neither be created nor destroyed. All of this energy, present in ourselves and in all of nature, is at our disposal to transform and alter to bring about the changes we desire in our lives. And we can transform it with our minds, because our minds are made of the same energy.

In order to make changes in the energy around you, you must first identify with it. Understand that everything is part of you, and you are part of everything. Feel this powerful connection with the people around you. They are made of the same energy, they fear the same things you fear, have the same hopes and similar desires. They may look different from you, but they are not. Feel a strong empathy for all that exists, suffer with other people's sorrows, imagine they are your own, partake of their joys, and do not begrudge them their fleeting moments of triumph or happiness. Above all, love everything and everyone because they are an extension of you. Then turn your attention to nature—identify with each grain of sand, each blade of grass, every tree and every flower; feel at one with the wind and the rain and the snow; love each creature, no matter how small or insignificant. Walk barefoot and bareheaded in the rain; pass your hands gently over a candle flame and feel the warmth of the fire—learn to control it and wield it as a force, as a part of you. Be one with the earth, the water, the wind, and the fire, the four elements that are present in all manifestations of life. When you have accomplished this, you will be ready to practice magic.

There are two keys to success in magic. One is faith, and the other is having no doubt. They may seem like the same thing, but they are not. Jesus, who was a master kabbalist, said to his disciples, "If you had as much faith as a mustard seed, you could say to the mountain, 'Move,' and it would move" (Matthew 17:20). He was not speaking metaphorically, he was speaking literally. Faith is the belief that you can do anything. It is an awesome power, the power of the mind. There is nothing you cannot do if only you believe you can do it. You can move mountains, you can alter a river's course, you can change weather patterns. One of the first exercises you can try to prove this is stopping the rain. Choose a day when rain has been predicted. Then state very strongly, "It will not rain today." Be absolutely certain that rain will not fall—think of clear skies and of the sun shining—then forget about it. One of the major premises of a magical statement is that in order to release it into the cosmos, you must not dwell upon it once you have expressed it. If you are totally sure it will not rain, it will not.

But it is not enough to have faith. You must also have no doubts. In another example of magical power, Jesus walked on the water to his disciples' boat in the middle of a storm. Peter, his oldest disciple, asked Jesus if he could also walk on the water. Jesus said, "Come." Peter began to walk on the water, but when the winds increased he became afraid and immediately sank beneath the waves. Jesus lifted Peter out of the water and asked, "Why did you doubt?" (Matthew 14:31).

This example shows that Peter had the magical power—the faith—to walk on water. But his faith—and, therefore, his magical power—failed him because he doubted. In magic, it is not only vital to believe you can do something, but you also must not doubt it. Your faith in your power to transform or change things must be absolute.

You must also learn how to hone your intuition and listen to your "inner voice." This is very important, because that is how you develop the power of clairvoyance. This power is latent in all human beings and is very well developed in some people. It is not a psychic or supernatural power, it is a very natural and common aspect of the human mind. Time, as we have seen, does not really exist. It is a human construct. That is why Einstein coined the term "space-time continuum." Time and space are the same thing; they are extensions of each other. That is why if we concentrate on "future" events we can foresee them and even create them.

As we have seen, everything is made of energy. This energy is of great importance in the practice of magic. What you must do is garner vast amounts of energy and then shape them and channel them toward your desired goal. You do this through the power of will, faith, and imagination, which in magic is known as visualization. You also need a focus for all this energy, and the focus in angel magic is the name of a specific angel.

Will, faith, and imagination are not easy to develop. They require self-control and determination. It is important to empower the will by controlling your natural instincts, and these, as we have seen, are to be found in the *Nephesh*, the seat of all desires, and natural impulses. These need to be firmly trained and controlled. Start by denying yourself things that you like and enjoy, like your favorite foods or your favorite television program. Do this for a long period of time, until you are firmly in control of your *Nephesh*. It is there to serve you, not the other way around. If you are overweight, determine to lose weight, and do not stop until you have reached your desired weight. If you suffer from a physical problem, instruct the *Nephesh* to correct it.

The best way to control your *Nephesh* is to look at the space between your eyebrows and give it a command. Repeat this every morning until you get the results you want. Doing this, I was able to cure myself of a very strong seasonal allergy. Each summer I suffered a severe reaction to ragweed, which is plentiful in New York from August to late September. Concentrating on the third eye every morning and telling the *Nephesh* to stop overreacting to the ragweed cured me of the allergy. Doing the same exercise, I also lost sixty pounds and lowered my blood pressure, which is now normal without the use of drugs, to my doctor's astonishment.

Part of the magical training includes keeping the body pure, avoiding the use of drugs, alcohol, and sexual excesses. A glass of wine or an occasional cocktail is fine, but do not overdo it. Most practicing magicians are vegetarians because they respect all life, and eating animal flesh is seen as cruelty toward nature. Older practitioners often chose celibacy as a way to enforce the body's purity and keep the mind focused. This is not an option for younger persons or those who are married, and should only be engaged in after a certain age.

It is also important to avoid all violent or negative emotions like anger, hatred, jealousy, and vengeance. Anyone who awakens these feelings in you controls you and robs you of immense quantities of energies. The result is imbalance and chaos in your life and the failure of your magical work.

When you have worked with your white and black mirrors successfully, have achieved control of your instincts through your *Nephesh*, and have learned to identify with nature and all that exists, you will start seeing results in your magical practices. You will also start noticing subtle but unmistakable signs of nature's growing rapport with you. To strengthen that rapport, walk barefoot in your home so you can keep a closer contact with earth and take an earth bath once a month. Mix some earth from your garden or backyard with bird seeds, flower petals, crushed bread crumbs, corn kernels, sugar, spices, and powdered incense. Spread a sheet on the floor of your bedroom, take off your clothes, face the east, and rub the mixture all over your body. Light a green candle and visualize the earth healed from all its problems—see the waters cleansed of all toxins, humanity at peace, and all animals safe in their secret nests and lairs. Feel you are one with the planet, and send it your love and your light. Then take a bath with a pure lanolin-based soap. This is a simple ritual for the earth that will leave you in great peace and balance. It will also help you develop a deep connection with angels and natural forces. Dispose of the earth mixture after use. You can use the same sheet each month.

In the practice of angel rituals, and indeed all magic rituals, there are several things to consider. First, all magic rituals are conducted facing the east, unless the ritual instructions call for another point of the compass. Second, the moon should be waxing unless otherwise indicated. The moon is waxing between the new moon and the full moon. It begins to wane immediately after the full moon until the night before the new moon. That night is known as the night of the black moon, and no ritual should be conducted at that time, as there are very negative energies present. It is important to have an astrological calendar to be sure of the moon phases.

Third, a circle must be cast from east to east in order to protect the ceremony and ensure there are no negative influences present. The person conducting the ritual should be barefoot, dressed in white, and have a magic wand to cast the circle. The circle can also be cast with the ficca, where the thumb of the dominant hand is held together between the index and the heart fingers (see appendix 6, figure 19).

If you use a wand to cast the circle, you must first consecrate it in the four elements. First, pass the wand over incense, which represents air, and say, "I consecrate you in the element of air." Second, pass the wand over the flame of a candle, and say, "I consecrate you in the element of fire." Third, sprinkle the wand with water, and say, "I consecrate you in the element of water." And fourth, place the tip of the wand on a small plate of uniodized salt, and say, "I consecrate you in the element of earth." Salt is always used as a symbol of the earth element.

By this time you should have your magical name. To learn this name, go to a river and step into the water only to your ankles. Close your eyes and say mentally, "I wish to know my magical or astral name." Immediately a name will come into your mind. Do not question the name, even if you do not like it. It is your true magical name. Do not reveal this name to anyone, for it has very definite powers to either help or hurt you. It is the essence of your being. Use it only when you do a ritual, to identify yourself to the forces you are working with. Remember, every spiritual being has a name, even God. That name is part of that force or entity. It is the same with your name. After you receive the name, take water from the river and pour it over your head three times, saying aloud, "I declare unto the cosmos that my astral name is...," and state the given name.

Before you attempt to do a ritual, you must be sure of what you wish to accomplish. It is important to ask for only one thing during each ritual; to ask for more will disperse the energies you have gathered, and you will not achieve any positive results. At this point it is necessary to define white versus black magic. In reality, magic is neutral. It is the person doing the magic that makes it white or black. To simplify things, you could say that white magic is any magic that will bring about positive results without harming anyone. Black magic is any magic that will affect others in a negative way, and that includes trying to force someone to do something against his or her will. Free will is a divine gift, and not even the Creator breaks this powerful mandate. Nor will his angels, and this means that if you want to do angel magic, that magic must be white.

Once you have decided what you want to accomplish through your magic ritual, you must decide which angel you will be invoking during the ceremony. The next chapter will provide a list of the seven great Archangels, their attributes, and everything they rule. Study the list well, and choose the appropriate angel. Remember, you must conduct the ritual during the waxing phases of the moon on the day ruled by that angel and on one of his hours. The angel hours are, as we have seen, 1 AM, 8 AM, 3 PM, and 10 PM.

You should gather as many of the angel's attributes as you are able. They must be placed upon your altar, which should face east. The attributes are very important, as these objects are filled with the energy you need to accomplish your goal. For that reason, they must be in harmony with the particular angel you have chosen.

It is also important to draw the angel's sigil or seal (see appendix 6) on a piece of cloth in the color associated with the angel (see chapter 6). This will help you connect with that particular entity. The cloth should be spread on the altar, with the attributes upon it. You should also place a small glass of sweet wine and a small bread roll upon the altar.

The Ritual of the Pentagram

Begin by purifying yourself during the twenty-four hours before the ritual. That includes fasting (taking only liquids) and abstaining from alcohol, drugs, tobacco, sex, and any negative behavior. Bathe carefully before the ritual, concentrating on ridding your body and your mind of all impurities. Dress in white (preferably in a long tunic) and be barefoot.

At exactly the angel's hour, to dispel any lingering negative vibrations, sprinkle salt water around the room where the invocation is to take place. Burn a mixture of the incenses ascribed to the angel on several pieces of charcoal, and pass the incense around the room. Then place a yellow candle in the east, a red candle in the south, a blue candle in the west, and a green candle in the north as symbols of the four elements: air, fire, water, and earth, respectively.

The Ritual of the Pentagram is very well known in the practice of magic. It is used to protect a person and to surround him with angelic energy during an invocation. It is a kabbalistic ceremony and invokes the power of God's holy names and those of the Archangels Raphael, Michael, Gabriel, and Uriel, who rule the four elements.

Start by facing the east and making the Kabbalistic Cross in the following manner:

- with your right hand (or left if you are left-handed),
  touch your forehead and say "*Atoh*" (In the name)

- point to your feet and say "*Malkuth*" (of the Kingdom)

- touch your right shoulder and say "*Ve-Geburah*" (and the power)

- touch your left shoulder and say *"Ve-Gedulah"* (and the Mercy)

- unite both hands in front of your chest and say *"Leolahm"* (Amen)

Point the wand (or the ficca), arm extended, toward a point in the east slightly higher than the head, and trace the invoking pentagram (shown in appendix 6, figure 23). As you do this, visualize that the lines of the pentagram are made of fire. When the pentagram has been formed, point the wand at its imaginary center and say in a loud and strong voice:

In the holy name of God, Yod Heh Vau Heh,
and the great Archangel Raphael, I seal this
circle in the east and the air element.

Without lowering the arm, turn right to the south, imagining that the wand is forming a line of fire from the east to the south. Trace another pentagram at the same level as the first, point to the center, and say:

In the holy name of God, Adonai, and the
great Archangel Michael, I seal this circle
in the south and the fire element.

Turn to the west, still tracing the fiery line that connects it to the south. Trace the third pentagram, point at the center, and say:

In the holy name of God, Eheieh, and the
great Archangel Gabriel, I seal this circle
in the west and the water element.

Continue to trace the imaginary line of fire until you reach the north. Form the pentagram again, point the wand at its center and say,

In the holy name of God, Agla, and the
great Archangel Uriel, I seal this circle
in the north and the earth element.

Return to the east, still tracing the imaginary line of fire, completing the circle, which is now surmounted by four blazing stars in its four cardinal points. Open your arms wide and say:

- - - - - - - - - - - -

175

DOING THE MAGIC

In front of me, Raphael.
Behind me, Gabriel.
To my right, Michael.
To my left, Uriel.
Facing me is the flaming pentagram
and behind me is the six-pointed star.

The six-pointed star is better known as the Star of David, which is formed of two interlaced triangles, one pointing upward and the other pointing downward. The upper triangle represents fire, and the lower triangle represents water.

After the four pentagrams have been traced, visualize the four Archangels on the four quarters of the flaming circle. In front of the eastern pentagram visualize Raphael draped in yellow and violet, with golden hair. In front of the southern pentagram visualize Michael in red and green, with hair like flame. In front of the western pentagram visualize Gabriel in blue and orange, with bronze-colored hair. And in the front of the northern pentagram visualize Uriel dressed in shades of lemon, olive green, brown, and black, with hair and beard black as night. Once the pentagrams are traced, you must always move deosil—that is, to the right—inside the circle, which you must not leave until the ceremony is ended.

At this point you can petition the angel of your choice, asking him to grant you the thing you desire, by saying the following:

In the name of the Creator of the universe, by
whom we both have been created, I ask you, great
Archangel (here mention the angel's name), to
grant that this, which I desire (mention the desire)
and which falls under your regency, be manifested
and realized in the material world in a natural
and positive form for my benefit and without
any danger to myself or to any other person.

This request is repeated in the four cardinal points, starting in the east. Then face the east again and say:

> *May this bread that I offer to you aid me*
> *in the manifestation of what I ask in joy*
> *and prosperity in the material world.*

Eat the bread with reverence, visualizing that what you have asked for has already come to pass. See it as if you were already enjoying it. Then raise the glass of wine and say:

> *May this wine that I offer to you aid me*
> *in the manifestation of what I ask in joy*
> *and prosperity in the material world.*

Drink the wine with equal reverence, visualizing that what you have asked has already come to pass. Then open your arms wide and say:

> *I give thanks to the Almighty Creator and the*
> *Archangel _____ for granting my desire.*

Repeat this in the four quarters. You must then retrace the pentagrams in the same order, but this time use the banishing pentagram, which is given in appendix 6, figure 23. Repeat the same names of God and the Archangels in the four points, but when you point to the center of the eastern pentagram, say:

> *I banish this circle in the east and the air element.*

Repeat the banishing in the south, the west, and the north, mentioning the appropriate element.

The angels are visualized with their backs to you, as they are now ready to depart. Face the east and say:

> *In the name of the Creator of the universe*
> *and the great Archangels Raphael, Michael,*
> *Gabriel, Uriel, and (name of the angel you*

invoked), this ritual is ended. I thank you for
your presence during this ritual and for granting
me my desire. I now say hail and farewell.

These words are repeated in the other cardinal points.

At this point, you must knock ten times on the altar to return your consciousness to the material world. You can then gather all the magical aids you used during the ritual and put them away to use in another ceremony. The candles must be put out without blowing on them, as blowing on a candle places the element of air in contradiction to the fire element.

This ritual, like all magical ceremonies and meditations, helps establish a deeper contact with the inner self, or unconscious, of an individual. The Archangels may be seen as archetypes of the collective unconscious of the human race. As such, they open a great vista of possibilities in our lives, creating new venues to express our innermost feelings and helping us accomplish our most important goals. What happens during each ritual is that we establish hidden connections with people and situations that help us materialize our visions, usually in the most simple and ordinary ways. It is a way to connect with each other on inner levels, which is what magic is basically all about.

CHAPTER 15

The Seven Great Archangels

I saw the angel in the marble
and carved until I set him free.

. . . .

MICHELANGELO

In the book of Revelation, John sees seven flaming torches in front of God's throne, which he identifies as the seven spirits of God. These seven spirits can also be identified with the seven princes of the Divine Presence and the seven great Archangels (Revelation 4:5).

These seven great Archangels are:

1. Gabriel

2. Raphael

3. Hanael

4. Michael

5. Kamael

6. Zadkiel

7. Cassiel

. . . .

As we saw earlier, these Archangels rule the seven days of the week and the hours of the day. According to the ancients, they also rule the seven heavens, the seven planets, seven of the ten sephiroth, and the twelve signs of the zodiac.

These archons can be propitiated through special rituals which must be conducted on their ascribed days and hours, using some of their attributes, such as numbers, colors, flowers, and preferred stones. The use of the angelic attributes is important to make the proper connection with the angels, as their spiritual vibrations are attuned to these objects. The following list provides the information necessary to perform angel magic associated with the seven great Archangels.

Gabriel

Rules the First Heaven, Shamaym; the Ninth Sphere, which is Yesod; and the moon. Gabriel's name means "God is my strength." His kabbalistic number is nine. His planetary colors are violet and silver. As ruler of the water element, Gabriel's colors are blue and orange, but these colors are not used when he is invoked. His ascribed day is Monday at 1 AM, 8 AM, 3 PM, and 10 PM. He rules the zodiac sign of Cancer. Gabriel rules all the liquids, especially water, milk, and wine; the circulation of the blood; foods; women; the family, especially children and the mother; fertility; long voyages; plants and nature; the mind; the brain; dreams; and psychic powers. The illnesses he rules are those affecting the lungs, the chest, the gastrointestinal tract, the uterus, and the stomach. Among his flowers are hyacinths, orchids, lilies, jasmine, gardenias, violets, and all white and purple blooms. Among his trees and plants are coconuts, melons, plums, yams, lentils, eucalyptus, mint, and chestnut and willow trees. His incenses are camphor and myrrh. Among his stones are beryl, moonstone, pearl, mother-of-pearl, chrysocola, selenite, white quartz, alexandrite, and alabaster. His metal is silver. The animals he rules are dogs, wolves, cows, hares, chickens, crustaceans and all aquatic animals, deer, elephants, bears, bulls, and owls.

· · · · · · · · · · ·

Raphael

Rules the Second Heaven, Raquie; the Eighth Sphere of the Tree of Life, Hod; and Mercury. Raphael's name means "God has healed." His kabbalistic number is eight. His planetary color is orange. As ruler of the air element, Raphael's colors are yellow and violet, but these colors are not used when he is invoked. Raphael is known as the angel who stands in the sun. His ascribed day is Wednesday at 1 AM, 8 AM, 3 PM, and 10 PM. He rules the zodiac signs of Gemini and Virgo. Raphael rules the intellect, studies, teachers, papers, contracts, books, communications, correspondence, medicine, doctors, and nurses. The caduceus is one of his symbols, as he is known as the divine physician. The illnesses he rules are epilepsy, meningitis, all nervous or mental ailments, and illnesses affecting the respiratory system, the nervous system, the arms, the mouth, the tongue, the pancreas, the gall bladder, the intestines, and the thyroid. His flowers and plants are the magnolia, lily of the valley, forget me not, lavender, parsley, elm tree, marjoram, mandrake, and all ferns. Among his fruits are oranges and almonds. His incenses are sandalwood, storax, gum arabic, and clove. His stones are carnelians, all the agates (especially lace agates), fire opals, celestites, aquamarines, and amazonites. The animals he rules are foxes, jackals, mules, giraffes, monkeys, parrots, and all flying insects, especially butterflies. His metals are quicksilver, silver, and aluminum.

Hanael

Rules the Third Heaven, Sagun; the Seventh Sphere of the Tree of Life, Netzach; and Venus. Hanael's name means "glory or grace of God." Hanael is a female entity. Her kabbalistic number is seven. Her planetary colors are emerald green and all pastel shades, especially pink and turquoise. Her ascribed day is Friday at 1 AM, 8 AM, 3 PM, and 10 PM. She rules the zodiac signs of Taurus and Libra. Hanael rules love and lovers, marriage, friends, pleasures, diplomacy, the arts, music, and the theater. The illnesses she rules are venereal diseases, AIDS, and those associated with the sexual organs, the ovaries, the throat, the hair and scalp, the veins, the kidneys, the lymphatic system, arthritis, and muscular spasms. Her flowers and plants are red roses, tulips, geraniums, vervain, myrtle, spearmint, apples, cherries, pears, and figs. Her incenses are storax, valerian, sandalwood, benzoin, and especially cinnamon. Her stones are opal, malaquite, emerald, corals, rodocrosite, jade, rose quartz, tourmaline, and aventurine. The animals she rules are the turtle dove, pigeons, flamingoes, turtles, spiders, and dolphins. Her metal is copper.

Michael

Rules the Fourth Heaven, Machen; the Sixth Sphere of the Tree of Life, Tiphareth; and the sun. Michael's name means "he who is like God." Because Michael and Raphael are both solar angels, they sometimes exchange the rulership of the sun and Tiphareth. In the Tree of Life Raphael is ascribed the sixth sphere of Tiphareth, but among the Archangels of the planets and the seven days of the week, Michael and Raphael switch places. In that system Michael rules Sunday and the sun because he also rules Leo, which is ruled by the Sun, while Raphael rules Wednesday and Mercury because he also rules Gemini and Virgo, which are ruled by Mercury. Therefore, as a planetary angel, Michael rules the sun. His ascribed day is Sunday at 1 AM, 8 AM, 3 PM, and 10 PM. His kabbalistic number is six. His planetary colors are yellow and gold. As ruler of the fire element, Michael's colors are red and green, but these elemental colors are not used when he is invoked. Michael rules the zodiac sign of Leo. He rules health, vitality, men, the father, executive positions, governmental issues, fame, publicity, everything that begins, and great wealth. The illnesses he rules are fevers and those associated with the heart, the back, the sides of the body, the eyes, the liver, and blood circulation. Among his flowers and plants are sunflowers, all yellow blooms, chamomile, ginger, mistletoe, heliotrope, laurel, pineapple, vanilla, saffron, and cinnamon. His incenses are copal and frankincense. His stones are sardonyx, sunstone, peridot, citrine, diamond, pyrite, ruby, tiger's eye, and amber. The animals he rules are all the wild cats—especially the lion, the tiger, the panther, and the leopard—as well as falcons, bees, all domestic cats, the bird of paradise, and mythical animals like the unicorn, the sphinx, the chimera, and the phoenix. His metal is gold.

Kamael

Rules the Fifth Heaven, Mathey; the Fifth Sphere of the Tree of Life, Geburah; and Mars. Kamael's name means "he who sees God." His kabbalistic number is five. His planetary color is red. His ascribed day is Tuesday at 1 AM, 8 AM, 3 PM, and 10 PM. Kamael rules war, the military, the police, fires and firefighters, enemies, judges, all court cases, wounds, accidents, enemies, and prisons. The illnesses he rules are high blood pressure, hemorrhages, diabetes, all contagious illnesses, inflammations, neuralgias, and illnesses associated with the blood, the bladder, the muscles, and the head, especially the face. The animals he rules are the ram, the scorpion, the snakes and all reptiles, as well as the eagle, the vulture, the basilisk, and the salamander. His flowers and plants are all red blooms (except red roses), geraniums, chrysanthemums, cacti, cumin, pepper, nicotine, all drugs, mustard, and garlic. His incenses are asafetida and dragon's blood. His stones are all the red stones like rubies and carnelians, topaz, garnet, diamond, thunderstone, bloodstone, obsidian, magnetite, and all magnets. His metal is iron.

Zadkiel

Rules the Sixth Heaven, Zebul; the Fourth Sphere of the Tree of Life, Chesed; and Jupiter. Zadkiel's name means "righteousness of God." His kabbalistic number is four. His planetary color is electric blue. His ascribed day is Thursday at 1 AM, 8 AM, 3 PM, and 10 PM. He rules the zodiac signs of Sagittarius and Pisces. Modern astrologers ascribe Neptune to Pisces, but in ancient times there were only seven planets, which were the sun and the moon (which are not really planets but luminaries), Mars, Mercury, Venus, Jupiter, and Saturn. Jupiter was designated as ruler of both Pisces and Sagittarius in those early times. That is why in planetary and angel magic Zadkiel, who rules Jupiter, is assigned the rulership of those two signs. Zadkiel rules finances, banks, loans, superiors, universities, world leaders (including kings, presidents, and religious leaders), captains of industry, gambling, the stock market, science, technology, expansion, prosperity, and abundance. The illnesses he rules are strokes, pleurisy, weight problems, varicose veins, and those associated with the teeth, the liver, the thighs, and the muscles. His flowers and plants are blooms in various shades of blue, sage, hyssop, the cedar, the oak, and the pine. His incenses are sarsaparilla, nutmeg, and frankincense. The animals he rules are the swan, the whale, the white bull, and the mythical centaur. His stones are lapis lazuli, azurite, sapphire, turquoise, amethyst, labradorite, meteorites, moldavite, and celestite. His metal is tin.

Cassiel

Rules the Seventh Heaven, Araboth; the Third Sphere of the Tree of Life, Binah; and Saturn. Cassiel is the angel of solitudes and fears, who shows forth the unity of the eternal kingdom. He sometimes exchanges places with Tzaphkiel, a female entity whose name means "contemplation of God" and who is assigned to Binah and the Shekinah. Both angels are associated with Saturn and Saturday, but among the planetary angels Cassiel is the angel ascribed to both Saturn and Saturday. Cassiel's kabbalistic number is three. His color is black. His ascribed day is Saturday at 1 AM, 8 AM, 3 PM, and 10 PM.

Cassiel rules time, wisdom, death, suffering, agriculture, inheritances, real state, building constructions, plumbers, secrets, and the unconscious. He rules the zodiac signs of Capricorn and Aquarius. Modern astrologers assign Uranus to Aquarius, but Uranus was unknown in ancient times. Saturn was the planet assigned to both Capricorn and Aquarius. Therefore, in planetary and angel magic, Saturn and Cassiel are ascribed to Aquarius as well as Capricorn. The illnesses ruled by Cassiel are rheumatism, leprosy, eczema, gout, arthrosclerosis, panic attacks, depression, chronic colds, and illnesses associated with the skin, the knees, and the bones. His flowers and plants are violets, belladonna, ebony, tamarind, pomegranates, the cypress tree, and opium. His incenses are myrrh and patchouli. The animals he rules are the peacock, the donkey, the goose, the goat, and the bat. His stones are obsidian, hematite, ebony, jet, onyx, basalt, silicon, tourmaline, sugilite, white quartz, aquamarine, and garnet. His metal is lead.

These are the seven great Archangels, their attributes, and the things they rule. As you have seen, some share the same attributes. There are three other Archangels who are important in angel magic. They are Uriel, the angel of the earth element and co-ruler of Aquarius with Cassiel; Sandalphon, the angel assigned to the tenth sphere of Malkuth and who is the protector and overseer of planet Earth; and Asariel, co-ruler of Pisces with Zadkiel, and one of the twenty-eight angels who rule the twenty-eight mansions of the moon.

Uriel

One of the seven princes of the Divine Presence and one of the angels of sanctification and repentance. He is a Seraph and a Cherub, one of the regents of the sun, and the Archangel of salvation. He rules the month of September, the north quarter, the earth element, and is co-ruler of Aquarius. Uriel's name means "fire of God." His number is eleven. His planetary colors are violet and aqua, all iridescent shades, and plaid. His ascribed day is Saturday at 11 PM. Uriel rules literature, good fortune, the riches of the earth, nuclear physics, atomic energy, explosions, electricity, aviation, intuition, astrology, and occultism. The illnesses he rules are leukemia and broken ankles. His flowers and plants are orchids, the fleur de lys, and all centenary or giant trees like the sequoia. His incenses are frankincense, galangal, and storax. His animals are macaws, cockatoos, birds of paradise, peacocks, and all birds of bright plumage. His stones are white quartz, amethyst, crisocolla, aquamarine, and sugilite. His metals are platinum, uranium, and all radioactive elements.

Sandalphon

Rules Malkuth, the tenth sphere of the Tree of Life. He is the protector and overseer of Earth. Sandalphon's name means "the wearer of sandals." He is the twin brother of Metatron and the master of heavenly song. He is regarded as one of the tallest archons in the celestial realms. He is also the angel of glory and the angel of prayer. Sandalphon is ruler of the planet Earth. His kabbalistic number is ten. His planetary color is green. His ascribed day is Sunday at 10 AM. Sandalphon rules the geology of the earth, earthquakes, mines and their ores, volcanoes and volcanic eruptions, seismic anomalies, the growth of plants, the fertilization of the soil, ecology, animal husbandry, global warming, and vegetarianism, and he also determines the sex of an unborn child or animal. His flowers and plants are all the plant species of the planet. His animals are all animal species, including the human race. He lays claim to all the stones, all the metals, and all the incenses. There are no specific illnesses associated with this angel.

Asariel

Co-ruler of Pisces. Asariel's name means "bound by God" (by oath). His number is twelve. His planet is Neptune. His planetary colors are pale lilac and blue-green. His ascribed day is Thursday at 12 AM. Asariel rules intuition, inspiration, clairvoyance, detectives, tsunamis, hurricanes, ships and shipwrecks, anesthesia, the deep unconscious, liquors, hallucinogens, frauds, the sea, and all river waters. The illnesses he rules are those associated with foot deformities. His flowers and plants are the lotus, water lilies, gardenia, freesia, anemones, seaweeds, lettuce, and watercress. The animals he rules are fish, amphibians, sea lions, seals, and penguins. His stones are tourmaline, amethyst, aquamarine, moldavite, coral, and seashells. His metals are silver and platinum.

As we have seen, the moon is very important in the practice of magic. Rituals for positive magic should always be performed during the waxing phases of the moon. The waxing phase begins with the new moon and ends with the full moon. The waning phase begins after the full moon and ends the night before the new moon, which is known as the night of the black moon. Each of these two phases lasts fourteen days. The twenty-eight days that form the two phases are known as the twenty-eight mansions of the moon. Each of these mansions is ruled by a different lunar angel. The first mansion of the moon is always the day of the new moon.

Following is a list of the twenty-eight angelic rulers of the lunar mansions:

Waxing Phase

1. Geniel (new moon)
2. Enediel
3. Anixiel
4. Asariel
5. Gabriel
6. Dirachiel
7. Scheliel
8. Amnediel
9. Barbiel
10. Ardifiel
11. Neciel
12. Abdizuel
13. Jazeriel
14. Ergediel

Waning Phase

1. Atliel (full moon)

2. Azeruel

3. Adriel

4. Egibiel

5. Amutiel

6. Kyriel

7. Bethnael

8. Geliel

9. Requiel

10. Abrinael

11. Aziel

12. Tagriel

13. Atheniel

14. Amnixiel

In order to give additional power to a ritual, it is recommended to invoke the name of the angel who rules the lunar mansion of the day of the ceremony. An astrological calendar like the one Llewellyn publishes every year is of great help in determining the lunar mansions. All you have to do is start counting the mansions beginning with the day of the new moon in any given month, which is the first mansion. This will tell you which mansion and which lunar angel rule the day of your ritual. If you are doing positive magic, that mansion will fall in one of the fourteen days of the waxing phase of the moon. Once you know the number of the mansion, you will also know the name of the lunar angel who rules it.

There is a ritual with the Archangel Gabriel that is designed to gather the great power of the new and the full moons. It calls for the preparation of a magical brew known as the Nectar of Levanah. Levanah is the Hebrew name for the moon.

The nectar is prepared by mixing light cream, white wine, sugar, and an egg white beaten until it thickens. The mixture is placed in a silver or blue goblet, and a moonstone is placed inside. A silver candle is lit in front of the goblet, and the Archangel Gabriel is invoked to bless the nectar and to grant the petitioner the power of the moon. The candle is allowed to burn for an hour, and then it is put out in the mixture, which is then drunk in the name of Gabriel. The ritual is conducted on the days of the new and the full moons. The same candle and moonstone are used when repeating the ritual.

A similar ritual is conducted to gather the powers of the sun, invoking the Archangel Michael, who rules it. The ritual uses the Nectar of Shemesh, which is the Hebrew name for the sun. The nectar is prepared by mixing a lightly beaten egg yolk, light cream, sugar, and red wine. The mixture is placed in a golden goblet, and a sunstone or citrine is placed inside. A golden candle is lit in front of the goblet, and the Archangel Michael is invoked to bless the nectar and grant the petitioner the powers of the sun. The candle is allowed to burn for an hour, and then it is put out in the mixture, which is drunk in the name of Michael. This ritual is conducted once a month, on the day when the sun enters a new sign. The candle and the stone can be reused when the ritual is repeated.

Every human interest or quality is ruled by a special angel. Among these angels are:

ABUNDANCE—Sophiel, Ilaniel, Barbelo

COMMUNICATIONS—Ambriel, Sabathiel

FAITH—Mebahiah, Isreal

HAPPINESS—Raphael, Sachial

HEALING, GOOD HEALTH—Raphael, Sabrael

HOPE—Derdeka, Drop

KNOWLEDGE——Raphael, Tarfiel

LOVE——Gabriel, Hanael

MERCY——Gabriel, Zadkiel, Tadhiel

MIRACLES——Michael, Raphael

OPTIMISM——Nachiel, Verchiel

PATIENCE——Anachiel, Oriphial

PROSPERITY——Hodiel, Kabniel, Zadkiel

PROTECTION——Abrid, Hanael

SERENITY——Metatron, Uretil

POWER——Kamael, Geburael

WILLPOWER——Nathanael, Seruph

WISDOM——Dina, Jophiel, Yefefiah

To petition one of these angels and ask for their divine gifts, the wish must be written using the letters of the angelic alphabet on a piece of unlined white paper. The paper is then burned over burning charcoals with a mixture of myrrh and frankincense. If the paper burns in its entirety, the angel has granted the request. This must be done facing the east within a magic circle and when the moon is waxing. (See appendix 6, figure 2 for examples of angelic alphabets.)

In the next chapter we will discuss the various rituals and magical works that can be done with the seven great Archangels.

CHAPTER 16

Angel Magic

We shall find peace. We shall hear angels.
We shall see the sky sparkling with diamonds.

· · · · · · · · · · · · ·

ANTON CHEKHOV

efore we can do angel magic, we must first know what angels
really are. Angels are patterns of cosmic energy, and they are
part of our collective unconscious and our ancestral memories.
What we do during an angel ritual is tap into this vast reservoir of energies, which are differentiated and personalized as angels and other cosmic forces. The same way we can recall memories of past events, we can
externalize into our conscious awareness those hidden aspects of our
minds that connect us with the cosmic forces that control and direct the
flowing energies of the universe. We can do this because these forces are
part of what Jung called the archetypes of the collective unconscious.
They are an intrinsic part of us, and each controls a different aspect of
physical reality. The anatomy of a ritual is designed to access that part of
our minds that corresponds to these cosmic energies and to release those

· · · · · · · · · · · ·

energies into the material world to bring about the things we need and desire to accomplish.

Across the centuries we have learned to categorize and differentiate these forces, anthropomorphizing them—that is, giving them a human physical appearance to help us visualize and contact them. We have assigned them attributes like numbers, colors, plants, and stones to link them to our earthly plane. Most importantly, we have discovered their interrelationship with the planets in our solar system, thus realizing their cosmic nature. Once we made the connection between these forces and the seven planets of the ancients, it was easy to identify them with the seven heavens, the seven angelic orders, and the seven great Archangels. It was a long process, and it was accomplished through meditation, visions, and revelation. We did not invent the angels. They revealed themselves to us.

Angel magic is essentially planetary magic. Every ritual designed to contact an angel requires knowledge of the planets they rule and the auxiliary forces that are connected with them. These auxiliary forces are the intelligences and the spirits that control the planets, and the seven Olympian spirits that represent them. They are called auxiliary because they help the Archangels in their work. Following are the intelligences and the spirits associated with the seven planets, the seven heavens, and their Archangels:

Planet	Heaven	Archangel	Intelligence	Spirit
Moon	Shamaym	Gabriel	Malkah ve Tarshi-sim Vead Ruachoth Schechalim	Chasmodai
Mercury	Raquie	Raphael	Tiriel	Taphthar-tharath
Venus	Sagun	Hanael	Hagiel	Kedemel
Sun	Machen	Michael	Nakhiel	Sorath
Mars	Mathey	Kamael	Graphiel	Bartzabel
Jupiter	Sebul	Zadkiel	Iophiel	Hismael
Saturn	Araboth	Cassiel	Agiel	Zazel

The intelligence of the planet is a beneficent entity of great power. The spirit of the planet is deemed negative but is, in reality, unbalanced energy. In planetary and angel magic, it is recommended to work with the intelligence of the planet and not with the spirit. It is possible to work with the intelligence of a planet without invoking or evoking its Archangel, as the Archangel oversees the work of the intelligence. In appendix 5 I will give rites of evocation for Hagiel, the intelligence of Venus, and Nakhiel, the intelligence of the sun. In rituals of invocation the entity contacted is asked to grant energies to the petitioner to accomplish his or her magical goal without manifesting physically. During a rite of evocation, however, the force is asked to materialize in front of the person conducting the ritual. See appendix 6, figure 27 for the planetary seals of intelligences.

The seven Olympian spirits are connected with the elemental forces as well as the planet. They are said to rule 196 Olympic provinces, representing the seven planets. The Olympic provinces are divided among them in multiples of seven:

Planet	Number of Provinces	Olympian Spirit
Moon	7	Phul
Mercury	14	Ophiel
Venus	21	Haggith
Sun	28	Och
Mars	35	Phaleg
Jupiter	42	Bethor
Saturn	49	Aratron

The Olympian spirits alternate their rulership of the heavens. Each rules for 490 years. The current ruler is Ophiel, who started his rulership in 1900 and will continue to rule until the year 2390. As Ophiel is a spirit of Mercury, the years of his rule should be marked by the intellect and many important discoveries. He will be followed by Haggith, who, as a spirit of Venus, should bring an era of love and peace to the earth. (See appendix 6, figure 25 for the sigils, or seals, of the Olympian spirits.)

The names of the Olympian spirits and their rituals were revealed in a book called the *Arbatel of Magic*, which appeared in Switzerland in 1575. It was originally written in Latin and was translated by Robert Turner in 1655. The original author is unknown. Each Olympian spirit is said to have legions of spirits at his or her command. Although the *Arbatel* has many inscriptions in Hebrew, its emphasis is decidedly Christian. The work was supposed to be composed of eight volumes, but only one of these has survived, and it is not known if the others were ever written. The surviving tome is known as the *Isagoge*.

According to the *Arbatel*, Olympian spirits have specific powers connected with the planets they rule:

PHUL—The Olympian spirit of the moon is said to give "familiars," or helping spirits, that belong to the water element. He is said to help human beings extend their lives for 300 years.

OPHIEL——The Olympian spirit of Mercury is said to give familiars of the air element. He teaches all the arts and converts quicksilver into the philosopher's stone.

HAGGITH——The Olympian spirit of Venus gives familiars of the earth element. She also makes people fair and beautiful and turns copper into gold and gold into copper.

OCH——The Olympian spirit of the sun gives familiars of the fire element. He is said to give 600 years of perfect health, bestow wisdom, teach medicine, and turn things into gold.

PHALEG——The Olympian spirit of Mars gives familiars of the fire element. He is known as the Prince of Peace. He is said to give honors in affairs of war.

BETHOR——The Olympian spirit of Jupiter gives familiars of the firmament. He can bestow fame upon an individual, help in finding treasures, and work with the spirits of the air element, which can materialize precious stones and heal all illnesses.

ARATRON——The Olympian spirit of Saturn gives powerful familiars. He is said to turn things into stone and turn treasures into coal and coal into treasures. He also teaches alchemy and magic, grants invisibility, prolongs life, and makes the barren fruitful.

The *Arbatel of Magic* is undoubtedly extravagant in the powers it ascribes to the Olympian spirits, but we must remember that this grimoire was written in the sixteenth century, when belief in supernatural occurrences was very common. An example of such beliefs is the story of Nicolas Flamel, who lived between the fourteenth and the fifteenth centuries. Flamel was a famed alchemist who is said to have made the philosopher's stone, which turns lead into gold. Flamel is also believed to have created the elixir of life, through which he and his wife, Perenelle, achieved immortality. The source of Flamel's knowledge was a book he purchased from a mysterious stranger and which was later identified as the original *Book of Abramelin the Mage*. Flamel and his wife allegedly decoded enough of the book to replicate its recipe for the philosopher's stone, producing first silver in 1382 and then gold. Whether this claim is true or not, the fact that Flamel and Perenelle were noted for their immense wealth and philanthropy later in life lends some credence to the story. Flamel is said to have died in 1418, but many believe his death was staged and that he is still alive. Flamel and Perenelle are important characters in the film *Indiana Jones and the Philosopher's Stone* and are mentioned in the novels *Foucault's Pendulum*, *The da Vinci Code,* and *Harry Potter and the Philosopher's Stone.*

Whether or not the Olympian spirits can deliver on the fantastic claims of the *Arbatel of Magic*, the book gives a ritual that can be used to invoke any of the big seven. It is clearly a ritual for the truly adventurous and those who assert that anything is possible with the suspension of belief.

First, the appropriate spirit must be chosen. Then the spirit's sigil is written on white, unlined paper. The ritual should be conducted during the waxing phase of the moon, on the day and the hour of the planet ruled by the chosen Olympian spirit. These days and hours have already been given, but I will repeat them here:

SUN—Sunday, 1 AM, 8 AM, 3 PM, 10 PM

MOON—Monday, same hours

MARS—Tuesday, same hours

MERCURY—Wednesday, same hours

JUPITER—Thursday, same hours

VENUS—Friday, same hours

SATURN—Saturday, same hours

It is recommended that the Invoking Ritual of the Pentagram be done before starting the ceremony. The person then holds the spirit's sigil in the right hand and says the following prayer:

*Omnipotent and eternal God, who hast ordained the
whole creation for thy praise and thy glory, as also
for the salvation of man, I beseech thee to send thy
spirit (here name the Olympian spirit), of the solar
order of (here name the spirit's planet), that he/
she may instruct me concerning those things about
which I design to ask him/her. Nevertheless, not
my will be done, but thine, through Jesus Christ,
thy only begotten son, who is our Lord, amen.*

The person then waits for a sign from the Olympian spirit, who may appear physically or send a clear omen of his or her presence. The person proceeds to address the spirit, making a request. When the request is granted, or even if it is not granted, a second prayer must be said to discharge the spirit and send him or her away:

*For as much as thou camest in peace and quietly,
having also answered unto my petitions, I give
thanks unto God, in whose name thou camest.
Now thou mayst depart in peace unto thy orders,
but return unto me again when I shall call thee
by thy name or by thy order or by thy office,
which is granted from the Creator, amen.*

The Banishing Ritual of the Pentagram is then performed. The *Arbatel* suggests the first hour of the day is the preferred time to do the invocation and admonishes the practitioner not to detain any of the Olympian spirits for more than an hour or it may become "familiarly addicted" to the person. That means it may want to stay permanently with the one who invoked it, which may prove rather disturbing, to say the very least.

As we have seen, the intelligences, the spirits, and the Olympian spirits of the seven planets fall within the regency of the seven great Archangels, whom they are compelled to obey as auxiliary spirits. Following is a sample ritual used to invoke the seven great Archangels. This is a very powerful and effective ritual if it is conducted exactly as it is given. The attributes of the Archangels are of vital importance and must be present during the ceremony.

It is important to choose the correct Archangel who rules the object of the person's desires if the ritual is to be successful. Although each Archangel rules his or her allotted day at 1 AM, 8 AM, 3 PM, and 10 PM, the preferred time is 1 AM, the first hour of the Archangel's day. The Archangels' attributes and the lunar angel that rules the day of the ritual were given in chapter 15; see appendix 6, figure 26 for the Archangels' seals, heavens, planets, and zodiac signs.

Gabriel

1. The ritual is conducted on a Monday at 1 AM. The altar should be covered with a violet or silver cloth and should face the east. Upon the altar are placed a crystal goblet filled with sweet white wine, a small bread roll, and a small bell.

2. A piece of white, unlined paper with Gabriel's sigil should be placed on the middle of the altar. The paper should be cut with nine sides, as nine is Gabriel's kabbalistic number. The sigil should be traced in violet ink. Several of Gabriel's attributes should be placed around the sigil to help establish a strong connection with the Archangel. Among these attributes should be an orchid, eucalyptus, mint leaves, a melon or a plum, a moonstone or a white quartz, and a piece of silver. A small image of a wolf or a crab should also be on the altar. (To use other attributes, see chapter 15.) A censer should be ready, filled with several burning charcoals and a mixture of camphor and myrrh, Gabriel's favored incense. Nine violet candles on their holders should be placed in a circle around the room. The candles should be unlit.

3. All these preparations must be ready before 1 AM. The person should wear a white tunic and must be barefoot. He or she should wear a diadem or a circlet of intertwined flowers. This helps establish the magical personality of the individual. Any jewelry worn must have

magical or talismanic symbolism. At exactly 1 AM, the candles are lit. The four elements are then passed around the circle, beginning at the east quarter. First, the censer is passed around the circle, and these words are said:

In the name of God and his angelic host,
I consecrate this circle in the air element.

The censer is placed on the floor in the east. Second, a large red candle, preferably glass-encased, is passed around the circle, and these words are said:

In the name of God and his angelic host,
I consecrate this circle in the fire element.

The candle is placed on the floor on the south quarter. Third, a large goblet of water is passed around the circle, and these words are said:

In the name of God and his angelic host,
I consecrate this circle in the water element.

The goblet is placed on the floor in the west quarter. Lastly, a small dish with salt is passed around the circle, and these words are said:

In the name of God and his angelic host,
I consecrate this circle in the earth element.

The person then stands in the center of the room facing the east and proceeds to do the ritual of the invoking pentagram. He or she may use a consecrated wand to cast the pentagrams and the circle, or the ficca, which is formed by placing the right thumb between the index and the middle fingers (left thumb if the person is left-handed). After the invoking pentagram, the person returns to the altar and opens the arms wide, shoulder high. He or she proceeds to invoke the Archangel five times, once in each of the four quarters, starting with the east and repeating the invocation upon returning to the east.

4. The bell is rung nine times, and Gabriel is invoked as follows:

> *Great Cherub, Virtue, power, Archangel, and angel*
> *Gabriel, who rules the First Heaven, Shamaym;*
> *the sephira of Yesod and the moon; and the*
> *water element: I call upon thee, mighty prince*
> *and archon, in the most holy name of Shaddai*
> *el Chai and with the blessing of the lunar angel*
> *(say the name of the lunar angel who rules the*
> *day of the ritual) to hearken unto my voice*
> *and answer my petition. Thou rulest what I so*
> *ardently need and desire: (name what you wish*
> *to accomplish). Call with a mighty voice thy*
> *auxiliary spirits: the powerful moon intelligence,*
> *Malkah ve Tarshi-sim Vead Ruachoth, and the*
> *powerful Olympian spirit of the moon, Phul, and*
> *their attending spirits, to carry on thy commands*
> *and bring to pass in the material world what I*
> *so ardently need and desire by (here a date must*
> *be given which should include the month, day,*
> *and year by which time the petition should be*
> *answered). I have placed upon my altar these*
> *humble offerings, which I hope will be agreeable*
> *to thee as testimonies of my love and gratitude.*
> *Accept them in divine mercy and transform their*
> *energies into the things I need and desire.*

5. The person remains in the east, eyes closed, visualizing the Archangel dressed in his planetary colors, shimmering with blinding light, his alabaster wings reaching to the ceiling, spread out, surrounding the person with the Archangel's blessing. At this point, the person should connect mentally with the Archangel and listen to his message. Very

often the person perceives many images rushing through his or her mind that are part of the Archangel's answer to the petition.

6. After the petition is answered, the person proceeds to discharge the Archangel, saying:

> *I thank thee, (name the angel), most precious and*
> *holy angel of God, for thy gracious presence during*
> *this ritual, for the presence of your auxiliary*
> *spirits and for answering my petition. Be always*
> *by my side and guide me always in the path of*
> *light that leads to our most beloved Creator, and*
> *may his/her blessings be always with you. And*
> *so I say to thee in the east, hail and farewell."*
> *(This is said in the east quarter and repeated in*
> *the other quarters, using the quarter's name.)*

7. The bread roll is eaten and the wine is drunk in the name of God and the Archangel.

8. The banishing pentagram is then done. The person says "This ritual is ended" and knocks ten times on the altar to earth the energies and to signify the conclusion of the ceremony. Ten is used because it represents Malkuth and the planet Earth. The various appurtenances of the ritual are gathered and put away. Candles are put out without blowing on them and discarded. Elements are also discarded.

The ritual is the same for the seven Archangels except for steps 1, 2, and 4, which describe the angels' offerings and their special invocations. Following are steps 1, 2, and 4 for the remaining Archangels.

Raphael

1. The ritual is conducted on a Wednesday at 1 AM. The altar should be covered with an orange cloth and should face the east. Upon the altar are placed a crystal goblet filled with sweet white wine, a small bread roll, and a small bell.

2. A piece of white paper with Raphael's sigil should be placed on the middle of the altar. The paper should be cut with eight sides, as eight is Raphael's kabbalistic number. The sigil should be traced in orange ink. Several of Raphael's attributes should be placed around the sigil to help establish a strong connection with the Archangel. Among these attributes should be lavender, marjoram, elm tree leaves, ferns, an orange, almonds, a piece of aluminum, and a lace agate. A small image of a butterfly should also be on the altar. (To use other attributes, see chapter 15.) A censer should be ready, filled with burning charcoals and a mixture of sandalwood, storax, gum arabic, and cloves, Raphael's favored incense. Eight orange candles on their holders should be placed in a circle around the room. The candles should be unlit.

3. See Gabriel's ritual.

4. The bell is rung eight times, and Raphael is invoked as follows:

> *Great Cherub and Archangel Raphael, who rules*
> *the Second Heaven, Raquie; the sephira Hod; the*
> *planet Mercury; and the air element: I call upon*
> *thee, mighty prince and archon, in the most holy*
> *name of Elohim Tzabaoth and with the blessing*
> *of the lunar angel (name of the lunar angel who*
> *rules the day of the ritual) to hearken unto my*
> *voice and answer my petition. Thou rulest what I so*
> *ardently need and desire: (name what you wish to*
> *accomplish). Call with a mighty voice thy auxiliary*
> *spirits: the powerful intelligence of Mercury, Tiriel,*

and the powerful Olympian spirit of Mercury,
Ophiel, and their attending spirits, to carry on
thy commands and bring to pass in the material
world what I so ardently need and desire by (here
a date must be given that includes the month,
day, and year by which time the petition should
be answered). I have placed upon my altar these
humble offerings, which I hope will be agreeable
to thee as testimonies of my love and gratitude.
Accept them in divine mercy and transform their
energies into the things I need and desire.

5—8. Steps are the same as in Gabriel's ritual.

Hanael

1. The ritual is conducted on a Friday at 1 AM. The altar should be covered with an emerald-green cloth and should face the east. Upon the altar are placed a crystal goblet with sweet red wine, a small bread roll, and a small bell.

2. A piece of white, unlined paper with Hanael's sigil should be placed on the middle of the altar. The paper should be cut with seven sides, Hanael's kabbalistic number. The sigil should be traced in green ink. Several of Hanael's attributes should be placed around the sigil, to help establish a strong connection with the Archangel. Among these attributes should be a red rose, vervain or myrtle, an apple, a rose quartz, and a piece of copper. A small image of a turtle, a spider, or a dove should also be placed on the altar. (To use other attributes, see chapter 15.) A censer should be ready with burning charcoals and a mixture of storax, valerian, sandalwood, benzoin, and cinnamon, Hanael's favored incenses. Seven green candles should be placed around the circle. The candles should be unlit.

3. See Gabriel's ritual.

4. The bell is ring seven times, and Hanael is invoked as follows:

> *Great Virtue and Principality Hanael, who rulest*
> *the Third Heaven, Sagun; the sephira Netzach;*
> *and the planet Venus: I call upon thee, mighty*
> *princess and archon, in the most holy name of*
> *Jehovah Tzabaoth and with the blessing of the*
> *lunar angel (name of the lunar angel who rules*
> *the day of the ritual) to hearken unto my voice*
> *and answer my petition. Thou rulest what I so*
> *ardently need and desire: (name what the person*
> *wants to accomplish). Call with a mighty voice*
> *thy auxiliary spirits: the powerful intelligence of*
> *Venus, Hagiel, and the powerful Olympian spirit*
> *of Venus, Haggith, and their attending spirits, to*
> *carry on thy commands and bring to pass in the*
> *material world what I so ardently need and desire*
> *by (here a date must be given, including the month,*
> *day, and year by which time the petition should*
> *be answered). I have placed upon my altar these*
> *humble offerings, which I hope will be agreeable*
> *to thee as testimonies of my love and gratitude.*
> *Accept them in divine mercy and transform their*
> *energies into the things I need and desire."*

5–8. Steps are the same as in Gabriel's ritual.

Michael

1. The ritual is conducted on a Sunday at 1 AM. The altar should be covered with a golden or yellow cloth. Upon the altar are placed a crystal goblet filled with sweet red wine, a small bread roll, and a small bell.

2. A piece of white, unlined paper with Michael's sigil should be placed on the middle of the altar. The paper should be cut with six sides,

Michael's kabbalistic number. The sigil should be traced in gold or yellow ink. Several of Michael's attributes should be placed around the sigil. Among these attributes should be yellow flowers, laurel, chamomile, mistletoe, cinnamon sticks, a pineapple, a citrine or amber, and a piece of gold. A small image of a lion or a tiger should also be placed on the altar. (To use other attributes, see chapter 15.) A censer should be ready, filled with burning charcoals and a mixture of copal and frankincense, Michael's favored incenses. Six yellow or gold candles should be placed around the circle. The candles should be unlit.

3. See Gabriel's ritual.

4. The bell is rung six times, and Michael is invoked as follows:

> Great Seraph, Virtue, and Archangel Michael, who
> rules the Fourth Heaven, Machen; the sephira
> Tiphareth; the Sun; and the fire element: I call
> upon thee, mighty prince and archon, in the
> most holy name of Jehovah Elo Ve Daath and
> with the blessing of the lunar angel (name of the
> lunar angel who rules the day of the ritual) to
> hearken unto my voice and answer my petition.
> Thou rulest what I so ardently need and desire:
> (name the desire). Call with a mighty voice thy
> auxiliary spirits: the powerful intelligence of the
> sun, Nakhiel, and the powerful Olympian spirit
> Och, and their attending spirits, to carry on thy
> commands and bring to pass in the material
> world what I so ardently need and desire by (here
> a date must be given, including the month, day,
> and year by which time the petition should be
> answered). I have placed upon my altar these
> humble offerings, which I hope will be agreeable
> to thee as testimonies of my love and gratitude.

Accept them in divine mercy and transform their
energies into the things I need and desire.

5–8. Steps are the same as in Gabriel's ritual.

Kamael

1. The ritual is conducted on a Tuesday at 1 AM. The altar should be covered with a red cloth and should face the east. Upon the altar are placed a crystal goblet filled with sweet red wine, a small bread roll, and a small bell.

2. A piece of white, unlined paper should be placed on the middle of the altar. The paper should be cut with five sides, Kamael's kabbalistic number. The sigil should be traced in red ink. Several of Kamael's attributes should be placed around the sigil to help establish a strong connection with the Archangel. Among these attributes should be red flowers (except red roses), a cactus, cumin, pepper, mustard seed, a garlic clove, a carnelian or a bloodstone, and a five iron nails, as iron is Kamael's metal. A small image of an eagle or a ram should also be on the altar. (To use other attributes, see chapter 15.) A censer should be ready, filled with burning charcoals and a mixture of dragon's blood resin and asafetida, Kamael's favored incenses. Five red candles on their holders should be placed around the circle. The candles should be unlit.

3. See Gabriel's ritual.

4. The bell is rung five times, and Kamael is invoked as follows:

> *Great Seraph and Power Kamael, who rules the*
> *Fifth Heaven, Mathey; the sephira Geburah; and*
> *the planet Mars: I call upon thee, mighty prince*
> *and archon, in the most holy name of Elohim*
> *Gebor and with the blessing of the lunar angel*
> *(name of the lunar angel who rules the day of the*
> *ritual) to hearken unto my voice and answer my*

petition. Thou rulest what I so ardently need and
desire: (name your desire). Call with a mighty voice
thy auxiliary spirits: the powerful intelligence
of Mars, Graphiel, and the powerful Olympian
spirit of Mars, Phaleg, and their attending spirits,
to carry thy commands and bring to pass in the
material world what I so ardently need and desire
by (here a date must given, including the month,
day, and year by which time the petition should
be answered). I have placed upon my altar these
humble offerings, which I hope will be agreeable
to thee as testimonies of my love and gratitude.
Accept them in divine mercy and transform their
energies into the things I need and desire.

5   8. Steps are the same as in Gabriel's ritual.

Zadkiel

1. The ritual is conducted on a Thursday at 1 AM. The altar should be covered with an electric blue cloth and should face the east. Upon the altar are placed a crystal goblet filled with sweet red wine, a small bread roll, and a small bell.

2. A piece of white, unlined paper with Zadkiel's sigil should be placed on the middle of the altar. The paper should be cut with four sides, in the form a square, as four is Zadkiel's kabbalistic number. The sigil should be traced in bright blue ink. Several of Zadkiel's attributes should be placed around the sigil to help establish a strong connection with the Archangel. Among these attributes should be blue flowers, sage, hyssop, pine cones, a lapis lazuli or an azurite, and a piece of tin. A small image of a swan or a whale should also be placed on the altar. (To use other attributes, see chapter 15.) A censer should be ready with burning charcoals and a mixture of sarsaparilla, nutmeg, and frankincense, Zadkiel's favored incenses. Four bright blue candles on

their holders should be placed around the circle. The candles should be unlit.

3. See Gabriel's ritual.

4. The bell is rung four times, and Zadkiel is invoked as follows:

> *Great Dominion and Archangel Zadkiel, who rules*
> *the Sixth Heaven, Zebul, and the sephira Chesed:*
> *I call upon thee, mighty prince and archon, in*
> *the most holy name of El and with the blessing*
> *of the lunar angel (name of the lunar angel who*
> *rules the day of the ritual) to hearken unto my*
> *voice and answer my petition. Thou rulest what*
> *I so ardently need and desire: (name the desire).*
> *Call with a mighty voice thy auxiliary spirits:*
> *the powerful intelligence of Jupiter, Iophiel,*
> *and the powerful Olympian spirit of Jupiter,*
> *Bethor, and their attending spirits, to carry on*
> *thy commands and bring to pass in the material*
> *world what I so ardently need and desire by (here*
> *a date must be given, including the month, day,*
> *and year by which time the petition should be*
> *answered). I have placed upon my altar these*
> *humble offerings, which I hope will be agreeable*
> *to thee as testimonies of my love and gratitude.*
> *Accept them in divine mercy and transform their*
> *energies into the things I need and desire.*

5–8. Steps are the same as in Gabriel's ritual.

Cassiel

1. The ritual is conducted on a Saturday at 1 AM. The altar should be covered with a dark navy blue cloth and should face the east. Upon the altar are placed a crystal goblet with sweet red wine, a small bread roll, and a small bell.

2. A piece of white, unlined paper with Cassiel's sigil should be placed on the middle of the altar. The paper should be cut in the form of a triangle, as three is Cassiel's kabbalistic number. The sigil should be traced in very dark blue ink. Several of Cassiel's attributes should be placed around the sigil. Among these attributes should be violets, a pomegranate, leaves from a cypress tree, a peacock feather, an obsidian, a hematite, a piece of basalt, and a piece of lead. A small image of a goat or a peacock should also be on the altar. A censer should be ready, filled with burning charcoals and a mixture of myrrh and patchouli, Cassiel's favored incenses. Three dark blue candles in their holders should be placed around the room. The candles should be unlit. (Note: The color black is assigned to the sephira Binah, Saturn, and Cassiel because it represents the dark void of space, but in reality space is not black but a very dark blue like the sky at night. That is why dark blue is used in rituals associated with Binah, Saturn, and Cassiel. Black candles should not be used in any angelic ritual, as black represents absence of color and therefore absence of light.)

3. See Gabriel's ritual.

4. The bell is rung three times, and Cassiel is invoked as follows:

> *Great Throne and Archangel Cassiel, who rules the*
> *Seventh Heaven, Araboth; the sephira Binah; and*
> *the planet Saturn: I call upon thee, mighty prince*
> *and archon, in the most holy name of Jehovah*
> *Elohim and with the blessing of the lunar angel*
> *(name of the lunar angel who rules the day of*

the ritual) to hearken unto my voice and answer
my petition. Thou rulest what I so ardently need
and desire: (here name the desire). Call with a
mighty voice thy auxiliary spirits: the powerful
intelligence of Saturn, Agiel, and the powerful
Olympian spirit Aratron, and their attending
spirits, to carry on thy commands and bring to
pass in the material world what I so ardently
need and desire by (here a date must be given,
including the month, day, and year by which time
the petition should be answered). I have placed
upon my altar these humble offerings, which I hope
will be agreeable to thee as testimonies of my love
and gratitude. Accept them in divine mercy and
transform them into the things I need and desire.

5—8. Steps are the same as in Gabriel's ritual.

It is important to be give a precise date by which time the petition should be granted, because time does not exist in the spiritual realms. If a date is not given during the ritual, the petition could take years to be answered, maybe longer than the person's lifespan.

This ritual is extremely effective, as the person connects with very deep levels of his or her unconscious mind when it is being conducted. The sigils, colors, numbers, geometric patterns, and attributes are symbols of the psychic energy the petitioner wishes to contact and release into his or her outer consciousness and the material world. This psychic energy is manifested as the angelic entity invoked, which is an archetypal force of the collective unconscious. The attributes are also concentrations of physical energy that may be transmuted into actual events through the symbolism encoded in the angelic archetype. This energy can be directed along specific channels controlled by the force invoked, which is an intrinsic part of the unconscious mind of the person conducting the ritual. We could then say that during a ritual the person is the angel and the one granting the petition.

Magic is an aphorism; it is a means to an end. Magic is simply a way to tap into our deep unconscious, releasing vast amounts of psychic energies that we can then transform into the things we need and want.

Angel magic works because angels are real. They exist in us and in the universe around us, as universal laws and as quanta of cosmic energy. They are part of our collective unconscious and, as such, they are intelligent, purposeful, and aware. The unconscious is a vast reservoir of inexhaustible energies. There are no limits to its power and its potential. Angels help us release this power because they are our links to the universal mind. They are our connection with the Divine, and through them we are one with God.

❖◀◆▶❖

Angel Imaging

It is necessary during the invocation or evocation of angels to visual-ize them in the forms that have been ascribed to them in traditional magic. These forms have been received by many people through visions, dreams, and revelations. None of the angels' eyes have whites; their eyes are made of one single color. Their faces are made of crystal planes of the color associated with the angel. They all have swords wreathed in fire and held by a girdle and a scabbard by their sides. Their wings are not always white. Some of their wings correspond to the color ascribed to the angel. Here is a list of the various Archangels and the images associated with them.

GABRIEL——As the ruler of the water element, Gabriel is envisioned as a man in his thirties with wavy brown hair reaching to his shoulders. His eyes are sea green and he wears a blue tunic with orange facings. As a planetary and kabbalistic Archangel of the moon, he appears as a beautiful young man with flowing lavender hair and deep violet eyes. His face is made of lavender crystal planes. He is dressed in a shimmering violet tunic trimmed with silver and mother-of-pearl. He wears a silver crown with nine stars interspersed with the lunar phases. He holds a silver trumpet in his hand, and his wings are lavender tipped with silver. When he speaks, his voice sounds like rippling waters. He wears silver sandals. Gabriel's demeanor is solemn and grave.

RAPHAEL——As the ruler of the air element, Raphael is envisioned as an adolescent with golden hair curling like a halo around his head. His eyes are blue, and he is dressed in yellow robes with violet facings. As a planetary and kabbalistic Archangel of Mercury, he appears as a beautiful young man with golden hair streaming down his shoulders. He has golden eyes, and his face is made of shimmering crystal planes with a pale orange hue. He wears a short orange tunic trimmed with gold and a gold belt encrusted with topaz stones. He also wears gold sandals with wings on the sides. Upon his head is a gold helmet topped with eight stars. He holds a golden caduceus in one hand, and his wings are golden. When Raphael speaks, his voice sounds like a whistling wind. He has an amiable countenance and a lovely smile.

HANAEL——She is not an elementary angel. As a planetary and kabbalistic Archangel of Venus, Hanael appears as a beautiful young woman with bright tomato-red hair flowing in curls down her back and shoulders. Her skin is white as snow, but her face is made of pale green crystal planes. Her eyes are emerald green. She wears a tunic of iridescent pastel hues trimmed with emeralds and fire opals. She wears a girdle of red roses and myrtle leaves interwoven with emeralds. Her crown is made of seven stars interspersed with red roses. Her wings are pale green, and she carries a white dove in her hand. She wears copper sandals. Her voice sounds like a gentle breeze. Her demeanor is pleasant, and she always smiles.

MICHAEL——As the ruler of the fire element, Michael is envisioned as a young man in his early twenties with bright red curls cascading to his shoulders. His eyes are green, and he wears a red tunic with green facings. As a planetary and kabbalistic Archangel of the sun, he appears as a dazzlingly beautiful young man with bright red hair tumbling upon his shoulders. There are innumerable small mouths on each hair strand, each praying to the Archangel and asking for his help. Michael is dressed in golden armor, studded with diamonds and rubies and a short golden tunic. He wears golden Roman sandals. His skin is golden, and he has emerald-green eyes. He wears a gold crown with six bright stars, and the solar orb in its center has fiery rays pouring outwardly. His face is made of golden crystal planes, and his wings are emerald green. When he speaks his voice sounds like a roaring fire, and small flames stream from his lips. Michael's demeanor is stern, and he never smiles.

KAMAEL——He is not an elementary angel. As a planetary and kabbalistic Archangel of Mars, Kamael appears as a powerful man in his mid-thirties with a grim visage. His hair is bright red, and his skin is also red. His face is made of reddish crystal planes, and his eyes are bright red. Kamael is dressed in engraved red leather armor covered with rubies and iron studs. His massive legs are encased in red leather leggings and he wears red leather sandals. His crown is made of iron spikes topped with five stars. His wings are ruby red, and he carries an iron maze in his hand. His voice rumbles like an erupting volcano. Kamael's demeanor is fierce, and he seldom smiles.

ZADKIEL——He is not an elementary angel. As a planetary and kabbalistic Archangel of Jupiter, Zadkiel appears as a jovial young man with a round, Cherubic face. His skin is pale blue, and so is his hair, which flows to his shoulders. Around his neck he wears a ruffle of bright blue tulle. His tunic is electric blue trimmed with amethyst and turquoise. His face is made of pale blue crystals, and his eyes are electric blue. His crown is made of lapis lazuli topped with four stars, and he wears sandals made of peacock feathers. Zadkiel's wings are blue, and he carries an eagle in his hand. His voice is soft and ripples with laughter. Zadkiel is a most amiable angel, and he always smiles.

CASSIEL——He is not an elementary angel. As a planetary and kabbalistic Archangel of Saturn, Cassiel appears as a regal older man with dark blue, almost black skin. His hair is dark blue and flows over his shoulders. His face is made of dark blue crystal planes, and his eyes are the color of sapphires. He wears a dark blue velvet tunic, almost black, trimmed with diamonds and onyx. He wears sandals made of lead and ebony. Cassiel's wings are dark blue, and he carries a lead goblet in his hand that is overflowing with red wine. His crown is made of lead filigree with three large stars. Cassiel's demeanor is grave, but his smile is kind.

URIEL——As the angel of the earth element, Uriel is envisioned as a handsome black man in his mid-forties with flowing black hair. He is dressed in a tunic of olive green, russet, lime, and black hues trimmed with jade and malachite. His face is made of black crystal planes, and his eyes are bright green. He wears a crown of green leaves and multicolored flowers topped with ten stars. His sandals are made of green leaves intertwined with flowers. Uriel carries in one hand a cornucopia flowing with gold and the fruits of the earth and an open book in the other. His wings are bright green, his demeanor is amiable, and he always smiles.

APPENDIX 2

Angel Signs

T he angelic presence may be felt in many ways. People who have conducted angel rituals or who have established a sensitive connection with them have reported a continuous subtle contact with these ethereal beings. Among the most common signs of an angelic presence is the constant finding of feathers in the most unexpected places, the pervasive fragrance of flowers or sweet aromas with no apparent source for their presence, a large concentration of fireflies where none appeared before, brightly colored butterflies, and special messages on billboards and even license plates. These signs appear when the person is under stress or is facing a dilemma that needs to be resolved.

A woman from Iowa who had been invoking the Archangel Michael and asking for his help after the disappearance of her daughter saw a billboard sign while driving to work. The sign said, "Your prayers are answered this day. Michael Works." The sign had been posted by a company called Michael Works that did home repairs. But that same afternoon the woman's daughter called her from Florida, where she had eloped with her boyfriend. She told her mother she was safe and had eloped because the family did not like her boyfriend. She was now married to him and felt the sudden urge to call her mother to tell her she was fine. Her new husband's name was Michael.

Another billboard sign saved a man from losing his job and possibly going to jail. This man had been persistently harassed by someone at work. One day he decided to end the harassment by giving his tormentor a thorough beating. As he drove to work with this grim determination fixed in his mind, he saw a white dove cross his field of vision and land on a billboard ahead of him. The message on the billboard was, "Violence leads nowhere. Try peace." This message flooded the man's consciousness with a great sense of relief. His anger seemed to dissolve, and he realized he had no desire to harm the person who had been attacking him. When he arrived at his office, he told his supervisor what had been going on in a calm and sensible manner. After an investigation of the harassment, which was corroborated by other employees, the culprit was dismissed and the man retained his job.

Sometimes signs appear for no specific reason and when least expected. Once I was driving on the Long Island Expressway when I saw a gold-colored Mercedes SUV move in front of me. I reduced speed to accommodate it, and then I saw its license plate: ELOHIM. This is the name of God as the Creator and also the name of one of the angelic choirs. I was instantly curious and kept my eyes on the SUV, wondering what it would do. We drove along for a while, and then it left the expressway at the exit I was going to take. I followed closely behind and then decided to get alongside the vehicle or in front of it so I could see the driver. But no matter how hard I tried, I could not get in front or on the side of the SUV. When we reached the first light, the vehicle made a swift right turn and disappeared. I was never able to see the driver.

This is not the only time I have seen angelic signs on car plates. Once I saw a plate that read AIN, which is God's first manifestation; other times I have seen plates with angel names like GABRIEL9 or HAN777, a reference to Hanael and her number, seven. Gabriel's number is nine. All of these times I have not seen the drivers' faces.

Feathers are perhaps the most important of the divine signs. Angels are anthropomorphized with human forms and wings. God is also conceived as a winged being. In Psalm 91:4 the psalmist says, "He shall cover you with his feathers, and under his wings shall thou trust." Some time ago, after a meditation, I saw a man and a woman behind my closed eyes. They were standing side by side and seemed to be joined at the shoulders. Their faces were human faces, nothing special about them, and I did not notice their clothing. They were just standing there. What I did notice was their wings. They were huge, and the two figures seemed to be sharing only one pair. There was a white wing behind the man and a black wing behind the woman. I was so startled by this vision that I gasped and opened my eyes. The images faded, and I had trouble understanding what I had seen. Had I seen a human manifestation of God, or was it my imagination? The next day I went through my daily routine and gave no further thought to my experience. Around two in the afternoon I went to pick up my correspondence, which my housekeeper always leaves on the dining room table. As I flipped through the letters I found a single feather among them. The feather was black-tipped with white along its entire length. I stared at the feather, stunned, and the vision of the previous night came flooding back into my mind. I called my housekeeper and asked her if she had seen the feather. She said she had not. She had picked up the letters from the floor, where they had lain after the mailman put them through the mail slot on the door. She had gathered them together and placed them on the table. When she had picked them up, there had been no feather among the letters.

Since that time I keep finding feathers in the most unexpected places. Sometimes I find them on my path on a busy sidewalk. Sometimes I find them in my car. Sometimes I find them on my desk. Sometimes they are big and other times they are small. They are nearly always white or black. Sometimes they are grey with white at one end and black at the other. As I was writing this section, I found a tiny white feather on the cover of my King James version of the Bible. I have no idea where it came from.

Each time I find a feather, I am about to do something important or make a vital decision. The feather seems to indicate I am on the right track. Several months ago I needed to have some repairs done to my car. I went to several shops, uncertain of where I should bring the car. When I got to the third shop, I found a large grey feather tipped with black and white at the main entrance. I immediately knew this was the place I was looking for. I left my car there that same day, and the work that was done was exactly what I had hoped for.

Fireflies are also seen by many people as angel signs, especially in times of great stress or hopelessness. There was a recent story on the Internet about a woman who had lost all of her savings in bad investments. She was practically destitute and feared she might lose her house. She prayed continuously to her guardian angel to help her find a solution to her problems. One night she walked out of her house into her backyard and found it blazing with hundreds of fireflies. So great was the light emitted by the creatures that the backyard seemed to be enveloped in phosphorescent green light. At that moment she felt that her guardian angel had answered her prayers. The next day the lawyer who was in charge of investigating her loss called to tell her that the company who handled her investments, fearing an indictment for fraud, had decided to return most of her money.

One of my students is a fervent believer in Hanael, as she was born under the sign of Libra, ruled by this Archangel. This person is allergic to perfume and flowers so she cannot offer red roses to Hanael, who rules them. Yet she says that all her visitors smell roses in her house, even though she cannot.

The smell of flowers, especially roses and lilies, has always been associated with angels. These fragrances appear most often during meditations and especially during angelic rituals. They are usually accompanied by a great sense of peace and harmony. Unusual and ethereal music and unexpected sounds without an obvious source are also associated with the angelic presence.

A very special angel sign is a dove flying directly over a person's head or over a car he or she is driving. This is usually an indication that the person is under angelic protection.

Large spider webs extending over an entire window or a doorway are also signs of divine protection. These signs are usually detected at night, and the web's threads tend to shimmer like silver strings. The next morning they are gone. Tiny golden spiders are an indication of the Shekinah's presence and of her blessing, as spiders are among her attributes.

To attune to the angelic presence is to find a source of constant solace in our lives. We feel that somehow we are not alone—that someone is nearby who cares, guides us, and protects us. I urge the reader to seek this presence. It is all around you. It is protective, it is loving, and it will never steer you wrong.

APPENDIX 3

Angel Spells

Although rituals are more dynamic and create greater amounts of energy that make results more obtainable, it is also possible to propitiate the Archangels through simple offers and spells. These can be very effective if the angelic offers include the entity's attributes. Following are several spells that have proven to be very effective in obtaining angelic help. The moon should always be waxing. Candles are anointed from the middle of the candle upward and from the middle downward. Do not rub the candle up and down, as it will disturb the candle's polarity.

HANAEL
A Spell for Love

Before doing this spell, consider that a person's free will must never be interfered with in any way. You can ask Hanael to help you in influencing a person to love you, not to force this person to care for you against their will.

The outcome of the spell depends on the person's attitude toward you. The spell should be done on a Friday at 10 PM. In a large bowl place myrtle, vervain, spearmint, seven red roses, cinnamon, and a perfect red apple. Surround the bowl with seven pieces of rose quartz. Burn cinnamon powder, storax, and valerian over a bed of charcoal. Pass the incense over the bowl. Inscribe the person's name on a long green taper and anoint with a mixture of mineral oil, powdered cinnamon, and sandalwood. Ask Hanael to influence this person in your favor and to see you in a romantic light. Light the candle seven minutes daily, repeating the petition. When the candle is finished, find an excuse to give this person the red apple. If he or she accepts it and eats it, Hanael has answered your request. Keep the rose quartz to strengthen the spell, and dispose of the rest of the ingredients.

URIEL
A Spell for Money

This spell should be done on a Sunday, as Uriel is a solar angel. The hour should be 10 PM. Mix earth with storax and frankincense, and place it in a crystal bowl. Surround it with alum, which is used for clarity and light. Under the bowl place a dollar bill. Over the earth mixture place eleven magnets. Burn storax and frankincense over a bed of coals. Pass the incense over the bowl. Anoint a long violet taper with a mixture of mineral oil, storax, and frankincense. Ask Uriel to multiply your money and attract it to you through the magnet's pull. Light the candle eleven minutes daily, repeating the petition, until the candle is finished. Wrap the magnets in the dollar bill and tie the bill with violet string. Carry this amulet with you always. Throw away the rest of the ingredients.

RAPHAEL
A Spell for Good Health

This spell should be done on a Wednesday at 10 PM. In a large bowl place parsley, marjoram, lavender, and six oranges. In the center of this offering put an agate. Over several charcoals burn sandalwood and cloves. Pass the incense over the offer and set it on the right side of the bowl. Inscribe an orange taper with Raphael's sigil and anoint it with a mixture of mineral oil and sandalwood. Ask Raphael to heal you or the person you are doing the spell for. Light the taper eight minutes daily, repeating the petition, until the candle is finished. Cut one of the oranges into six sections, which should be eaten by the person who is ill. The other oranges and the herbs should be left in a park near the person's house. The agate should be carried by the person always.

A Spell for Fame and Fortune

This spell should be done on a Sunday at 10 PM. Fill a large bowl with honey, as Michael rules bees. Surround the bowl with six yellow flowers. Inside the honey place something made of gold and six pieces of amber. Burn copal and frankincense over a bed of charcoals. Pass the incense over the bowl. Ask Michael to bring you fame and fortune. Inscribe a golden taper with Michael's sigil and anoint it with a mixture of mineral oil, vanilla extract, and frankincense. Light it six minutes every day, repeating the petition, until the candle is finished. Throw the six yellow flowers outside your house, encircling the place. Each day dip the middle finger of your right hand in the honey, lick it, and say that in the name of Michael, as you taste the honey so will you taste fame and fortune.

A Spell to Win a Court Case

This spell should be done on a Tuesday at 10 PM. Fill a large bowl with five red flowers (not roses) and cover them with pepper, cumin, powdered mustard, and garlic powder. Burn asafetida and dragon's blood resin over several charcoals. Surround the bowl with either five magnets or five thunderstones. Pass the incense over the bowl. Ask Kamael to give you the power to win your case. Inscribe Kamael's sigil on a tall red taper and anoint with a mixture of mineral oil, mustard, and ground pepper. Light the candle five minutes daily, repeating the petition, until the candle is finished. The day of the court case, boil five iron nails in water with the red flowers. Wash your hands in the liquid, and place the magnets or thunderstones in your pocket or your handbag before you leave for the courthouse.

ZADKIEL

A Spell to Secure Employment

This spell should be done on a Thursday at 10 PM. The name of the company where employment is desired is written on a piece of blue paper. The paper is placed on a bright blue cloth and covered with sage, hyssop, and pine needles. In the center of this mixture place an amethyst. Burn nutmeg, sarsaparilla, and frankincense over a bed of charcoals and pass the incense over the cloth. Ask Zadkiel to secure your employment with that company. Surround the cloth with four blue tapers inscribed with Zadkiel's sigil and anointed with mineral oil, powdered nutmeg, and sarsaparilla. Burn the candles four minutes daily, repeating the petition, until they are finished. The day of the interview with that company, tie the herbs and the paper with the company's name in the blue cloth and secure it with four knots. Leave it near the building where the company is located. Carry the amethyst in your pocket or handbag during the interview.

CASSIEL

A Spell to Sell a Property

The spell should be done on a Saturday at 10 PM. Place a copy of the property's keys in a bowl filled with earth from the property. Over the earth and the key place three white quartz, a pomegranate, and a piece of lead. Under the bowl place a dollar bill. Burn myrrh and patchouli over a bed of charcoals, and pass the incense over the bowl. Ask Cassiel to help you sell the property profitably. Inscribe a dark blue taper with Cassiel's sigil, and anoint it with a mixture of mineral oil, myrrh, and patchouli. Light the candle three minutes daily, repeating the petition, until it is finished. Wrap the key in the dollar bill, and carry it in your pocket or handbag. Bury the white quartz, the lead, and the pomegranate in the property, and sprinkle the earth over them.

GABRIEL
A Spell for Fertility

This spell should be done on a Monday at 10 PM. Fill a goblet with milk, and place a moonstone inside the milk. Put the goblet on a dish filled with lentils, mint, and eucalyptus leaves. Surround it with nine lilies or nine orchids. Burn camphor and myrrh over a bed of charcoals, and pass it over the offering. Ask Gabriel to grant you the gift of fertility. Inscribe a silver taper with Gabriel's sigil and anoint it with a mixture of mineral oil, powdered camphor, and myrrh. Light the candle for nine minutes and drink the milk. Do this daily, filling the goblet with fresh milk each day and repeating the petition, until the candle is finished. The flowers and the other offerings are strewn outside the house.

Rites of Passage

The Ritual of the Spring or Vernal Equinox

The spring equinox marks the true beginning of the year, as the earth awakens from its prolonged winter slumber. During an equinox, both fall and spring, the day and night are of equal length. This rite is conducted to ensure a healthy and prosperous new year for the earth and all those that inhabit it, as well as for the person conducting the ceremony. The day of the spring equinox is March 20, but the ritual is celebrated on the eve of the festival at 12 midnight. The sign of Aries begins with the spring equinox. As Aries is a fire sign, the ritual is celebrated in the name of Archangel Michael, who rules the fire element, and the angel of spring, Spugliguel.

You should wear white clothing during the ritual and be barefoot. Start the ritual by consecrating the room with the four elements. First, consecrate it with the air element. This is represented by incense. In this case, because Michael is the Archangel associated with the spring equinox, burn copal and frankincense, Michael's favored incenses, and pass the mixture around the room, saying, "I consecrate this place in the air element." Then take a red candle, which represents the fire element, and pass it around the room, saying, "I consecrate this room in the fire element." Sprinkle water around the room, saying, "I consecrate this room in the water element." Lastly, put some salt on a small dish and pass it around the room, saying, "I consecrate this room in the earth element."

Spread a red cloth on the middle of the floor and place upon it several red flowers, a tray of seasonal fruits, several small cakes, a goblet of sweet red wine, and a large red cinnamon-scented candle. Make a circle around the room with a magic wand or the ficca, starting in the east and turning around clockwise until you return to the east. While you are drawing the circle, say, "This circle is blessed and protected against all negative energies." Remember to move always clockwise within the circle after it has been cast.

Stand facing the east and lift the red candle, saying, "In the name of the Creator of the universe; the Archangel Michael, ruler of the fire element; and the angel Spugliguel, the ruler of spring, may the spring season that begins today bring peace among nations, a stable world economy where wealth is distributed equitably among all peoples, justice for all the earth's inhabitants, and may the world, including myself and my loved ones, be blessed with positive energies and new life." Repeat the same words in the south, west, and north of the circle.

Take the tray of fruits, cakes, and wine, and stand facing the east. Lift the tray and say, "In the name of the Creator of the universe; the Archangel Michael, ruler of the fire element; and the angel Spugliguel, the ruler of spring, may these humble offerings be a symbol of abundance and prosperity in this new spring season and during the entire zodiac year that begins today." Repeat the same words in the south, west, and north of the circle. Then sit down on the floor, facing the east, and eat some of the fruits and cakes and drink the wine.

Stand again facing the east and draw another circle from east to east, saying, "I now banish this circle in love and peace."

Share the remaining fruits and cakes with your family and friends. The other objects used in the ritual may be disposed of.

The Ritual of the Summer Solstice

The summer solstice is celebrated on June 21. This is the longest day of the year and is best known as midsummer. After the summer solstice, the days will shorten and the sun begins to work backwards, retreating across the sky. For that reason, bonfires are lit on the summer solstice to ensure the sun's return. It is a time to give thanks for nature's bounties and a time to plant seeds and flowers. The ritual is conducted on the eve of the solstice at 12 AM. Because the sign of Cancer begins on June 21 and Cancer is a water sign, the Archangel Gabriel, who rules Cancer and the water element, is invoked during the ritual, together with the angel Tubiel, who rules summer.

You should wear white clothing and be barefoot during the ritual. Start by consecrating the room with the four elements, as explained in the rite for the spring equinox. The incense in this case should be a mixture of camphor and myrrh, Gabriel's favored incenses.

Spread a purple cloth on the floor and place upon it several white lilies, a bowl with lentils, several packets of flower and vegetable seeds, nine yams, a tray with seasonal fruits, several small cakes, a goblet filled with sweet white wine, and a bowl filled with mineral water. Cast the circle as explained in the rite for the spring equinox.

Stand facing the east, lift the bowl of mineral water, and say, "In the name of the Creator of the universe; the Archangel Gabriel, ruler of Cancer and the water element; and the angel Tubiel, ruler of the summer, may the summer season that begins today bring peace, harmony, new fertility, clarity of mind, an overflow of compassion, and an abundance of food and sustenance to the world and all that inhabit it, including myself and my loved ones. May our waters be clean and plentiful and perfectly controlled for our enjoyment, and may peace and harmony bless the planet." Repeat the same words on the south, west, and north of the circle. Then spray the mineral water around the circle.

Take the tray of fruits with some of the lentils, one of the yams, the seeds and the wine, and face the east. Lift the tray and say, "In the name of the Creator of the universe; the Archangel Gabriel, ruler of Cancer and the water element; and the angel Tubiel, ruler of summer, may these humble offerings ensure that there will always be food for the hungry and drink for the thirsty, and an overflow of abundance and prosperity in our planet in this new summer season and during the entire zodiac year." Repeat the same words in the south, west, and north of the circle.

Sit on the floor facing the east, eat some of the fruits and cakes, and drink the wine. Banish the circle. Share the remains of the offering with family and friends. The next day, plant the seeds. Dispose of the rest of the objects used during the ritual.

The Ritual of the Fall Equinox

The fall equinox is celebrated on September 22, but the ritual is conducted on the eve of the equinox at 12 AM. The ritual is celebrated to heal the earth and to give thanks for its many bounties, as well as to ensure a plentiful harvest. The sign of Libra, an air sign, begins with the fall equinox. The Archangel Raphael, who rules the air element, and the angel Torquaret, who rules the fall, are invoked during the ritual.

You should wear white and be barefoot. Start by consecrating the room with the four elements, as explained in the rite for the spring equinox. The incense should be a mixture of storax, sandalwood, and cloves.

Spread a yellow cloth on the floor and place upon it ferns; yellow flowers; a bowl filled with a small squash, acorns, and pine cones; and a tray with seasonal fruits, nuts, several small cakes, and a goblet filled with cider.

Cast the circle and stand facing the east. Lift the bowl with the squash, the acorns, and the pine cones, and say, "In the name of the Creator of the universe; the Archangel Raphael, ruler of the air element; and the angel Torquaret, who rules the fall, I give thanks for the many bounties of the earth and ask that the planet be healed of all its infirmities. May the temperature of the earth return to normalcy; may the ozone layer remain sealed; may the earth's axis, the tectonic plates, and the magma beneath the volcanoes remain stable; may the waters be cleansed and return to their normal levels; and may this new harvest that approaches be ample and plentiful so that all who inhabit our planet, including myself and my loved ones, find sustenance now and during the rest of the year, and may they continue to be blessed by the earth's bounties." Repeat the same words in the south, west, and north of the circle.

Take the tray of fruits, cakes, nuts, and the cider, and face east. Lift the tray and say, "In the name of the Creator of the universe; the Archangel Raphael, who rules the air element; and the angel Torquaret, who rules the fall, may these humble offerings be a symbol of healing for the earth and all that inhabit it, and of a plentiful harvest during this fall season and during the entire zodiac year." Repeat the same words in the south, west, and north of the circle. Sit down on the floor, eat some of the fruits and the cakes, and drink the cider. Banish the circle. Share the fruits and cakes with family and friends. Leave the nuts, the acorns, and the pine cones in a park. Dispose of the other objects used in the ritual.

The Ritual of the Winter Solstice

The winter solstice is celebrated on December 21, but the ritual is conducted on the eve of the solstice at 12 AM. The winter solstice is the shortest day of the year. It is also known as the Saturnalia because the sign of Capricorn, ruled by the planet Saturn, begins on this solstice. The ritual is celebrated to mark the beginning of the end of the zodiac year and to emphasize the passage of time, ruled by Saturn. After the winter solstice the earth falls into a profound sleep, during which it rests from its labors and renews its strength in preparation for a new cycle of life. Deep within its nurturing womb, seeds are waiting to spring forward with new life, and all of nature remains in a state of suspended animation. Gifts are traditionally exchanged at this time because a cycle has come to a successful end and it brings with it the promise of a new beginning. Because Capricorn is an earth sign, the Archangel Uriel, who rules the earth element, is invoked during the ritual, together with the angel Attarib, who rules winter.

As with the other rituals, you should wear white and be barefoot. Start by consecrating the room as explained in the rite for the spring equinox. The incense should be a mixture of galangal, frankincense, and storax.

Spread a green cloth on the floor and place upon it several orchids; dry leaves; a bowl filled with berries, wheat, rye, and corn kernels; a tray with dried fruits, several small cakes, and a goblet of warm mulled wine, prepared by heating red wine, cinnamon, vanilla, cloves, and sugar. Cast the circle.

Stand facing the east, raise the bowl with the berries and the grains, and say, "In the name of the Creator of the universe; the Archangel Uriel, ruler of the earth element; and the angel Attarib, ruler of winter, may the winter season that now begins bring closure to all of the earth's ailments and to all our past troubles, and may this cycle that ends now be a herald of renewed hope and renewal to the planet and all that inhabit it, including myself and my loved ones." Repeat the same words in the south, west, and north of the circle.

Take the tray of dried fruits, cakes, and wine, and face the east. Lift the tray and say, "In the name of the Creator of the universe; the Archangel Uriel, ruler of the earth element; and the angel Attarib, ruler of winter, may these humble offerings be a symbol of rest and solace in the winter months and of hope for renewal and new life in the next zodiac year." Repeat the same words in the south, west, and north of the circle. Sit down on the floor, eat some of the fruits and cakes, and drink the mulled wine. Banish the circle.

Share the remaining fruits with family and friends. Leave the berries and the grains in a park. Dispose of the other objects used in the ritual.

Evocation

In contrast with invocation, where an entity is asked to grant protection or a specific wish to the petitioner, an evocation summons the entity, who is asked to manifest visibly in front of the person. An example of an evocation is the ritual dedicated to Hagiel, the intelligence of Venus, which now follows.

The Rite of Hagiel

Hagiel is the intelligence of Venus and an angel of love. This is a well-known rite of evocation, given originally by German kabbalist Franz Bardon in his book *Magical Evocation*. This is a powerful ritual that may result in very visible and auditory phenomena.

This is a ritual for love—not to force another person to love the petitioner against his or her will, but rather to know what love really is and to bring it to the person's life bountifully and naturally.

The version I will give here has been simplified to make it more accessible to the reader, who may not be familiar with the complexities of kabbalistic magic, but it is still very powerful and extremely effective.

The ingredients required for the performance of the ritual are the following:

- a censer with several pieces of charcoal
- powdered cinnamon

- a green light bulb that should illuminate the area of the ritual

- a piece of green cardboard cut in the form of a heptagon (seven sides), with the seal of Hagiel drawn upon it in green ink (see appendix 6, figure 27)

- a green tunic

- a length of copper wire where a malachite or a green stone is inserted, to be worn around the neck

- a piece of green cloth cut in the shape of a triangle about two feet long from tip to base

- 4 green candles

- a small cake

- a glass of sweet wine

The ritual is conducted on a Friday at 10 PM, the day and the hour of Venus. The moon should be waxing. Before the ritual, sprinkle the room with salt water for purification. You should then bathe, don the green tunic, and anoint your forehead and temples with cinnamon oil. Put on the copper necklace with the green stone, turn off the lights, and turn on the green bulb. This should suffuse the room in a green haze. On the floor to the east of the room, place the green triangle. On top of the triangle place the heptagonal piece of cardboard with Hagiel's seal. Around the triangle, in the form of a cross, light the four green candles, which represent the four cardinal points. Place some cinnamon on the burning charcoals and pass the censer around the room. Keep the censer near you and add more cinnamon throughout the ritual to keep the scent alive, as this is one of the most powerful attributes of the Venus sphere.

Cast the circle with a magic wand or the ficca, starting in the east and moving to the south, west, north, and back to the east. Say, "In the name of the Creator of the universe and the angels of the four elements, this circle is protected against all negative energies." Visualize a stream of golden light around the area as you draw the circle.

EVOCATION

Begin to evoke Hagiel to manifest visibly inside the green triangle. This is done three times. The first time Hagiel's name is said mentally seven times, visualizing her as she descends from the Venus sphere into the triangle. The second time her name is uttered softly, almost inaudibly, also seven times. The third time her name is called out seven times in a loud, ringing voice, asking her to materialize in the triangle. During the three evocations the wand or the ficca must be pointed at the triangle.

If you have followed the instructions exactly and with strong willpower, the image of Hagiel will start to take form within the triangle. This image is a mental projection from the petitioner's unconscious, and it is very real.

Hagiel manifests as an ethereally beautiful woman with snowy skin and tomato-red hair. Her eyes are green, and she is naked from the waist up. She wears a skirt of blue-green material, similar to satin, embroidered with pink roses. Upon her head rests a copper crown shaped with turrets like a tower. Her voice is musical, and her attitude is sweet and amiable. The impression received by the petitioner when such a vision appears can only be described as earth-shaking, but it is important to remain calm and continue with the ritual. At this moment, you may ask Hagiel any questions related to love matters or to grant a special favor. This she is invariably willing to do. If she grants a petition, it is assured that what was asked will come to pass. After she has answered your questions, thank her and bid her hail and farewell. Eat the cake and drink the wine to anchor the energies released by the ritual.

If Hagiel does not appear in the triangle, there was insufficient energy created by the ritual or some important element was left out. But some type of phenomenon will still be experienced, like strange and unearthly music, banging sounds, oscillating lights, or strange vibrations.

After the appearance of Hagiel, or when it is obvious that she will not appear, the ritual is ended. The circle is banished by saying, "In the name of the Creator of the universe and the angels of the four elements, this circle is banished, and the ritual is ended." The candles are put out, and the room is cleared. The various objects may be kept to be used in a similar ritual later on.

The Rite of Nakhiel

The rites of evocation are similar, and the ritual dedicated to Nakhiel follows the rite of Hagiel's structure closely. Nakhiel is the intelligence of the sun and is evoked for the acquisition of money during difficult financial situations. The ingredients used during the ritual are the following:

- a censer filled with several pieces of charcoal

- a mixture of copal and frankincense

- a large yellow light bulb that should illuminate the area of the ritual

- a piece of yellow cardboard cut in the form of a hexagon (six sides), with Nakhiel's seal drawn upon it with gold-colored ink (see appendix 6, figure 27)

- a yellow or gold tunic

- a gold chain with a yellow stone (like a topaz, citrine, or amber), to be worn around the neck

- a piece of yellow cloth cut in the form of a triangle about two feet long from tip to base

- 4 yellow candles

- a small cake

- a glass of sweet white wine

The ceremony is conducted on a Sunday at 10 PM, the day and hour of the sun. The moon should be waxing. Begin by sprinkling the room with salt water for purification. Bathe, don the yellow tunic, and anoint your forehead and temples with oil of vanilla. Put on the gold necklace with the yellow stone, turn off the lights, and turn on the yellow bulb. This should suffuse the room in a yellow haze. Place the yellow cloth triangle in the east corner of the room. On top of it place the hexagonal cardboard with Nakhiel's seal. Around the triangle, in the form of a cross, light the four candles, which represent the four cardinal points. Place some of the incense over the charcoals and pass it around the room. Keep the censer near you and keep adding incense to it, as the aroma of copal and frankincense acts as a powerful attraction for solar entities.

Cast the circle as described in the rite of Hagiel. Begin to evoke Nakhiel to manifest visibly inside the yellow triangle. This is done three times. The first time Nakhiel's name is said mentally six times. Then it is pronounced in a low voice six times. Lastly, it is pronounced aloud, also six times, asking him to materialize in the triangle. During the three evocations, the wand or ficca should be pointed at the triangle.

If the instructions are followed exactly, the image of Nakhiel will start to form inside the triangle. Nakhiel manifests as a beautiful adolescent with golden skin and golden curly hair. His eyes are amber-colored. He wears a crown of laurel leaves surrounded by solar rays and is dressed in a short gold tunic cinched at the waist by a gold belt encrusted with yellow crystals. He wears gold Roman sandals, and his feet never touch the ground. When he appears, he floats over the triangle with one foot pointing downward and the other leg bent at the knee. His entire frame is enveloped in golden flames. His voice sounds like crackling fire, and his demeanor is grave yet kind.

You may ask Nakhiel any questions related to money matters or to grant a special favor, which he is nearly always certain to grant. If he grants the petition, it will come to pass within six days, as he works very swiftly. If he does not grant the petition, he will say why. After he has answered your questions, thank him and bid him hail and farewell. Eat the cake and drink the wine to anchor the energies. Banish the circle as given in the rite of Hagiel, put out the candles, and clear the room.

If Nakhiel does not appear in the triangle, there was insufficient energy created by the ritual or some important element was left out.

But some type of phenomenon will still be experienced, like unearthly music, oscillating lights, banging sounds, or strange vibrations.

The other planetary intelligences can also be evoked using the instructions given in the rite of Hagiel or the rite of Nakhiel but changing the planetary attributes, such as colors, numbers, incenses, metals, and stones. These are the same as the attributes ascribed to the seven Archangels.

APPENDIX 6

Illustrations

FIGURE 1. Hebrew alphabet.

א	ב	ג	ד	ה	ו	ז	ח	ט
Aleph (A)	Beth (B)	Gimel (G)	Daleth (D)	Heh (H)	Vau (V)	Zayin (Z)	Cheth (CH)	Teth (T)
Ox	House	Camel	Door	Window	Peg, Nail	Weapon	Enclosure	Serpent
1	2	3	4	5	6	7	8	9
י	כ	ל	מ	נ	ס	ע	פ	צ
Yod (I)	Caph (K)	Lamed (L)	Mem (M)	Nun (N)	Samekh (S)	Ayin (O)	Pe (P)	Tzaddi (TZ)
Hand	Palm of Hand	Ox Goad	Water	Fish	Support	Eye	Mouth	Fishing Hook
10	20	30	40	50	60	70	80	90
ק	ר	ש	ת	ך	ם	ן	ף	ץ
Qoph (Q)	Resh (R)	Shin (SH)	Tau (TH)	Final Caph	Final Mem	Final Nun	Final Pe	Final Tzaddi
Back of Head	Head	Tooth	Sign of the Cross					
100	200	300	400	500	600	700	800	900

* Although there are only twenty-two letters in the Hebrew alphabet, five of these letters have final versions, which are also of importance.

The Misterious Characters of Letters deliver'd by Honorious call'd the Theban Alphabet

A B C D E F G H I K L M

N O P Q R S T V X Y Z

The Characters of Celestial Writing.

Lamed Caph Jod Theth Cheth Zain Vau He Daleth Gimel Beth Aleph

Tau Shin Res Kuff Zade Pe Ain Samech Nun Mem

The Writing call'd Malachim.

Caph Jod Theth Cheth Zain Vau He Daleth Gimel Beth Aleph

Pesh Kuff Zade Pe Ain Samech Samech Schin Tau Nun Mem Lamed

The Writing call'd Passing the River.

Lamed Caph Jod Theth Cheth Zain Vau He Daleth Gimel Beth Aleph

Tan Schin Resh Kuff Zade Pe Ain Samech Nun Mem

FIGURE 2 (OPPOSITE PAGE). Four versions of the angelic alphabet, which are very similar to the Hebrew alphabet. From top to bottom: Theban, Celestial, Malachim, and Passing the River. The alphabet of the angels is often used to write petitions to the angels, which are then burned in the flame of a white candle. Petitions should be made on the day and hour of the angel invoked.

FIGURE 3. The Tetragrammaton, which is written from right to left.

Heh — Vau — Heh — Yod

FIGURE 4. The transliterated Shemamphora gives the correct pronunciation of the seventy-two names of God. Each of the four lines of the Shemamphora falls under the aegis of one of the four letters of the Tetragrammaton (Yod Heh Vau Heh, or YHVH).

Y

K	L	H	H	M	I	H	L	A	H	K	A	L	M	O	S	I	V
L	A	Q	R	B	Z	H	A	L	Z	H	K	L	H	L	I	L	H
I	V	M	I	H	L	O	V	D	I	Th	A	H	Sh	M	T	I	V
18	17	16	15	14	13	12	11	10	9	8	7	6	5	4	3	2	1

H

M	K	L	I	V	L	A	R	Sh	I	H	N	Ch	M	I	N	P	L
N	V	H	Ch	Sh	K	V	I	A	R	A	Th	H	L	I	L	H	V
D	Q	Ch	V	R	B	M	I	H	Th	A	H	V	H	I	K	L	V
36	35	34	33	32	31	30	29	28	27	26	25	24	23	22	21	20	19

V

N	N	O	H	D	V	M	O	O	S	L	V	M	H	I	R	Ch	A
I	N	M	Ch	N	H	I	Sh	R	A	L	V	I	H	I	H	O	N
Th	A	M	Sh	I	V	H	L	I	L	H	L	K	H	Z	O	M	I
54	53	52	51	50	49	48	47	46	45	44	43	42	41	40	39	38	37

H

M	H	I	R	Ch	A	M	D	M	O	I	V	M	H	I	N	P	M
V	I	B	A	B	I	N	M	Ch	N	H	M	Tz	R	I	M	V	B
M	I	M	H	V	O	Q	B	I	V	H	B	R	Ch	L	M	I	H
72	71	70	69	68	67	66	65	64	63	62	61	60	59	58	57	56	55

The *pronounciation* of the seventy-two names is as follows:

1. Vehu; 2. Yeli; 3. Sit; 4. Aulem; 5. Mahash; 6. Lelah; 7. Aka; 8. Kahath; 9. Hezi; 10. Elad; 11. Lav; 12. Hahau; 13. Yezel; 14. Mebha; 15. Heri; 16. Haquem; 17. Lau; 18. Keli; 19. Levo; 20. Pahel; 21. Nelak; 22. Yiai; 23. Melah; 24. Chaho; 25. Nethah; 26. Haa; 27. Yereth; 28. Shaah; 29. Riyi; 30. Aum; 31. Lekab; 32. Vesher; 33. Yecho; 34. Lehach; 35. Keveq; 36. Menad; 37. Ani; 38. Chaum; 39. Rehau; 40. Yeiz; 41. Hahah; 42. Mik; 43. Veval; 44. Yelah; 45. Sael; 46. Auri; 47. Aushal; 48. Miah; 49. Vaho; 50. Doni; 51. Hachash; 52. Aumem; 53. Nena; 54. Neith; 55. Mabeh; 56. Poi; 57. Nemem; 58. Yeil; 59. Harach; 60. Metzer; 61. Vamet; 62. Yehah; 63. Aunu; 64. Machi; 65. Dameb; 66. Menak; 67. Aiau; 68. Chebo; 69. Raah; 70. Yekem; 71. Haiai; and 72. Moum.

FIGURE 5. The angel Shemamphora gives the seventy-two names of the angels associated with it.

The Cabala.

Shewing at one View the Seventy-two Angels bearing the name of God Shemhamphora.

כליאל	לאויה	הקמיה	הריאל	מבהאל	יזלאל	ההעיה	לאויה	אלדיה	הזיאל	כהתל	אכאיה	ללהאל	מהשיה	עלמיה	סיטאל	יליאל	והויה
Caliel	Levriah	Hakamiah	Hariel	Mebahel	Ielael	Hahiah	Lauiah	Aladiah	Haziel	Cahethel	Akhaiah	Lelahel	Mahasiah	Elemiah	Sitael	Ieliel	Vehuiah
מנדאל	כוקיה	להחיה	יהויה	ושריה	לכבאל	אומאל	רייאל	שאהיה	ירתאל	האאיה	נתהיה	ההייה	מלהאל	ייייאל	נלכאל	פהליה	לוויה
Monadel	Chavakiah	Lehahiah	Iehuiah	Vasariah	Lecabel	Omael	Reiiel	Seehiah	Ierathel	Haaiah	Nithhaiah	Hahuiah	Melahel	Ieiaiel	Nelchael	Pahaliah	Leuuiah
ניתאל	ננאאל	עממיה	ההשיה	דניאל	והואל	מיהאל	עשליה	עריאל	סאליה	ילהיה	וולייה	מיחאל	הההאל	ייזאל	רהעאל	חעםיה	אניאל
Nithael	Nanael	Imamiah	Hahaziah	Daniel	Vehuel	Mihael	Asaliah	Ariel	Sealiah	Ielahiah	Vevaliah	Michael	Hahahel	Ihiazel	Rehael	Haamiah	Aniel
מוםיה	הייאל	יבמיה	ראהאל	הבויה	איעאל	מנקאל	דמביה	מחיאל	ענואל	יההאל	ומבאל	מצראל	הרהאל	יילאל	נממיה	פויאל	מבהיה
Mevamaih	Haiaiel	Ibamiah	Rochel	Habuiah	Eiael	Menkl	Damabiah	Mochael	Annauel	Iahhel	Umabel	Mitzrael	Harahel	Ieilael	Nemamaih	Poiel	Mebahiah

FIGURE 6. Tree of Life.

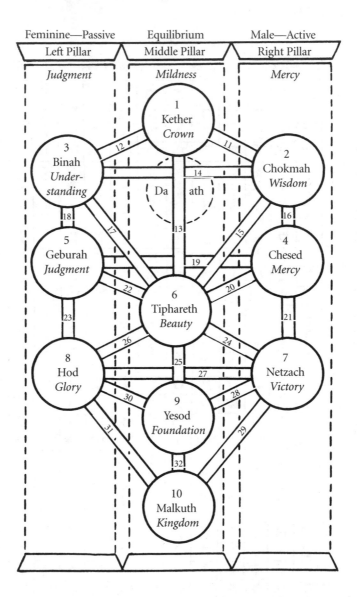

FIGURE 7. Adam Kadmon. This figure represents the body of God as the created universe.

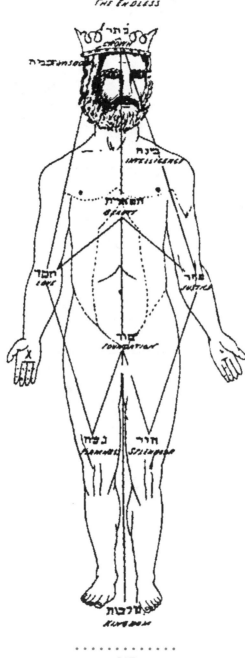

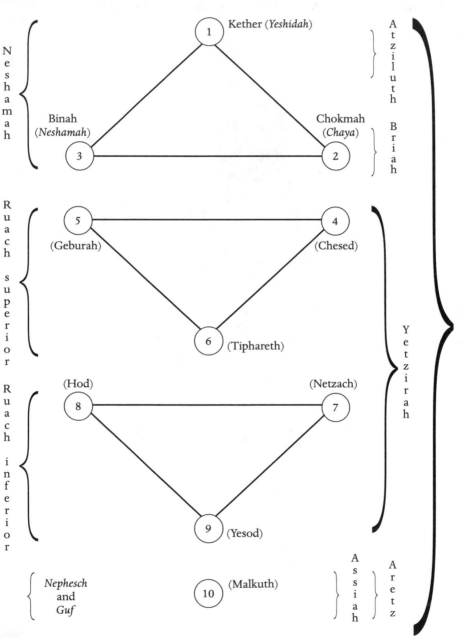

FIGURE 8 (OPPOSITE PAGE). The structure of the soul. The soul has six parts. The first is the *Guf* (the body), the second is the *Nephesch* (the instincts), and the third is the *Ruach* (the emotions), divided into Inferior and Superior Ruach. The fourth is the *Neshamah* (our higher self). The fifth and sixth are the *Chaya* and *Yeshidah*, our highest connection with God. Only the *Neshamah* is accessible to us in the material world. The higher two are beyond human contact.

FIGURE 9. Pentagram.

FIGURE 10. Star of David.

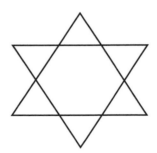

APPENDIX 6

FIGURE 11. The five Platonic solids (polyhedra), with Metatron's Cube at the top left.

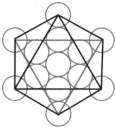
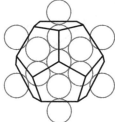
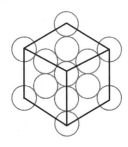
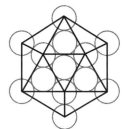

FIGURE 1 2 . Metatron's cube.

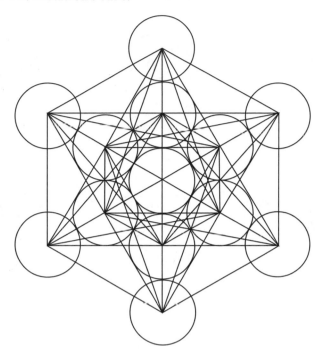

APPENDIX 6

FIGURE 13. Six days of Creation and the Seed of Life.

  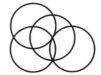

  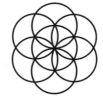

FIGURE 14. Fruit of Life.

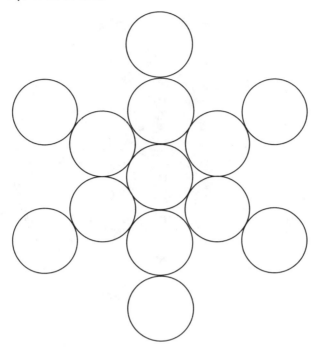

FIGURE 15. Flower of Life.

FIGURE 16. Tree of Life from Flower of Life.

FIGURE 17. Solar spectrum.

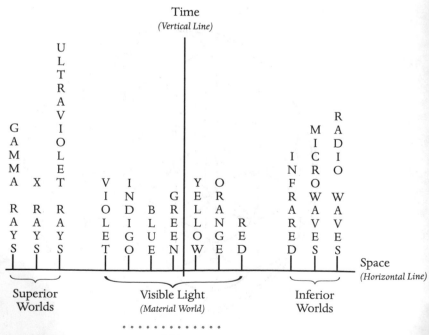

FIGURE 18. Space-time continuum.

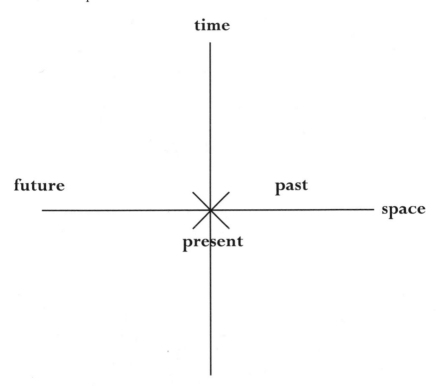

FIGURE 19. Ficca.

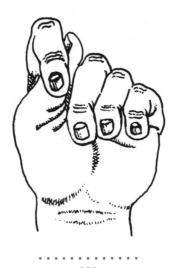

FIGURE 20. Inverted pentagram, left, and regular pentagram, right.

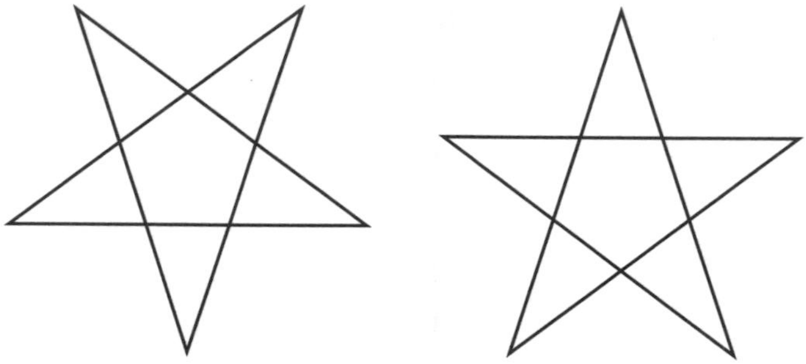

FIGURE 21. Hours and days of planets and angels. Note that the name of Kamael is misspelled as Samael, but Kamael is the angel that rules those hours.

Hours Day.	Angels and Planets ruling SUNDAY.	Angels and Planets ruling MONDAY.	Angels and Planets ruling TUESDAY.	Angels and Planets ruling WEDNESDAY.	Angels and Planets ruling THURSDAY.	Angels and Planets ruling FRIDAY.	Angels Plane rulin SATURI
	Day.	*Day.*	*Day.*	*Day.*	*Day.*	*Day.*	*Day*
1	☉ Michael	☽ Gabriel	♂ Samael	☿ Raphael	♃ Sachiel	♀ Anael	♄ Cassi
2	♀ Anael	♄ Cassiel	☉ Michael	☽ Gabriel	♂ Samael	☿ Raphael	♃ Sachi
3	☿ Raphael	♃ Sachiel	♀ Anael	♄ Cassiel	☉ Michael	☽ Gabriel	♂ Sama
4	☽ Gabriel	♁ Samael	☿ Raphael	♃ Sachiel	♀ Anael	♄ Cassiel	☉ Micha
5	♄ Cassiel	☉ Michael	☽ Gabriel	♂ Samael	☿ Raphael	♃ Sachiel	♀ Anael
6	♃ Sachiel	♀ Anael	♄ Cassiel	☉ Michael	☽ Gabriel	♂ Samael	☿ Raph
7	♂ Samael	☿ Raphael	♃ Sachiel	♀ Anael	♄ Cassiel	☉ Michael	☽ Gabri
8	☉ Michael	☽ Gabriel	♁ Samael	☿ Raphael	♃ Sachiel	♀ Anael	♄ Cassie
9	♀ Anael	♄ Cassiel	☉ Michael	☽ Gabriel	♂ Samael	☿ Raphael	♃ Sachi
10	☿ Raphael	♃ Sachiel	♀ Anael	♄ Cassiel	○ Michael	☽ Gabriel	♂ Sama
11	☽ Gabriel	♂ Samael	☿ Raphael	♃ Sachael	♀ Anael	♄ Cassiel	☉ Micha
12	♄ Cassiel	☉ Michael	☽ Gabriel	♂ Samael	☿ Raphael	♃ Sachiel	♀ Anael
Hours Night	*Night.*	*Night.*	*Night.*	*Night.*	*Night.*	*Night.*	*Nigh*
1	♃ Sachael	♀ Anael	♄ Cassiel	☉ Michael	☽ Gabriel	♂ Samael	☿ Rapha
2	♂ Samiel	☿ Raphael	♃ Sachiel	♀ Anael	♄ Cassiel	☉ Michael	☽ Gabri
3	☉ Michael	☽ Gabriel	♂ Samael	☿ Raphael	♃ Sachiel	♀ Anael	♄ Cassie
4	♀ Anael	♄ Cassiel	☉ Michael	☽ Gabriel	♂ Samael	☿ Raphael	♃ Sachi
5	☿ Raphael	♃ Sachiel	♀ Anael	♄ Cassiel	☉ Michael	☽ Gabriel	♂ Samae
6	☽ Gabriel	♂ Samael	☿ Raphael	♃ Sachiel	♀ Anael	♄ Cassiel	☉ Micha
7	♄ Cassiel	☉ Michael	☽ Gabriel	♂ Samael	☿ Raphael	♃ Sachiel	♀ Anael
8	♃ Sachiel	♀ Anael	♄ Cassiel	☉ Michael	☽ Gabriel	♂ Samael	☿ Rapha
9	♂ Samael	☿ Raphael	♃ Sachiel	♀ Anael	♄ Cassiel	☉ Michael	☽ Gabri
10	☉ Michael	☽ Gabriel	♂ Samael	☿ Raphael	♃ Sachiel	♀ Anael	♄ Cassie
11	♀ Anael	♄ Cassiel	☉ Michael	☽ Gabriel	♂ Samael	☿ Raphael	♃ Sachie
12	☿ Raphael	♃ Sachiel	♀ Anael	♄ Cassiel	☉ Michael	☽ Gabriel	♂ Samae

FIGURE 22. Abbreviation of Vade Retro Satanas (VRSNS...) on the reverse of a Saint Benedict medal.

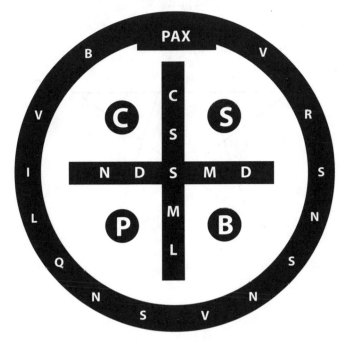

FIGURE 23. Invoking pentagram, left, and banishing pentagram, right.

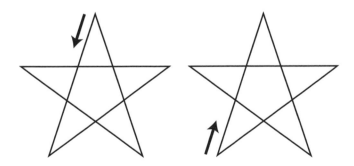

FIGURE 24. Elements in the pentagram.

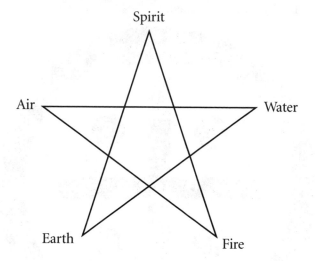

FIGURE 25. Sigils or seals of Olympian spirits.

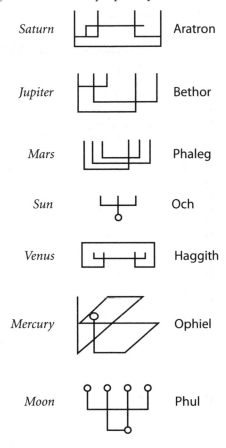

Saturn — Aratron

Jupiter — Bethor

Mars — Phaleg

Sun — Och

Venus — Haggith

Mercury — Ophiel

Moon — Phul

FIGURE 26. Seals or sigils of the seven great Archangels with their heavens, planets, and zodiac signs.

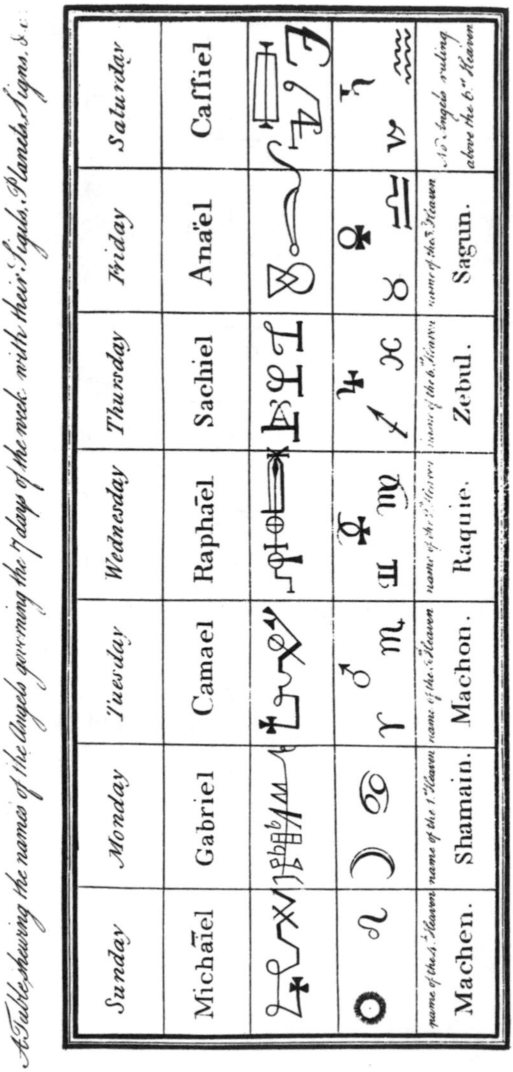

A Table shewing the names of the Angels governing the 7 days of the week, with their Sigils, Planets, Signs, &c.

	Sunday	Monday	Tuesday	Wednesday	Thursday	Friday	Saturday
	Michäel	Gabriel	Camael	Raphäel	Sachiel	Anäel	Caffiel
name of the 7 Heaven	Machen.	Shamain.	Machon.	Raquie.	Zebul.	Sagun.	above the 6.th Heaven

FIGURE 27. Seals of intelligences of Venus, top, and Mars, bottom.

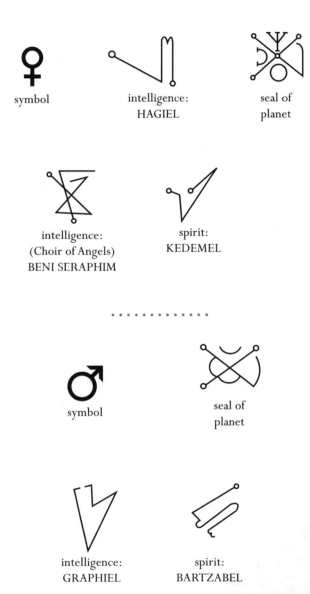

symbol

intelligence:
HAGIEL

seal of
planet

intelligence:
(Choir of Angels)
BENI SERAPHIM

spirit:
KEDEMEL

symbol

seal of
planet

intelligence:
GRAPHIEL

spirit:
BARTZABEL

FIGURE 27, CONTINUED. Seals of intelligences of the moon, top, and Mercury, bottom.

symbol

spirit:
CHASHMODAI

seal of
planet

intelligence of the intelligences of the moon: MALCAH BETARSHISIM VE-AD RUACHOTH HA-SCHECHALIM

spirit of the spirits of the moon: SHAD BARSCHEMOTH HASCHARTATHAN

. . . .

symbol

seal of
planet

intelligence:
TIRIEL

spirit:
TAPHTHARTHARATH

. . . .

FIGURE 27, CONTINUED. Seals of intelligences of Saturn, top, and Jupiter, bottom.

symbol

seal of
planet

spirit:
ZAZEL

intelligence:
AGIEL

. . . .

symbol

seal of
planet

spirit:
HISMAEL

intelligence:
YOPHIEL

. . . .

FIGURE 27, CONTINUED. Symbol and seals of the sun.

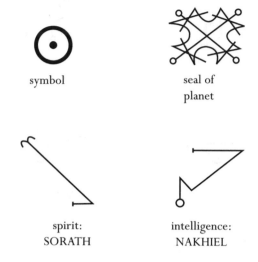

symbol

seal of
planet

spirit:
SORATH

intelligence:
NAKHIEL

Bibliography

Abano, Peter de, *The Heptameron*, Philadelphia, 1987.

Adler, M., *The Angels and Us*, New York, 1982.

Agrippa, Cornelius, *Three Books of Occult Philosophy*, Inwood, NY, 1945.

Akiba, Rabbi, *Alphabet of Rabbi Akiba*, New York, 1956.

Alighieri, Dante, *The Divine Comedy*, New York, 1958.

Ambelain, Robert, *La Kabbale Pratique*, Paris, 1951.

The Apocrypha, New York, 1962.

Aquinas, Thomas, *Basic Writings* (comprising *Summa Theologica* and *Summa Contra Gentiles*), New York, 1941.

Augustine, *City of God*, New York, 1958.

Bamberger, Bernard J., *Fallen Angels*, Philadelphia, 1956.

Bardon, Franz, *Magical Evocation*, London, 1977.

Barrett, Francis, *The Magus*, London, 1924.

Benet, Stephen V., *Selected Works*, New York, 1942.

The Bible, The Authorized or King James Version, New York, 1963.

Blake, William, *All Religions Are One*, London, 1936.

Blavatsky, H. P., *The Secret Doctrine*, California, 1952.

Book of the Angel Raziel (Sepher Raziel or Raziel-ha-Malach), credited to Eleazar of Worms, in Hebrew, Warsaw, 1881; in English, *Book of Angel Rezial*, trans. Stephen Savedow, New York, 2000.

Book of Enoch or Enoch I, trans. R. H. Charles, Oxford, 1912.

BIBLIOGRAPHY

Book of Jubilees, trans. R. H. Charles, London, 1927.

Book of the Secrets of Enoch or Enoch II, trans. R. H. Charles, Oxford, 1911.

Briggs, C.V., *The Encyclopedia of Angels*, New York, 1997.

Buber, Martin, *Tales of Angels, Spirits and Demons*, trans. D. Antin and J. Rothenbderg, New York, 1938.

Budge, E. A. Wallis, *Amulets and Talismans*, New York, 1961.

————, *Book of the Dead*, London, 1910.

Bunson, M., *Angels A to Z*, New York, 1996.

Burham, S., *A Book of Angels*, New York, 1990.

Butler, E. M., *Ritual Magic*, New York, 1959.

Cabell, James B., *The Devil's Dear Own Son*, New York, 1949.

Chaldean Oracles of Zoroaster, trans. Sapere Aude, New York, 1976.

Christopher, J., C. Spence, and J. Rowan, *The Raccolta, or a Manual of Indulgences*, St. Athanasius Press, 2003.

Clement of Alexandria, *Stromata, in Anti-Nicene Fathers*, New York, 1925.

Cohen, C., *God and the Universe*, London, 1946.

Connell, J.T., *Angel Power*, New York, 1995.

Connolly, D., *In Search of Angels*, New York, 1993.

Cordovero, Moses, *Orchard of Pomegranates*, London, 1960.

Cumont, F., *The Mysteries of Mithra*, London, 1978.

Daniels, J., *Clash of Angels*, New York, 1930.

Davenport, B., *Deals with the Devil*, New York, 1958.

Davidson, Gustav, *A Dictionary of Angels*, New York, 1967.

Davies, Paul, *About Time*, New York, 1996.

————, *God and the New Physics*, New York, 1984.

————, *The Mind of God*, New York, 1993.

BIBLIOGRAPHY

de Claremont, Lewis, *The Ancient's Book of Magic*, New York, 1989.

De Plancy, Collins, *Dictionnaire Infernal*, New York, 1976.

Dialogues of Plato, trans. B. Jowett, New York , 2008.

Dionysius the Aeropagite (Pseudo-Dionysius), *The Mystical Theologie and The Celestial Hierarchies*, trans. Shrine of Wisdom, Surrey, England, 1949.

Einstein, Albert, *Relativity: The Special and the General Theory*, Princeton, 2010.

Eleazar of Worms, *Hilkot Metatron*, London, 1989.

Euclid, *The Thirteen Books of the Elements*, New York, 1956.

Flowers, S. Edred, *Fire and Ice: Magical Teachings of Germany's Greatest Secret Order*, 1995.

Fodor, Nandor, *Encyclopedia of Psychic Science*, New York, 1966.

Folger, Tim, "Science's Alternative to an Intelligent Creator: the Multiverse Theory," *Discover Magazine*, 2008 (http:// discovermagazine.com/2008/dec/10-sciences-alternative -to-an-intelligent-creator#.UL_MyI72gfE).

Fox, M., and R. Sheldrake, *The Physics of Angels*, New York, 1996.

Frazer, James, *The Golden Bough*, New York, 1951.

Freud, Sigmund, *The Complete Psychological Works*, New York, 2009.

Gamow, George, *The Thirty Years That Shook Physics: The Story of Quantum Mechanics*, New York, 1985.

Garland, Trudi H., *Fascinating Fibonaccis: Mystery and Magic in Numbers*, New York, 1987.

Gilmore, G. D., *Angels, Angels, Everywhere*, New York, 1981.

Ginsburg, Christian D., *The Essenes/The Kaballah*, London, 1956.

Ginzberg, Louis, *Legends of the Jews*, Philadelphia, 1954.

Gollancz, Hermann, *Key of Solomon*, London, 1965.

. . . .

González-Wippler, M., *Dreams and What They Mean to You*, St. Paul, 1990.

————, *A Kabbalah for the Modern World*, St. Paul, 1974.

————, *What Happens After Death*, St. Paul, 1996.

Greene, B., *The Elegant Universe: Superstrings, Hidden Dimensions*, New York, 2000.

Grimorium Verum, ed. and trans. Joseph H. Peterson, 2007.

Guazzo, F., and M. Summers, *Compendium Maleficarum*, New York, 2010.

Gurd, J. M., "A Case of Foreign Accent Syndrome," *Neuropsychologia* 26(2), 1998.

Gurdjieff, G., *All and Everything / Beelzebub's Tales to His Grandson*, New York, 1964.

Guth, Alan H., *The Inflationary Universe*, New York, 1998.

Hammond, G., *A Discourse of Angels*, London, 1979.

The Harper Collins Study Bible, New York, 1973.

Hartmann, Franz, *Magic, White and Black*, Chicago, 1910.

Harvey, H., *The Many Faces of Angels*, California, 1986.

Hawking, Stephen, *A Brief History of Time*, New York, 1998.

————, *The Grand Design* (with L. Mlodinow), London, 2010.

Hawkings, Edward, *The Poetical Works of John Milton*, Oxford, 1978.

Hebrew Book of Enoch, or Enoch 3, trans. H. Odeberg, Cambridge, 1928.

Heil, G., and A. M. Ritter, *Pseudo-Dionysius Areopagita*, New York, 1991.

Hermes Trismegistus, *The Divine Pymander*, ed. Shrine of Wisdom, Surrey, England, 1955.

Heywood, Thomas, *The Hierarchy of the Blessed Angels*, London, 1987.

The History and Practice of Magic, ed. Paul Christian, New York, 1963.

. . . .

BIBLIOGRAPHY

Hoyle, Fred, *Intelligent Universe*, New York, 1988.

Iamblichus, *On the Mysteries of the Egyptians, Chaldeans, and Assyrians*, trans. T. Thomas, New York, 1989.

Jastrow, Robert, *God and the Astronomers*, New York, 1977.

Jung, Carl Gustav, *The Archetypes and the Collective Unconscious*, New York, 1997.

Jung, Leo, *Fallen Angels in Jewish, Christian and Mohammedan Literature*, Philadelphia, 1969.

Jungman, G., "Supersymmetric Dark Matter," *Physics Review* 267, 1996.

Kaplan, Aryeh, *Inner Space: Introduction to Kabbalah, Meditation and Prophecy*, New York, 1990.

————, *The Living Torah*, New York, 1981.

————, *Meditation and Kabbalah*, New York, 1995.

————, *Sefer Yetzirah*, New York, 1997.

King, L. W., *Babylonian Magic and Sorcery*, London, 1998.

The Koran, New York, 2001.

Langdon, E., *Essentials of Demonology*, London, 1949.

de Laurence, L. W., *The Legemeton (The Lesser Key of Solomon)*, includes *The Almadel* and *The Pauline Art*, New York, 1957.

Leadbeater, C. W., *The Astral Plane*, India, 1963.

Lederman, L., *The God Particle*, New York, 1993.

The Lesser Key of Solomon / Goetia / The Book of Evil Spirits, ed. L. W. de Laurence, New York, 1978.

Levi, Eliphas, *The History of Magic*, trans. A. E. Waite, London, 1963.

————, *The Occult Philosophy*, New York, 1997.

————, *Transcendental Magic*, trans. A. E. Waite, Philadelphia, 1923.

Lewis, J. R., and E. D. Oliver, *Angels A to Z*, Michigan, 1996.

Lost Books of the Bible and the Forgotten Books of Eden, New York, 1930.

· · · · · · · · · · · ·

BIBLIOGRAPHY

Luria, Rabbi Isaac, *The Ten Luminous Emanations*, Israel, 1969.

Luzzatto, M. H., *Mesillat Yesharim (The Path of the Upright)*, Philadelphia, 1936.

Magnus, Albertus, *The Book of Secrets*, London, 1933.

Maimonides, Moses, *The Guide to the Perplexed*, trans. M. Friedlander, New York, 1956.

————, *Mishnah Thora*, New York, 1922.

Malchus, Marius, *The Secret Grimoire of Turiel*, London, 1960.

Malleus Maleficarum (The Hammer of Witches), trans. Montague Summers, London, 1948.

Mathers, S. L. MacGregor, *The Almadel of Solomon*, London, 1976.

————, *The Book of the Sacred Magic of Abra-Melin the Mage*, Chicago, 1939.

————, *The Kabbalah Unveiled*, London, 1987.

Mead, G. R. S., *Fragments of a Faith Forgotten*, New York, 1960.

Milton, John, *Paradise Lost*, New York, 2003.

The Mishnah, trans. Herbert Danby, Oxford, 1956.

Moore, Thomas, *The Loves of Angels*, London, 2001.

The New English Bible, Oxford and Cambridge, 1961.

Newton, Isaac, *The Principia: Mathematical Principles of Natural Philosophy*, New York, 2007.

Orlov, Andrei, *The Enoch-Metraton Tradition*, 2005.

Paracelsus, *Four Treatises*, Baltimore, 1949.

Parente, Pascal P., *The Angels*, Indiana, 1957.

Penrose, Roger, *The Road to Reality: A Complete Guide to the Laws of the Universe*, New York, 2007.

Plato, *Timaeus*, New York, 2007.

Poe, Edgar Allan, *The Complete Works*, New York, 2001.

BIBLIOGRAPHY

Rawles, B. *Sacred Geometry Design Sourcebook*, 1997.

Rees, Martin, *Just Six Numbers: The Deep Forces That Shape the Universe*, New York, 2001.

Regamey, R. P., *What Is An Angel?* New York, 1969.

Regardie, Israel, *A Garden of Pomegranates*, St. Paul, 1969.

———, *The Golden Dawn*, St. Paul, 1986.

Salkeld, John, *A Treatise of Angels*, London, 1967.

Scholem, Gershom, *Jewish Gnosticism, Merkabah Mysticism, and Talmudic Tradition*, New York, 1941.

Sepher Yetzirah (Book of Formation), trans. William Postel, Paris, 1982.

Serres, M., *Angels: A Modern Myth*, Paris, 1995.

Snell, Joy, *The Ministry of Angels, Here and Beyond,* New York, 1959.

Steiner, Rudolf, *The Mission of Archangel Michael*, New York, 1961.

———, *The Work of the Angels in Man's Astral Body*, London, 1960.

Susskind, Leonard, *The Cosmic Landscape: String Theory and the Illusion of Intelligent Design*, New York, 2005.

Swedenborg, Emanuel, *Heaven and Its Wonders and Hell*, New York, 1956.

Taylor, T. L., *Messengers of Light*, California, 1990.

Tipler, F. J., *The Physics of Immortality*, New York, 1994.

Trachtenberg, Joshua, *Jewish Magic and Superstition*, New York, 1939.

Trimble, Virginia. "Existence and Nature of Dark Matter in the Universe," *Annual Reviews of Astronomy and Astrophysics*, 1987.

Trithemius, J., *Of the Heavenly Intelligences,* London, 1936.

Waite, Arthur Edward, *The Book of Ceremonial Magic*, New York, 1961.

———, *Grand Grimoire*, New York, 2001.

Ward, Peter, and Donald Brownlee, *Rare Earth: Why Complex Life is Uncommon in the Universe*, New York, 2003.

BIBLIOGRAPHY

Welsh, Robert G., *Azrael and Other Poems*, New York, 1989.

West, Robert H., *Milton and the Angels*, Georgia, 1955.

Westcott, W. W., *Book of Formation (Sepher Yetzirah)*, London, 1956.

Wheatley, J. D., *The Nature of Consciousness: Scientific Verification and Proof of Logic God Is*, New York, 2001.

Williams, Charles, *War in Heaven*, New York, 1950.

Woit, Peter, *String Theory: An Evaluation*, New York, 2001 (http://www.math.columbia.edu/%7Ewoit/strings.pdf).

Yadin, Yigael, *War Between the Sons of Light and the Sons of Darkness*, Jerusalem, 1956.

Young, M., *Angel in the Forest*, New York, 1945.

The Zohar, ed. Gershom Scholem, New York, 1949.

To Write to the Author

If you wish to contact the author or would like more information about this book, please write to the author in care of Llewellyn Worldwide and we will forward your request. Both the author and the publisher appreciate hearing from you and learning of your enjoyment of this book and how it has helped you. Llewellyn Worldwide cannot guarantee that every letter written to the author can be answered, but all will be forwarded. Please write to:

Migene González-Wippler
c/o Llewellyn Worldwide
2143 Wooddale Drive
Woodbury, MN 55125-2989

Please enclose a self-addressed stamped envelope for reply,
or $1.00 to cover costs. If outside the USA, enclose an
international postal reply coupon.

Many of Llewellyn's authors have websites with additional information and resources. For more information, please visit our website:

WWW.LLEWELLYN.COM